Battlefield Tourism

TOURISM SECURITY-SAFETY AND POST CONFLICT DESTINATIONS

Series editors: Maximiliano E. Korstanje and Hugues Seraphin

Since the turn of the century, the international rules surrounding security and safety have significantly changed, specifically within the tourism industry. In the age of globalization, terrorism and conflict have moved beyond individual high-profile targets; instead, tourists, travelers, and journalists are at risk. In response to this shift, the series invites authors and scholars to contribute to the conversation surrounding tourism security and postconflict destinations.

The series features monographs and edited collections to create a critical platform which not only explores the dichotomies of tourism from the theory of mobilities but also provides an insightful guide for policymakers, specialists, and social scientists interested in the future of tourism in a society where uncertainness, anxiety, and fear prevail.

Tourism Security-Safety and Post Conflict Destinations explores research approaches and perspectives from a wide range of ideological backgrounds to discuss topics such as:

- Studies related to comparative cross-cultural perceptions of risk and threat
- Natural and human-caused disasters
- Postdisaster recovery strategies in tourism and hospitality
- Terror movies and tourism
- Aviation safety and security
- Crime and security issues in tourism and hospitality
- Political instability, terrorism, and tourism
- Thana-tourism
- War on terror and Muslim tourism
- The effects of global warming on tourism destinations
- Innovative quantitative/qualitative methods for the study of risk and security issues in tourism and hospitality
- Virus outbreaks and tourism mobility
- Disasters, trauma, and tourism
- Apocalyptic theories and tourism as a form of entertainment

Advisory Board

Rami Isaac
Breda University of Applied Sciences, Netherlands

Stanislav Ivanov
Varna University of Management, Bulgaria

Metin Kozak
Dokuz Eylul University, Turkey

Sharad K. Kulshreshtha
North Eastern Hill University Shillong Meghalaya, India

Dominic Lapointe
University of Quebec at Montreal, Canada

Duncan Light
Bournemouth University, UK

Claudio Milano
The Autonomous University of Barcelona, Spain

Andreas Papatheodorou
University of Aegean, Greece

Cesar Augusto Oliveros
University of Guadalajara, Mexico

Daniel Olsen
Brigham Young University, USA

Alexandros Paraskevas
Oxford Brookes University, UK

Lorri Pennington Gray
University of Florida, USA

Arie Reichel
Ben-Gurion University of the Negev, Israel

Claudia Seabra
University of Coimbra, Portugal

Anukrati Sharma
University of Kota, India

Richard A. Sharpley
University of Central Lancashire, UK

Jonathan Skinner
University of Roehampton, UK

Geoffrey Skoll
Buffalo State College, USA

Marta Soligo
University of Nevada, USA

Dallen Timothy
Arizona State University, USA

Abraham Pizam
University of Central Florida, USA

Peter Tarlow
Texas A&M University, USA

Marcelo Tomé de Barros
State University of Fluminense, Brazil

Diego R. Toubes
University of Vigo, Spain

Rodanthi Tzanelli
University of Leeds, UK

Ghialy Yap
Edith Cowan University, Australia

Battlefield Tourism

EDITED BY

ONUR AKBULUT

Muğla Sıtkı Koçman University, Türkiye

YAKIN EKIN

Akdeniz University, Türkiye

MEHMET EMRE GÜLER

İzmir Katip Çelebi University, Türkiye

AND

ÖZGÜR SARIBAŞ

İzmir Katip Çelebi University, Türkiye

United Kingdom – North America – Japan – India – Malaysia – China

Emerald Publishing Limited
Emerald Publishing, Floor 5, Northspring, 21-23 Wellington Street, Leeds LS1 4DL

First edition 2024

British Library Cataloguing in Publication Data
A catalogue record for this book is available from the British Library

ISBN: 978-1-83909-991-5 (Print)
ISBN: 978-1-83909-990-8 (Online)
ISBN: 978-1-83909-992-2 (Epub)

Printed and bound by CPI Group (UK) Ltd, Croydon, CR0 4YY

INVESTOR IN PEOPLE

Contents

List of Contributors

Fatih Çavuşoğlu	Kutahya Dumlupinar University, Türkiye
Onur Akbulut	Muğla Sıtkı Koçman University, Türkiye
Yakın Ekin	Akdeniz University, Türkiye
Mehmet Emre Güler	İzmir Katip Çelebi University, Türkiye
Buğcan Güvenol	İzmir Katip Çelebi University, Türkiye
Johan Hattingh	Central University of Technology, South Africa
Pınar Işıldar	Dokuz Eylül University, Türkiye
Kaan Kasaroğlu	İzmir Katip Çelebi University, Türkiye
Eben Proos	Central University of Technology, South Africa
Simge Kömürcü Sarıbaş	İzmir Katip Çelebi University, Türkiye
Özgür Saribas	İzmir Katip Çelebi University, Türkiye
Özay Emre Yildiz	Dokuz Eylul University, Türkiye

Section 1

Special Interest Tourism

Introduction

The concept of special interest in tourism (SIT) operations has been frequently observed in the tourism literature after the social and environmental deteriorations created by mass tourism applications because mass tourism applications generally result in huge number of visitors. As a consequence of these massive tourist mobilities, the concept of visitor management revealed. In order to manage the destinations in a sustainable manner, some precautions are utilized such as carrying capacity, destination lifecycle, and environmental impact assessment. Moreover, destinations needed the product diversification through creating new sorts of tourism which is conceptualized as alternative tourism.

Most of the alternative tourism types have a fundamental of special interest such as battlefield tourism, adventure tourism, dark tourism, etc. For this reason, before examining the battlefield tourism as the topic of the book, editors decided to launch into the peculiar features of the special interest tourism. In this respect, this section is dedicated to shed light on the conceptualization of special interest tourism, some related definitions, similarities, and distinctions with alternative tourism. Sustainability is also the crucial issue for the evolution and development of special interest tourism.

SIT can reflect postmodern production philosophies such as consumer-oriented production, tailor-made products, and sustainability in the tourism sector (Uluçeçen, 2011). However, two essential elements are needed to define a leisure activity as SIT. One is that individuals devote a specific time to realize their interests. The other is that providing efficient and satisfactory supply for such events gains a commercial dimension (Trauer, 2006). Thus, what is essential for SIT is the availability and decisiveness of the interest that leads the person to travel (Tanrısevdi, 2009).

The following chapters in this section discuss the theory-based SIT, the benefits and limitations of SIT, and identification of the gap in the literature respectively.

Chapter 1

Theory-Based Special Interest Tourism

Yakın Ekin

Akdeniz University, Türkiye

Abstract

Special interest tourism (SIT) is a specialized type of tourism. People aim to visit destinations with a specific theme through this type of tourism. During SIT consumption, they create or develop peculiar interests and participate individually or in groups. In this respect, SIT is a concept that reflects some trends. These trends developed toward satisfying different interests rather than those developed around mass tourism. In other words, SIT emerges as an alternative movement to mass tourism based on general interests. Soon after mass tourism gained extensive dimension, alternative tourism, ecotourism, and SIT concepts emerged. These concepts altered the style of tourism operations. Diversified tourism operations have transformed conventional tourism into experience-based tourism activities. Presentations of these types of experiences are frequently in the form of special interests. The content of this chapter encompasses the fundamental concepts forming the SIT. An overview of the terminology – such as alternative tourism, sustainable development, and sustainable tourism – is the scope of this chapter. Moreover, criticisms and some trends in SIT are the leading subtopics. Some examples of academic research about SIT in Turkey are listed in the current study. This list was compiled from the information gathered from the Council of Higher Education National Thesis Center Database records.

Keywords: Special interest tourism; alternative tourism; sustainability; sustainable development; sustainable tourism; theory-based

Introduction

Leisure-based trips *en masse* might date back as early as the industrial revolution. Increasing disposable income of the visitors and more leisure time contributed to developing individual and group movements. Moreover, with the help of social

Battlefield Tourism, 3–20

Copyright © 2024 Yakın Ekin

Published under exclusive licence by Emerald Publishing Limited

doi:10.1108/978-1-83909-990-820241002

factors like international cultural interactions, convenience, and conformity in transportation technology, various facilities were created and built for tourists. As a result, tourism spread rapidly worldwide, especially after World War II. This massive human mobility has primarily targeted certain mass tourism destinations. Afterward, the adverse effects of large masses on destinations in the tourism development process, such as environmental and visitor management issues, were widely observed. In addition, rapid changes and transformations have begun in the consumer demand for tourism products. In this direction, alternative tourism types have started to appear in the tourism market as a new option instead of mass tourism.

Some academic sources synonymously use alternative and special interest tourism (SIT) types. In others, scholars tried to define these two concepts separately, with some minor differences in accessibility in daily life or offering extraordinary experiences. On the other hand, some scholars generally regarded SIT as distinct in the leisure travel categories because the activity of such an interest is dominant and determinant when selecting the destination. There are many divergences and enlargements within the scope of defining the concept of SIT. Nonetheless, the significant and fundamental motive to participate in SIT remains the activity of interest (MacKay, 2016).

Recently, a wide variety of SIT vacations have been disposable worldwide. The SIT product might be a tour of ghettos of World War II, some mountaineering activities, or visits to some contemporary postconflict areas. This diversity has been generated owing to the growing alternatives in leisure, culture, and other interests. Such interests consequently unveil a considerable number of niche products. Tourists, therefore, would sooner live their niche and visual experiences. The consumption models and the development of interest indicate the diversification in leisure choices through late modernity (Douglas et al., 2001).

The international tourism market shows some changes in the needs and motivations of tourists. There has been a specialization in travelers' preferences and habits of consumption. Such travelers are searching for living cultures, natural landscapes, and authenticity with a growing awareness of the responsible use of cultural and natural resources. Therefore, the international tourism market trends are oriented toward the search for thematic products. These trends emphasize the enjoyment of natural areas and local culture. Subsequently, the current situation is favorable for the creation/promotion of alternative and responsible tourism products. In this sense, the configuration of a specialized, competitive, and qualified offer is especially relevant for the sustainable development of tourist activity.

When dealing with SIT and its development, it is crucial to start with sustainability. Sustainability has a wide range of applications. Moreover, it is a new perception and sensitivity with deeper meanings and interpretations (Uluçeçen, 2011). Nevertheless, as the current book's topic is tourism, the author(s) restricted the framework to sustainable tourism and ecotourism. Sustainable development and ecotourism are distinct concepts. The concept of ecotourism refers to a segment within the tourism sector. However, overall sustainability principles are valid in tourism activity, management, company, and project, whether conventional, alternative, or specialized. In order to shed light on SIT, summarized definitions of some concepts will be in focus in the Sustainability, Sustainable Tourism, and Alternative Tourism Versus SIT section.

Sustainability, Sustainable Tourism, and Alternative Tourism Versus SIT

Many of the tourism authorities in the world agree on the risks caused by mass tourism. Some tourism operations endanger the future of natural resources. Therefore, policymakers suggested environment-friendly and sustainable tourism development. The fundamental objective of such a development is to overcome the destruction of resources. Sustainable tourism development requires an environmental movement consisting of inspection, monitoring, implementation, and control in this context (Akoğlan Kozak & Bahçe, 2009).

Sustainability might reduce the environmental effects of economically irregular and unbalanced resource use. This movement includes all relations between tourism operations and the environment, such as inputs, outputs, and effects of production activities on soil, ecology, and society. Those resources that serve as tourist attractions should be inherited appropriately by future generations. It is one of the mere qualifications of sustainable tourism. This fact is the fundamental reason for the emergence of alternative and sustainable tourism types. New-generation consumers have focused on less harmful tourism products to the environment and nature. The preferences of differentiated and transformed consumers have forced tourism professionals to reconsider the products that harm the environment and culture. Hence, reproduction and reshaping of the processes would be required.

Environment-friendly and ecotourism applications in tourism have become fashionable among tourism consumers. In some cases, many new-generation consumers regarded these sorts of tourism as a requirement. Since these consumers check the certifications of such environmental protection and preservation, from this perspective, they look for alternative options for mass tourism. Furthermore, they pursue their interests by fulfilling their leisure time through new style tourism products. Therefore, more tailor-made, personalized, and flexible tourism products are necessary for the tourism market (Uluçeçen, 2011).

The terminology of alternative tourism provides a generic conception for researchers in the tourism industry. In order to qualify a tourism type as an alternative, one should state its antagonism to the conventional package tours led by massive movements of people. Furthermore, economic, sociocultural, and environmental concerns are in focus in alternative tourism projects. Here, the objective of the tourism type is not to have negative impacts or to create positive impacts on the resources used and the places visited.

Consumers' travel experiences have become more sophisticated than ever. Subsequently, their decision-making process regarding which tourism activity to select among diversified alternative tourism types has become more complex. For this very reason, great alternatives presented by SIT are available in the world tourism market. Conventional tourism trips share the previously dominant position in the tourism business with SIT trips. However, relatively lower pax characterizes SIT trips. SIT diminishes the harm provoked by the massive mobility of traditional tourism operations. Hence, SIT possesses a specific position in the alternative tourism market from this viewpoint.

SIT was previously accepted as the synonym of alternative tourism and included in these classifications. However, SIT has started to take its place, especially in niche markets, as a type of tourism in this area, where different services are on the stage. Within the scope of diverse participant motives comprised, contribution to the specialization of alternative tourism, and the role in forming a new tourist profile, SIT is worth being classified as a different terminology of alternative tourism. As if that were not enough, one cannot claim that all the alternative tourism types possess or encompass a unique or special interest. Some alternative tourism products exist due to general interest in tourism purposes (Uluçeçen, 2011).

SIT refers to the customization of goods and services in the tourism industry. These offerings and presentations meet the fashionable demands of individuals and smaller groups. By doing so, tourism is to accomplish the requirements of the new demand's specific needs. SIT presents rewarding, enriching, adventuresome, and informative experiences. This vast spectrum varies from tea and coffee tours to specific battlefield visits or favela tourism operations such as visits to slums.

Special Interest Tourism (SIT)

The concept of SIT can reflect postmodern production philosophies such as consumer-oriented production, tailor-made products, and sustainability in the tourism sector (Uluçeçen, 2011). However, two essential elements are needed to define a leisure activity as SIT. One is that individuals devote a specific time to realize their interests. The other is that providing efficient and satisfactory supply for such events gains a commercial dimension (Trauer, 2006). Thus, what is essential for SIT is the availability and decisiveness of the interest that leads the person to travel (Tanrısevdi, 2009).

Mass tourism products cannot satisfy the development of environmental and social awareness. They cannot ensure individualization, escape from crowds, and personal development. For this reason, SIT is growing gradually due to new trends, such as changing tourist expectations (Yıldız, 2009). SIT is a concept identified by the desire to partake in tourism chiefly through a particular interest (Weiler & Hall, 1992). Such tourism also requires the supply of personalized tourism outputs stimulated by the specific interests of persons and groups (Douglas et al., 2001).

SIT is a growing trend in the travel industry. Unlike traditional tourism, SIT focuses on a theme or interest, allowing travelers to delve deeper into their passions and hobbies. This type of travel can be tailored to almost any interest, including history, food, art, wildlife, sports, and more. There are numerous types of SIT, including adventure tourism, cultural tourism, ecotourism, culinary tourism, and more.

SIT caters to its demand through occasional contact with people having similar lifestyles, pleasures, or common viewpoints. For instance, a specific gastronomy tour might coincide with the region's famous chefs, farm and market visitation, and tasting local cuisine. Similarly, a battlefield tour may present access to warfare sites, ensuring more information about the battles and conflicts.

Another advantage of SIT is that it can be customized to meet individual preferences and requirements. Consumers can form their tour routes according to interests, programs, and purchasing power. Tour levels might alter according to diverse tastes and choices, such as exploring organic wines, biodynamic wines, or rare vintages. SIT may make some contribution to regional development and local economy. It can create employment opportunities, support local businesses, and increase cultural exchange. Additionally, SIT may help preserve and protect cultural and natural resources as it often highlights sustainability and responsible tourism practices.

SIT, on the other hand, brings about some obstacles. One of the primary concerns is a possible case of overtourism. Excessive consumers might accumulate in a particular SIT destination. Hence, the potential negative consequences are overcrowding, environmental degradation, and cultural homogenization. Many SIT practices now address not well-known destinations, maintain sustainable practices, and prioritize local cultural exchange.

As SIT operations meet essential or average health and cleanliness standards, there is almost no need for luxury facilities and services. Therefore, SIT generally finds application in less developed regions. It is a type of tourism shaped by natural and cultural resources offering specialized products that give manufacturers and intermediaries a significant competitive advantage. It is a type of tourism product that can reach tourism consumers and niche markets with a tendency to individualize and change expectations. Mass tourism products often have substitutions; however, in SIT products, there is no or limited substitution (Yıldız, 2009).

Management of SIT

In the past tourism development phases, tourists were homogeneous. Therefore, researchers might anticipate their behaviors more quickly. Such participants of tourism mobility of that time enjoyed having trips with the pax of tens or hundreds of people. These visits were organized in a detailed schedule hour by hour. The consumer paid the price of the package in advance. This type of consumption was merely fashionable. Nonetheless, contemporary tourists are more impulsive and raging.

SIT and niche tourism highlight and focus on individual preferences. Visitors of such types generally perceive that they are out of the mundane of the mass and ordinary tourism experiences. In other words, they feel they are in a specific and tailor-made environmental bubble (Urry & Larsen, 2011) of their interests and choices. Moreover, some isolated communities' cultures and traditions are becoming a part of staged authenticity. One might observe the superficial formation of even never-existing traditions for consumption in new-age tourism demand.

SIT is associated with various forms that fit into a new tourism perspective. This sort of tourism practice links supply and demand in a language. Such a language invites us to consider a different reading on tourist travel motivations. SIT demand requests new proposals for tourist services capable of giving an account of the cultural and environmental identity of the chosen destination. Such a demand not only values a punctual service but puts a note on an entire territorial environment, in other words, a landscape that shows its history (such as the passage of time, customs, and changes), human geography, social activity, and economy. SIT is a macro category. Thus, it encompasses specific typologies. SIT encompasses wildlife safaris, yoga retreats, culinary tours, art and architecture tours, and cultural immersion experiences. Fashionable examples are cultural heritage, battlefield tourism, and faith tourism. Sport, health, event, business, cruise, nature-based, educational, scientific, cultural trips, adventure, urban, rural, cultural, ethnographic, heritage tourism, and ecotourism may be on the long SIT list. SIT requires careful organization, accurate-detailed information service, and expert guides.

SIT combines various elements of equipment and specific infrastructure facilities. In addition, resources and local heritage, such as crafts and gastronomy, are also part of the product. Incorporating efficient measures consistent with the sustainable development proposal is fundamental for its realization. At the same time, respecting the rural communities and creating benefits for them are the other objectives.

Since it is a broad category, SIT encompasses multiple aspects that require adequate training and preparation of human resources, a detained supply and territory planning, a holistic quality approach, and optimal intersectoral coordination. A series of specificities particular to each tourism type is also needed. In this sense, specialized marketing and commercialization aspects are fundamental to achieving the objectives of each type of SIT.

SIT contributes to improving the resources with high development potential, the diversification of destinations, and their service offerings. Moreover, the seasonal adjustment and continuous innovation of tourism products are also the benefits of SIT. A large part of the SIT consists of nature tourists who demand products related to the natural environment. These parts encompass tourists visiting a destination to experience and enjoy nature.

One may also find tourists with interests dedicated to studying or observing species of flora or fauna. Nature-based tourism has rapidly developed since the early 1990s by appearing in many documentaries, clubs, and specialized publications. In addition, magazines, books, and tourist guides are frequent incentives for such travels, particularly in the United States, Canada, and European markets.

Visitors come to a tourism destination from different regions of the world. Destinations are to attract the interest of increasingly sophisticated travelers. The visitors possess access to an enormous amount of information in the phase of destination selection. In order to guide the SIT market about contemporary visitors, United Nations World Tourism Organization announced some of the main tourist trends. It states that there will be polarizations in tourist tastes. According to that fact, while some tourists seek comfort, others pursue their interests. Tourists will gravitate more toward unexplored places. Visitor attraction focuses on new types of tourism and places. Elements of product development are expected to be entertaining, exciting, and educational (UNWTO Tourism: 2020 Vision, 1999).

Emerging and nontraditional markets often identify SIT operations. International markets offer many segments, which ensure their residents greater possibilities to travel abroad than in the past. This fact leads to numerous tourist destinations nationwide, regionally, and locally striving to capture the interest.

An example of a nontraditional market is high-risk tourism. The desire to travel from people is so strong that it often outweighs any possible concern about external threats. Tourism was uncertain after 9/11 in New York and the tsunami in 2004. International trips suffered an initial retraction but did not stop being carried out and experienced redirections toward tourist destinations that guarantee a climate of safety for their visitors. On the other hand, a tourist trend revealed traveling to destinations with terrorism and natural disaster problems. The main objective is for observation, research, and study purposes. There are also streams of tourists traveling to areas in extreme poverty to learn about these kinds of realities.

Tourism demand has become polarized among those who wish to travel to destinations that ensure comfort (and even some luxury, image, and status) and those who want to travel for adventure or cultural tourism, which is linked to local communities and in which extreme comfort is not an essential factor. It is essential to define the product according to the market to capture and structure it within an intelligent, sustainable development policy with benefits for all agents of the tourism system.

Information technologies and communications will become predominant for information quests, reservations, and online purchases of travel services. Increasingly, the buyer's market will be determinant in trips. This issue will lead to campaigns achieving sustainable tourism development. One may see the reflections in a reorientation of destination marketing. This orientation will focus on generating a brand image demonstrating social and environmental awareness.

Moreover, entertainment, excitement, and education will be trendy. These global trends constitute remarkable opportunities for the design of tourism products. Therefore, renovation and innovation in destinations are of concern in SIT. Incorporating quality elements and generating value-added services will further develop the product. The product offers nature and living culture capable of satisfying the information requirements and specialized experiences the new tourist profile seeks (Antonietti & Lo Bello, 2019).

Since the trend in international travel is increasing independent travel and relatively decreasing package tour participation, it is impossible to know or calculate the SIT dimensions precisely. Moreover, many SIT participants travel independently. For this reason, it does not seem very easy to calculate the absolute and accurate data related to SIT (Akoğlan Kozak & Bahçe, 2009).

Future Market Insights (FMI) announced leisure and adventure-based trips are increasing the SIT market. The demand for SIT business is expected to develop quickly between 2022 and 2032 with a forecast of 3.48 to 26.92 billion dollars. Special interest demand is wealthier, more educated, and allocentric. According to the FMI report, France and the United Kingdom lead in SIT. Thanks to this achievement of the two countries, Europe is the biggest shareholder of the SIT pie. Environment-based tourism applications weigh in at SIT operations. Sustainability concerns of the demand will be the critical factor for the enlargement of SIT (Future Market Insights, 2022).

Activities presenting experiences are the notable features of SIT. The key segments in the FMI report underline activity-based, educational, discovery, hobbies, relaxation, health, and therapy. This report has focused on the competition in South Asia. This country emerged as an attraction center that possesses a destination appeal. The feature of the product is the choice of tailor-made tours by the consumers. According to the report, travel motivations and social media influence drive the SIT. Australia promises an exquisite and unique wildlife tour. Adventure tourism share is growing. Leisure travel is the key factor for tourism. Saudi Arabia holds a large share of religious tourism. Educational tourism has become a booming business in China. Besides these country-based instances, sustainable tourism is slowly seeping into overall tourism operations. Consequently, niche places would be searched by destination developers. Hence, SIT practices would expand.

Criticisms of SIT

SIT is one concept that expresses awareness, sustainability, and quality in world tourism. Nonetheless, it is also exposed to some criticisms based on these sensitivities. Typical mistakes associated with mass tourism should not be made in SIT operations. There exists a capacity problem in the SIT business. The quest for new experiences within the scope of SIT threatens existing investments and creates pressure on infrastructure elements such as roads, transportation systems, and accommodation investments. In SIT projects, it is necessary to determine the carrying capacities, legally audit them, carry out environmental planning, and request environmental impact assessment reports from investors (Akoğlan Kozak & Bahçe, 2009).

Another criticism is that SIT facilitates access to ecologically sensitive areas. It is frequently probable that SIT also may lead to some harm to flora and fauna. Additionally, the potential conflict is likely between SIT entrepreneurs and local stakeholders. Due to misuse of resources, SIT operations can give negative results like mass tourism. By pursuing undiscovered places and different cultures, SIT consumers cause a rise in demand for such emerging destinations and cultures after a short exploration period. Hence, a massive movement of visitors is very likely. This new mass tourism, considered environmentally friendly, may cause much more harm to the natural environment in the long run since SIT also offers the world's most sensitive ecosystems for consumption (Roney, 2002). Therefore, the consumers and sellers of SIT should reflect their environmental consciousness and ethics in implementing SIT operations to avoid being new to mass tourism.

Policymakers should monitor the economic, social, and cultural alterations caused by tourism entrepreneurship in an emerging destination. Otherwise, the regional development plans through SIT would result in an increase in quantity rather than quality. In other words, the number of arrivals would exponentially increase, whereas the unbalanced growth seems utilitarian for some stakeholders. Nevertheless, such growth might be beneficial solely and exclusively in the short run. Moreover, this growth would likely make immigration and population density worse.

The inconsistencies between what is intended to be done and what is realized are the source of these criticisms. Although the tourism cake in the world is large, new destinations and new initiatives that are joining every day create a high level of competition in this sector. To avoid making some international or supranational initiatives hegemonic in this area, unfair competition in the market should be eliminated. This dominance should also be prevented in SIT operations for the healthy progress of the competition.

A Basic Classification of SIT Research Topics in Turkish Higher Education

This part of the chapter lists a brief and simple categorization of the SIT research topics. In so doing, the author would like to indicate the fields of study regarding this broad concept. This list is a snapshot of the SIT research topic studied in Turkiye. As seen in Table 1.1, the terminology of SIT is used restrictedly in MA theses and PhD dissertations. In most of the research, the determination of the case rather than the conception and empirical proof is dominantly observed. The keyword search is realized as "special interest tourism" and SIT in the Council of Higher Education, National Thesis Center Database.

Such research topics dominantly enhance the utilization for highlighting a differentiated tourism type rather than emphasizing the term's organization, characteristics, pros, and cons. As stated in Table 1.2, selected research fields are indicated predominately as 28 of them being about tourism. Runner-up keywords of the research are business administration and sports, having the name in five and two topics. In total, there are 40 topics extracted from the thesis list because some of the dissertations possess more than one keyword related to SIT.

The classification of the research topics according to the tourism types reveals that gastronomy tourism has popularity in terms of SIT research in Turkiye. As a wealthy country in almost every tourism type, dark, sports, adventure, cultural, and event tourism are the other forms of tourism investigated in graduate studies. The distribution is listed in Table 1.3.

Table 1.1. SIT Research Topics in Turkish Higher Education.

Author	Year	Topic	MA/PhD
Sunar, H.	2017	Sadness tourism within the scope of special interest tourism and examples from Turkiye	MA
Yalçınkaya, B.	2021	Evaluation of submarine tours in Antalya within the scope of special interest tourism	MA
Aşan, K.	2018	Neo-tribes in tourism: An ethnographic study of cycling special interest groups	PhD
Ağlamaz-Susup, A. E.	2018	A systematic approach to improve gastronomy tourism in the city of Izmir	PhD
Yalçın, Ç.	2003	Spain & Turkiye: Trends toward SIT from mass tourism	MA
Mazman, H. Y.	2020	Evaluation of participation motivations of participants visiting Nene Hatun Historical National Park within the scope of Nov. 9	MA
Asan, H.	2020	The effect of the emotional labor of adventure tourism employees within the framework of professional personality on job satisfaction	PhD
Yücesoy, S.	2018	Dark tourism as a tourism product: Prison museum example	MA
Erşen, G.	2017	Determination of İzmir Karaburun gastronomy tourism product routes via geographic information systems	MA
Söyler, S.	2016	The relationship among trekking as a serious leisure activity in tourism, environmental identity, and life satisfaction	MA
Gürsay, M. S.	2014	Geotourism and sustainability in Kızılcahamam – Çamlıdere Geopark	MA
Baştemur, C.	2013	The cultural and natural landscape traces of Architect Sinan's route	PhD
Akkil, A.	2021	Analysis of the factors affecting the loyalty of festival visitors. Sample of Gaziantep Gastronomy Festival	MA
İnce, Ö.	2020	Investigation of entertainment factories in the scope of dark tourism: Deep Fear Park example	MA

Table 1.1. *(Continued)*

Author	Year	Topic	MA/ PhD
Yazgeç, G.	2019	Analysis of leisure satisfaction and happiness levels of individuals participating in nature and adventure recreation: Sample of Fethiye destination	MA
Oğurtanı, C.	2019	Photographing wild animals in their natural habitats	MA
Boztoprak, F.	2019	The effect of gastronomy tourism on the identity and branding of the city; Erzurum example	MA
Temiz, T.	2019	The importance of products having geographical indication for gastronomy tourism: The case of Konya	MA
Kocabaş, E.	2019	Identifying the destination brand equity through festivals within the framework of gastronomy tourism: The case of Gaziantep	MA
Yalçın, V.	2019	Outdoor sports tourism in Sakarya	MA
Özdemir-Akgül, S.	2019	A neurotourism approach to hospitality operations: A study on domestic and foreign tourist perceptions	PhD
Mandal, M.	2018	The role of chiefs in the development of sustainable gastronomy tourism in Turkiye	MA
Kasap, M.	2018	Determination of satisfaction levels of local and foreign tourists regarding Trabzon and Rize destinations	MA
Yetimoğlu, S.	2017	A research on authentic practices and authentic marketing in restaurant enterprises: Sample of İstanbul	MA
Akkuş, O.	2015	Evaluation of Mersin – Aydıncık district and its environs in terms of culture tourism potential	MA
Üner, E. H.	2014	The evaluation of gastronomic tourism potential of Turkiye within the framework of all-inclusive system	MA
Akyurt Kurnaz, H.	2013	The importance of dark tourism on domestic tourism (Domestic tourism's demand): The case of Çanakkale	MA

(Continued)

Table 1.1. *(Continued)*

Author	Year	Topic	MA/PhD
Özçelik, H.	2012	Gallipoli-Waterloo comparison through tourism potential analysis in Turkiye	MA
Ekin, Y.	2011	Festivals within the context of event tourism and a research about social impacts of Antalya Altın Portakal Film Festival on residents	PhD

Source: Compiled by the author from the Council of Higher Education, National Thesis Center.

Table 1.2. Field of Study Distribution of Graduate Theses About SIT.

Tourism	28
Business Administration	5
Sports	2
Landscape Architecture	1
Performing and Visual Arts	1
Nutrition and Dietetics	1
Geography	1
Sociology	1

Source: Compiled by the author from the Council of Higher Education, National Thesis Center.

Table 1.3. The Classification of the Research Topics According to the Tourism Types.

Gastronomy Tourism	9
Dark Tourism	6
Sports Tourism	4
Adventure Tourism	3
Cultural Tourism	2
Event Tourism	2
Geotourism	2
Neurotourism	1
Destination-Based Evaluation	1

Source: Compiled by the author from the Council of Higher Education, National Thesis Center.

Conclusion

Applications of experience economy have transformed the tourism industry, too. Massive movements and package-oriented products must be altered or reformed regarding the newcomer generations' individual-based and specific demands. In other words, the tourism industry is to adapt to demand requirements and adapt to organize brand new specialized tours. Leisure and recreation are, of course, the very nature of tourism. Nevertheless, they are not efficient for the overall satisfaction of the new demand. This inefficiency is due to the need for product differentiation after the traditional mobility of vast proportions of the population, especially the Western population. Such a new type of demand requested some senses and actions of experience more and more. Therefore, higher standards and quality enhancement regarding experience are vital in developing and assessing SIT because the demand for SIT generally addresses tourism product innovations, mainly encompassing a specific experience. Destinations should keep track of experience-based tourism resources to present them and combine them with the conception of SIT. While doing so, authenticity preservation is a must not to become a pseudo-event through staged authenticity.

In cases where the destinations have ample tourism resources, lodging services of high quality, aggressive marketing, and advertisement techniques, upholding ancillary services, and notably enthusiastic approval of the state, the tourism experts do not need to perform backbreaking work. However, the situation would be challenging if these features were lacking. Frequently, this issue will promote what the destination possesses in its tourism inventory. Appealing landscape, sometimes kind welcoming, and hospitality might be the pull factor. Hence, destinations should target consumers who look for what they already have.

Additionally, this inventory that pulls the new type of consumers should have the characteristics of special interest. Generally, such a type of demand does not require luxurious amenities. Instead, these consumers are keen on the beautiful and natural reality. In other words, special interests are fulfilled in return for a reasonable cost (Kruja & Gjyrezi, 2011).

Tourism activity is going through uncertainty and vulnerability at a global level after COVID-19. This fact has led governments, associations of tourism service providers, chambers of commerce, and international organizations to think about strategies for tourism recovery. Different destinations will have different behaviors in response to changes in tourist preferences. This struggle is coupled with greater diversification in tourism products to avoid crowds. Therefore, there is the possibility that tourism associated with nature and its different modalities (rural tourism, agritourism, community-based tourism, indigenous tourism, adventure tourism, ecotourism, among others), as well as other segments – such as cultural tourism, health tourism, or gastronomic tourism – are positioned as the most popular and alternative in opposition to mass tourism.

Consequently, the demand for less congested and more sustainable destinations will coincide with travelers' concerns for health security in accommodation facilities and food. Thus, the vacation choice will give preference to rural environments, which also influences the interest in carrying out agricultural production activities, managing natural resources and the territory, and preparing food and agricultural crafts through experiential workshops.

The interaction between tourism, the environment, and local cultures, together with the great potential of activity tourism for the conservation of nature and the fight against poverty, is reflected in the concept of sustainable tourism, referring to the practice of a tourist activity that respects the environment and economically beneficial for local host communities (Alba Sud, 2020).

So far, a general conclusion of the SIT conception was tried to be underlined. As the book's topic is battlefield tourism, in the conclusion part, the connection between SIT and battlefield tourism should be stated. Mobilities and visits of people to the destinations where battles took place are included in the classifications of SIT. Moreover, this type of tourism has a growing demand, especially in the battlefields in Europe. Battlefields and even ruined towns visited are ancient phenomena that began with World War I. Nevertheless, during the interwar, it aroused a certain mistrust, even rejection. It weakened as locals erased the scars of war from the landscapes, except in areas frequented by Commonwealth nations.

The values and meaning attributed to remembering the restaging of the battlefields by local actors put tourism in touch with the present. Tourism activities based on history are experiencing a thorough alteration owing to the historiographical renewals. Both places of destruction and creation, places of commemoration and exhibition, places of recollection and entertainment, and historical sites, which are the subject of a promotion policy, refer to hybrid representations and uses. Artists, historians, and more and more scenographers and technicians confront their representations in the construction of desirability (Hertzog, 2012).

Apparently, SIT is a growing trend that allows travelers to explore their interests and passions more deeply. By connecting with like-minded people, customizing their itineraries, and supporting local communities, travelers can have a more meaningful and authentic travel experience. If the operation is mounted within a responsible tourism scope, SIT can positively influence consumers and residents.

In conclusion, theory-based approaches provide a framework for understanding tourists' behavior in SIT. Motivation theory, push and pull theory, experience economy theory, and destination image theory are some theoretical frameworks applied to SIT. Understanding the theories that underpin SIT is essential for tourism destinations to develop and market customized tourism products that cater to the needs and interests of different tourist segments.

In summary, SIT is characterized by its focus on niche markets, authentic experiences, education, sustainability, community-building, customization, and effective marketing. These fundamentals contribute to the growth and development of SIT as a vital and unique segment within the broader tourism industry.

References

Ağlamaz-Susup, A. E. (2018). *İzmir'de gastronomi turizminin geliştirilmesine yönelik sistemsel bir yaklaşım* (Doctoral dissertation, Aydın Adnan Menderes Üniversitesi Sosyal Bilimler Enstitüsü Turizm İşletmeciliği Ana Bilim Dalı, Aydın, Turkiye). https://acikbilim.yok.gov.tr/handle/20.500.12812/251577

Akkil, A. (2021). *Festival ziyaretçilerinin sadakatlerini etkileyen faktörlerin analizi: Gaziantep Gastronomi Festivali örneği* (Master's thesis, Gaziantep Üniversitesi Sosyal Bilimler Enstitüsü Gastronomi ve Mutfak Sanatları Ana Bilim Dalı, Gaziantep, Turkiye). https://tez.yok.gov.tr/UlusalTezMerkezi/tezSorguSonucYeni.jsp

Akkuş, O. (2015). *Mersin – Aydıncık ilçesi ve çevresinin kültür turizmi potansiyeli açısından değerlendirilmesi* (Master's thesis, Atılım Üniversitesi Sosyal Bilimler Enstitüsü Turizm Yönetimi Ana Bilim Dalı, Ankara, Turkiye). https://acikbilim.yok.gov.tr/handle/20.500.12812/58735

Akoğlan Kozak, M., & Bahçe, S. (2009). *Özel ilgi turizmi.* Detay Yayıncılık.

Akyurt-Kurnaz, H. (2013). *Hüzün turizminin iç turizme (İç turizm talebine) etkisi: Çanakkale örneği* (Master's thesis, Muğla Sıtkı Koçman Üniversitesi Sosyal Bilimler Enstitüsü Turizm İşletmeciliği Ana Bilim Dalı, Muğla, Turkiye). https://tez.yok.gov.tr/UlusalTezMerkezi/tezDetay.jsp?id=vj5H6BCyKk5zT4lv2rJ6Lg&no=2bbwqw-AxX_A0UQpQbZDOg

Alba Sud. (2020). *Turismo de Intereses Especiales, espacio rural y alimentación en tiempos del COVID-19.* https://www.albasud.org/noticia/es/1217/turismo-de-intereses-especiales-espacio-rural-y-alimentaci-n-en-tiempos-del-covid-19

Antonietti, B., & Lo Bello, S. (2019). *Introducción al turismo: el turismo de intereses especiales.* https://utntyh.com/wp-content/uploads/2019/05/Turismo-de-Intereses-Especiales.pdf

Aşan, K. (2018). *Turizmde yeni kabileler: Bisiklet özel ilgi grupları üzerine etnografik bir araştırma* (Doctoral dissertation, Anadolu Üniversitesi Sosyal Bilimler Enstitüsü Turizm İşletmeciliği Ana Bilim Dalı, Eskişehir, Turkiye). https://tez.yok.gov.tr/UlusalTezMerkezi/tezDetay.jsp?id=4BjiXo2RoY8Wuwq38no=r6iRtWdTYw&CmgvMNgJPpdLl764w

Asan, H. (2020). *Macera turizmi çalışanlarının mesleki kişilikleri çerçevesinde gösterdikleri duygusal emeğin iş tatminine etkisi* (Doctoral dissertation, Sivas Cumhuriyet Üniversitesi Sosyal Bilimler Enstitüsü İşletme Ana Bilim Dalı, Sivas, Turkiye). https://tez.yok.gov.tr/UlusalTezMerkezi/tezDetay.jsp?id=_Nx6ODwDjPxOqNJQmBKvvQ&no=C0mFvLNDuN3OJmvs8EDxFw

Baştemur, C. (2013). *Mimar Sinan rotasının doğal ve kültürel peyzaj izleri* (Doctoral dissertation, Ankara Üniversitesi Fen Bilimleri Enstitüsü Peyzaj Mimarlığı Ana Bilim Dalı, Ankara, Turkiye). https://dspace.ankara.edu.tr/xmlui/handle/20.500.12575/34654

Boztoprak, F. (2019). *Gastronomi turizminin kentin tanıtımı ve markalaşmasına etkisi; Erzurum örneği* (Master's thesis, Gazi Üniversitesi Eğitim Bilimleri Enstitüsü Aile Ekonomisi ve Beslenme Eğitimi Ana Bilim Dalı, Ankara, Turkiye). https://tez.yok.gov.tr/UlusalTezMerkezi/tezDetay.jsp?id=OxHAAFf3E47GDD5RunHT4g&no=INv5RSYO7eHPppTERjXcsA

Douglas, N., Douglas, N., & Derret, R. (2001). *Special interest tourism.* Pennsylvania State University; John Wiley & Sons.

Erşen, G. (2017). *İzmir Karaburun Yarımadası gastronomi turizmi ürününe yönelik rotalarının coğrafi bilgi sistemleri ile belirlenmesi* (Master's thesis, Anadolu Üniversitesi Sosyal Bilimler Enstitüsü Turizm İşletmeciliği Ana Bilim Dalı, Eskişehir, Turkiye). https://earsiv.anadolu.edu.tr/xmlui/handle/11421/2941

Future Market Insights – FMI. (2022). *Special interest tourism market outlook 2022–2032.* https://www.futuremarketinsights.com/reports/special-interest-tourism-sector-overview-and-analysis

Gürsay, M. S. (2014). *Kızılcahamam – Çamlıdere Jeoparkı'nda jeoturizm ve sürdürülebilirlik* (Master's thesis, Atılım Üniversitesi Sosyal Bilimler Enstitüsü Turizm İşletmeciliği Ana Bilim Dalı, Ankara, Turkiye). https://tez.yok.gov.tr/ UlusalTezMerkezi/tezDetay.jsp?id=beHvnGNEKH6j9j9GvX6cpQ&no=-cHg4m Y2kPTTFBhYg0AX0A

Hertzog, A. (2012). Tourisme de mémoire et imaginaire touristique des champs de bataille. *Via Tourism Review*, *1*(1), 1–16. http://journals.openedition.org/ viatourism/1276. https://doi.org/10.4000/viatourism.1276

İnce, Ö. (2020). *Karanlık turizm kapsamında eğlence fabrikalarının incelenmesi: Deep Fear Park örneği* (Master's thesis, İstanbul Ticaret Üniversitesi Sosyal Bilimler Enstitüsü Turizm İşletmeciliği Ana Bilim Dalı Turizm İşletmeciliği Bilim Dalı, İstanbul, Turkiye). https://tez.yok.gov.tr/UlusalTezMerkezi/tezDetay.jsp? id=BZAJqfl9lkUdy7Lb19EMsw&no=3JpwSAsaAAwrJvYI_ygwuw

Kasap, M. (2018). *Yerli ve yabancı turistlerin Trabzon ve Rize destinasyonlarına ilişkin memnuniyet durumlarının belirlenmesi* (Master's thesis,Gaziantep Üniversitesi Sosyal Bilimler Enstitüsü Turizm İşletmeciliği Ana Bilim Dalı, Gaziantep, Turkiye). https://acikbilim.yok.gov.tr/handle/20.500.12812/419249?show=full

Kocabaş, E. (2019). *Gastronomi turizmi çerçevesinde destinasyon marka değerinin festivaller aracılığıyla belirlenmesi: Gaziantep örneği* (Master's thesis, İstanbul Üniversitesi Sosyal Bilimler Enstitüsü Turizm İşletmeciliği Ana Bilim Dalı, Gaziantep, Turkiye). https://tez.yok.gov.tr/UlusalTezMerkezi/tezDetay.jsp? id=3LFb6tIctMKq_jOeic9Vuw&no=hD7eQSSql86QZcehn5FKlg

Kruja, D., & Gjyrezi, A. (2011). The special interest tourism development and the small regions. *Turizam*, *15*(2), 77–89.

MacKay, K. J. (2016). Special interest tourism. In J. Jafari & H. Xiao (Eds.), *Encyclopedia of tourism*. Springer Cham. https://doi.org/10.1007/978-3-319-01384-8_187

Mandal, M. (2018). *Türkiye'de sürdürülebilir gastronomi turizminin gelişmesinde mutfak şeflerinin rolü* (Master's thesis, Atılım Üniversitesi Sosyal Bilimler Enstitüsü Turizm İşletmeciliği ve Otelcilik Ana Bilim Dalı Turizm İşletmeciliği Bilim Dalı, Ankara, Turkiye). https://tez.yok.gov.tr/UlusalTezMerkezi/tezDetay.jsp? id=nABIKGq5l_nX5yJs9EXaZQ&no=X4xHK1W_PIAOAC0_NVeSXg

Mazman, H. Y. (2020). *Geleneksel 9 Kasım etkinlikleri kapsamında Nene Hatun Tarihi Milli Parkını ziyaret eden katılımcıların katılım motivasyonlarının değerlendirilmesi* (Master's thesis, Atatürk Üniversitesi Sosyal Bilimler Enstitüsü Turizm İşletmeciliği ve Otelcilik Ana Bilim Dalı, Erzurum, Turkiye). https://acikbilim.yok. gov.tr/handle/20.500.12812/57277

Oğurtanı, C. (2019). *Yaban hayvanlarının doğal yaşam ortamlarında fotoğraflanması* (Master's thesis, Haliç Üniversitesi Sosyal Bilimler Enstitüsü Fotoğraf ve Video Ana Sanat Dalı Fotoğraf ve Video Sanat Dalı, İstanbul, Turkiye). https://tez.yok. gov.tr/UlusalTezMerkezi/tezDetay.jsp?id=CGEr6Pp7UydDF2jVCMYrBw&no= W6ALGFJtJFcC0nFYWmGSOQ

Özçelik, H. (2012). *Gelibolu-Waterloo karşılaştırması yoluyla Türkiye'de keder turizmi potansiyeli analizi* (Master's thesis, Akdeniz Üniversitesi Sosyal Bilimler Enstitüsü Turizm İşletmeciliği ve Otelcilik Ana Bilim Dalı, Antalya, Turkiye). https://tez.yok. gov.tr/UlusalTezMerkezi/tezDetay.jsp?id=9j59CH17-uOvwNV2Lq9S_g&no=6S PV7Xit2g2-nZTtZwLubg

Özdemir-Akgül, S. (2019). *Konaklama işletmelerinde yeni bir yaklaşım nöroturizm: Yerli ve yabancı turist algısı üzerine bir araştırma* (Doctoral dissertation, Selçuk Üniversitesi Sosyal Bilimler Enstitüsü Turizm İşletmeciliği Ana Bilim Dalı Turizm İşletmeciliği Bilim Dalı, Konya, Turkiye). https://tez.yok.gov.tr/UlusalTezMerkezi/ tezDetay.jsp?id=J-rby1ZtUqYsmZ_TbLs9xA&no=WZWinUsNYYRFYdZXrx W9ug

Roney, S. A. (2002). Fordizmden Post Fordizme Geçiş Sürecinin Turizme Yansımaları: Kitle Turizmi ve Alternatif Turizm. *Anatolia: Turizm Araştırmaları Dergisi, 13*(1), 9–14.

Söyler, S. (2016). *Turizmde ciddi serbest zaman faaliyeti olarak doğa yürüyüşleri, çevre kimliği ve yaşam doyumu ilişkisi* (Master's thesis, Dokuz Eylül Üniversitesi Sosyal Bilimler Enstitüsü Turizm İşletmeciliği Ana Bilim Dalı Turizm İşletmeciliği Bilim Dalı, İzmir, Turkiye). https://acikbilim.yok.gov.tr/handle/20.500.12812/552483

Sunar, H. (2017). *Özel ilgi turizmi olarak hüzün turizmi ve Türkiye'den örnekler* (Master's thesis, Selçuk Üniversitesi Sosyal Bilimler Enstitüsü Seyahat İşletmeciliği Ana Bilim Dalı, Konya, Turkiye). https://tez.yok.gov.tr/UlusalTezMerkezi/tezDetay.jsp? id=hK7wiCL_Aa8SuyMANhhizA&no=Eu9zu-9xR7niBBUUZAJ6bA

Tanrısevdi, A. (2009). Türk özel ilgi gezginleri sansasyon arama özelliği sergilemekte midir? *Ege Akademik Bakış, 9*(4), 13.

Temiz, T. (2019). *Konya örneğinde coğrafi işaretli ürünlerin gastronomi turizmi açısından önemi* (Master's thesis Selçuk Üniversitesi Sosyal Bilimler Enstitüsü Turizm İşletmeciliği Ana Bilim Dalı, Konya, Turkiye). https://tez.yok.gov.tr/ UlusalTezMerkezi/tezDetay.jsp?id=lycMS1Ze5WwVq2Km8EMZOg&no=VV42 sRFRKzm6StaRbq9X3g

Trauer, B. (2006). Conceptualizing special interest tourism – Frameworks for analysis. *Tourism Management, 27*(2), 183–200.

Uluçeçen, T. H. (2011). *Özel ilgi turizmi: Kapsamı, çeşitleri ve Türkiye'de uygulanabilirliği* (Master's thesis, TC Kültür ve Turizm Bakanlığı Dış İlişkiler ve Avrupa Birliği Koordinasyon Daire Başkanlığı, Ankara, Turkiye). https://silo.tips/ download/zel-lg-turzm-kapsami-etler-ve-trkye-de-uygulanablrl

Üner, E. H. (2014). *Her şey dahil sistemde Türkiye gastronomi turizmi potansiyelinin değerlendirilmesi* (Master's thesis, Atılım Üniversitesi Sosyal Bilimler Enstitüsü Turizm Yönetimi Ana Bilim Dalı, Ankara, Turkiye). https://tez.yok.gov.tr/ UlusalTezMerkezi/tezDetay.jsp?id=w28geHsjpWv0kB3nA8RIOg&no=oomKU8 qZtHhm9MMSq_9QBg

UNWTO. (1999). *Tourism: 2020 vision* (Executive Summary English version online only). https://www.e-unwto.org/doi/epdf/10.18111/9789284403394?role=tab

Urry, J., & Larsen, J. (2011). *The tourist gaze 3.0.* Sage.

Weiler, B., & Hall, C. M. (1992). *Special interest tourism: In search of an alternative.* Belhaven Press.

Yalçın, Ç. (2003). *Kitle turizminden özel ilgi turizmine yönelişte İspanya ve Türkiye* (Master's thesis, İstanbul Üniversitesi Sosyal Bilimler Enstitüsü Turizm İşletmeciliği Ana Bilim Dalı, İstanbul, Turkiye). https://tez.yok.gov.tr/ UlusalTezMerkezi/tezDetay.jsp?id=RV8l7zBmhGjubUANTGUx5w&no=9f1FY kEWypCDfGNCsREaxQ

Yalçın, V. (2019). *Sakarya'da doğa sporları turizmi* (Master's thesis, Sakarya Üniversitesi Sosyal Bilimler Enstitüsü Coğrafya Ana Bilim Dalı, Sakarya, Turkiye). https://acikerisim.sakarya.edu.tr/handle/20.500.12619/90250

Yalçınkaya, B. (2021). *Antalya'daki denizaltı turlarının özel ilgi turizmi kapsamında değerlendirilmesi* (Master's thesis, İstanbul Üniversitesi Sosyal Bilimler Enstitüsü Turizm İşletmeciliği Ana Bilim Dalı, İstanbul, Turkiye). https://tez.yok.gov.tr/ UlusalTezMerkezi/tezSorguSonucYeni.jsp

Yazgeç, G. (2019). *Doğa ve macera rekreasyonu etkinliklere katılan bireylerin serbest zaman doyum ve mutluluk düzeylerinin incelenmesi: Fethiye destinasyonu örneği* (Master's thesis, Manisa Celal Bayar Üniversitesi Sosyal Bilimler Enstitüsü Rekreasyon Ana Bilim Dalı, Manisa, Turkiye). https://tez.yok.gov.tr/Ulusal TezMerkezi/tezDetay.jsp?id=4086SMXngwAGX-u5lf3U7g&no=U2WshKUZKlZ rGHNo5sTqxA

Yetimoğlu, S. (2017). *Restoran işletmelerinde otantizm uygulamaları ve otantik pazarlama üzerine bir araştırma: İstanbul örneği* (Master's thesis, Necmettin Erbakan Üniversitesi Sosyal Bilimler Enstitüsü Turizm İşletmeciliği Ana Bilim Dalı, Konya, Turkiye). https://acikerisim.erbakan.edu.tr/xmlui/handle/20.500. 12452/3543

Yıldız, Ö. E. (2009). *Türkiye'de şarap turizmi: Çeşme örneğinde ürün geliştirme modeli* (Doctoral dissertation, Dokuz Eylül Üniversitesi Sosyal Bilimleri Enstitüsü, Turizm İşletmeciliği Ana Bilim Dalı, İzmir, Turkiye). https://acikerisim.deu.edu.tr/ xmlui/handle/20.500.12397/11108

Yücesoy, S. (2018). *Turistik bir ürün olarak keder turizmi: Müze hapishaneler örneği* (Master's thesis, Erciyes Üniversitesi Sosyal Bilimler Enstitüsü Turizm İşletmeciliği Ana Bilim Dalı, Kayseri, Turkiye). https://tez.yok.gov.tr/UlusalTezMerkezi/tezDetay. jsp?id=-xjvwa4Dos3ngV_Uy8bfTg&no=KimaSDLKc_L6mO0M0NH2mA

Chapter 2

The Benefits and Limitations of Special Interest Tourism

Özay Emre Yildiz

Dokuz Eylul University, Türkiye

Abstract

Although the definition and classification of special interest tourism may prove difficult or misleading, certain tourist attractions, motives, and scale clearly indicate the niche markets of those individuals specifically interested in certain activities and destinations. The nature, benefits, and limitations of special interest tourism can readily be studied in contrast with mass tourism. The former largely indicates creative recreation, a search for meaning, existential authenticity, cocreation of transformative experiences, and satisfaction of higher needs. The visitor engages in the self, the novel cultural center, and the environment in a deeper sense, resulting in self-improvement/realization, cultural integration, strong sense of place, memorable experiences, and ultimately competitive advantage for the destination. These cases of tourism activity offer product diversification, alleviate tourism congestion and are also usually less detrimental and more sustainable for the destination. However, the small scale and impermanence of special interest tourism appeal may raise questions of profitability, where planning and product development require more time and resources, and this singular item production is not standardizable as in mass tourism. The search and conveyance of meaning in special interest tourism may also lead to a pretentious over-glorification, shrinification, or museification of the destination. Lastly, unethical motivations or potentially dangerous activities may be associated with some forms of special interest, which should clearly be discouraged.

This chapter discusses the basic motivations, benefits, and limitations of special interest tourism, largely in opposition with mass tourism.

Keywords: Special interest; mass tourism; tourist motivations; types of tourism product; creative tourism; tourist experience

Battlefield Tourism, 21–32

Copyright © 2024 by Emerald Publishing Limited

All rights of reproduction in any form reserved

doi:10.1108/978-1-83909-990-820241003

Introduction

Tourism, as a human endeavor, has been developing in such a manner that challenges humans' basic method of studying and giving meaning to environment and existence, which heavily relies on creating and imparting knowledge through denomination, definition, classification/categorization, association, and separation. This process of compartmentalization, which has successfully helped humans to survive as a species overall the planet, and develop increasingly complex forms of civilization, is largely dependent on a simple binary logic that is rooted in the basic survival orientation of reward versus punishment.

Tourism, due to (factors including) its inherent dynamism and fluidity, unparalleled range of consumer activities, and emerging cultural interactions, has proven impossible to be defined, classified, and delineated in a universal, static, explicit, and objective fashion. This is even more apparent in special interest tourism.

Tourism still needs to be defined and classified. Proper and common terminology and language, consistent terms, and concepts should be employed to study tourism and to measure and classify tourism activity. This is crucial once the economic impact of tourism is considered. Receiving regions and countries rely on concrete and reliable statistical information, on which they will develop tourism policies and planning, and coordinate marketing efforts (Olalı, 1990). As a field of production, tourism is by no means an industry of competing products or a standalone sector of economy (Olalı & Timur, 1988), rather an interconnected web of service providers (Lickorish & Jenkins, 1999) including producers of tourism characteristics and supporting products (UNWTO, 2010) and governing bodies functioning in collaboration to cater to the vast array of visitors' needs. Tourism is also the economy resulting from the exchange of value. As a human, activity tourism refers to the multidimensional activities of visitors and the social interactions throughout tourism travel (Goeldner & Ritchie, 2009).

The study of tourism as an interdisciplinary social science has had its fair share of this binary approach. Two-dimensional vector models, bell curves, and similar approaches have always proven useful in quantification, simplification, and classification of the broad motives and activities of consumers and producers. As early as 1943, Maslow proposed tension-reducing versus arousal-seeking motives (for travel) (Maslow, 1943). The following hierarchy of needs model, besides being cited to no end, is specifically valuable for the discussion of special interest tourism, in its separation of *lower* vital needs of the simple human from the *higher* cultural needs of the civilized counterpart (Maslow, 1954). Gray (1970) specifies two opposing forces in wanderlust versus sunlust, and Cohen (1972) improves on the duality of opposing motives to propose fear versus curiosity. Especially important is the introduction of an "environmental bubble", which offers the (illusion of) safety of familiarity to the visitor outside of their comfort zone. MacCannell (1973) discusses the tourism settings, separating the front stages, the economic environment of the destination, where interactions focus on service delivery, commercial activity, and staging of cultural appearances from the back stages, the habitats of local culture, where day-to-day, authentic cultural interactions take place. The tourist-pilgrim seeks the highest form of authenticity possible and is supposed to be dismayed by the blatant staging of culture. They therefore need to leave their environmental bubble to venture in back stages.

Plog's typology (1974) based on the duality of tourist motivation has proven to be one of the most seminal, where the adventurist allocentric tourist is at the one extreme and the psychocentric, in their environmental bubble, is at the other. The "ordinary" mid-centric tourist forms the bulk of the bell curve as well as the majority of the tourist market (Plog, 2001). Dumazedier's (1974) separation of passive versus active recreation (and the latter's associations to creative tourism) is yet another indispensable duality in the discussion of special interest tourism. Regarding the separation of tourist motives, Dann's (1977) anomie versus ego enhancement and the recurring push–pull model (Crompton, 1979) are also worthy of mention.

Cohen improves on Plog's and MacCannell's approaches and offers five different modes: recreational/diversionary/experiential/experimental/existential (1979a, 1979b). Iso Ahola's (1982) application of "personal escape/personal seeking" to tourist motivations and Fischler's (1988) neophilia versus neophobia propositions are other valuable typologies for the discussion at hand.

Reviewed as a whole, the typologies tend to approach tourist motivations on a continuum of dedication. On the one hand stands the caricature of the modern person who consciously wishes to passively relax within the confines of their own environmental bubble and has no interest in the cultural or natural environment of the destination. On the other hand, we have the dedicated pilgrim-tourist in search of escapism, meaning and absolute authenticity, self-improvement or even realization, transformation, and complete integration in the new cultural center (MacCannell, 1973; Thomas, 2010). The visitor may wish to escape, however temporarily, from their own cultural center, in which the individual has lost the sense of individuality and meaning, and which more often than not serves as a source of social pressure and stress. In such instances, the individual may wish to experience new cultural centers with varying degrees of motivation for integration.

Mass Tourism Versus Special Interest Tourism

Based on the previous efforts of binary classification, the search for definition and localization of special interest tourism is in order. We are inclined to study special interest tourism and mass tourism in antonymy, and exhibiting contrasting/opposing features, as offered by the typologies mentioned above. While this approach (of comparing apples to smartphones) is not in any sense accurate, it simplifies the discussion and serves the purpose.

The development and rapid growth of modern tourism is mostly (due to) mass tourism. Before mass tourism, leisure travel was reported to be a luxury afforded by a minuscule percentage of the population, basically serving special interests and higher needs. Instigated by the Industrial Revolution and brought to fruition by WWII, due to changing social and economic conditions and clearly exploded by commercial and civil airline transport and the internet, tourism has massified

(İçöz, 2007). The classical tourism approach equals to mass tourism, character-ized by the standardization of products, services, processes, architecture, land-scape etc., minimization of costs and benefiting from economies of scale, and inevitably, large groups of tourists (İçöz, 2005). Mass tourism is associated by very large and multinational airline carriers, tour operators, and chains of hotels operating in a monopolistically competitive market (Olalı, 1990). Special interest tourism looks suspiciously a lot like the service providers' response to tourism demand that has grown increasingly dismayed, underwhelmed, and under-satisfied by mass tourism's overly standardized offer.

It must be noted that neither mass tourism nor special interest tourism is a categorization of statistical significance. Broad classification of tourism forms based on main purpose of travel is proposed to classify tourism trips for statistical purposes, separating personal (holidays, leisure and recreation, VFR, religion, etc.) from business tourism. "Types of tourism product" offer a finer classification based on various aspects of tourist activity such as motivation, selection of destination, accommodation and centers of interest, including culinary tourism, agro-tourism, health tourism, etc. (UNWTO, 2010). The latter classification does not offer clear separation of motives and bears little, if any, statistical significance largely due to overlapping purposes and activities within a single trip, but it is nevertheless invaluable for marketing purposes.

Some types of tourism product are widely recognized to be classified within the scope of mass or special interest tourism; however, this type of clear-cut classi-fication will undoubtedly be misleading. This approach to special interest tourism as an umbrella term to include certain types of tourism product in absolute terms may function to a large extend for some products with self-serving titles, including ornithology or botanical tourism. However, any case of tourism activity will be unique and may or may not exhibit features of special interest or mass tourism. Therefore, the umbrella term is better off containing common *themes* of special interest, appealing to a well-defined (but poorly quantifiable) niche market, passionately and specifically interested in those themes (Kruja & Gjyrezi, 2011).

The special interest tourist will be highly and specifically motivated in their expectation and search of meaning, existential authenticity, and fulfilling higher needs such as self-improvement, and the degree of dedication is useful in sepa-rating cases of soft and hard special interest tourism (Rittichainuwat, 2018; Steiner & Reisinger, 2006). Soft special interest tourism is where the visitor is not necessarily expected to develop a new, vital, specific skill, or expertise in the special interest associated with such tourism (Trauer, 2006). Hard special interest tourism indicates motives including self-actualization, self-enrichment, self-renewal, self-expression, and social integration (Stebbins, 1996).

Where cases of mass tourism differ from its special interest counterpart can be summarized in three major areas: scale, activity, and cost. Special interest inherently implies a much smaller scale. Any commercially rational demand from a specifically interested niche market may create special interest travel and in time evolve to be considered as a type of tourism product/case of special interest tourism (Kruja & Gjyrezi, 2011). As examples of types of tourism product usually associated with special interest, rural tourism is defined by Eurostat to be the activities of a person taking a tourism trip and staying in rural areas, *without mass tourism* (1998). Cases of dark tourism, including ghost tourism, suicide tourism, and also battlefield tourism, are characterized by a special and unusual form of curiosity, a desire for empathy, and self-identification with the victims of atrocities (Ashworth & Hartmann, 2005).

The tourism activity in special interest tourism is almost always more clearly defined, personalized, and appealing to the visitor in a much higher degree. Tours therefore need to be extremely well planned and tailored to the tastes of special interest. Special interest tourism related destinations also seem to differ, offering direct personal contact with richer (natural and cultural) environments, the luxury of tranquility, pleasure of (shared) experiences of authentic spectacle, discovery, learning, and challenge (Kruja & Gjyrezi, 2011).

As a result of the first two differences, costs per unit seem to be much higher in special interest tourism where singular production and delivery of service is needed, while mass tourism has all to do with repetition and economies of scale. Special interest tourists usually search for unique and unrepeatable experiences, develop a social network within a smaller group (niche market) sharing similar and specialist interests, and are the specific target audience for those specialist service providers who cater for travelers with such niche interests (Weiler & Hall, 1992).

Benefits of Special Interest Tourism

It would be misleading to consider, based on the contrasts stated above, and also the following discussion of benefits, that special interest tourism is to *replace* mass tourism. The major form of tourism has been and is continuing to be mass tourism, generating the bulk of the trillions of US dollars in export revenues from tourism.

Special interest tourism offers *alternatives* to mass tourism. Where the appeal of special interest tourism generates the main motivation for tourism travel for niches, it mostly provides supporting elements to the rest of the tourist market engaging in activities related to mass tourism (Olalı & Timur, 1988).

Where mass tourism has received the majority of criticism is sustainability. However, to propose special interest tourism is categorically sustainable and mass tourism is not would be a major overstatement. Mass tourism has endured, and its demand has sustained. Mass tourism is here to stay. However, cases of mass tourism development have more often than not proven to be less than sustainable for the destination.

In contrast, special interest tourism is generally, maybe even mistakenly, perceived to generate lower negative impacts than mass tourism does. However, it must be stated that a variety of factors and time determine the nature and severity of the impacts, including tourism planning and implementation, visitor numbers, degree of congestion, behavior of visitors, service providers (local), government, and local population. The form of tourism attraction and fragility of the cultural and natural environment must also be considered (ARTN, 2020; Stange & Brown, 2011).

Limits of acceptable change model is one planning tool that takes most of these factors into account (Stankey et al., 1984).

However, blaming any type of tourism product, or deeming one form of tourism development absolutely safe, would be inherently wrong. Sustainability of tourism development depends on time and numerous factors and is largely case dependent. In theory, a well-planned and managed development of mass tourism might be less intrusive than one of special interest. However, experience mostly suggests otherwise.

Where special interest offers the highest promise is the ease of congestion through product diversification. Where mass tourism tends to create crowding in certain locations and times, special interest tourism simply does not, due to its very nature of smaller scale.

Such discussions of the effects of overcrowding and the resulting social movement have reached their pinnacle in overtourism (Selby, 2016). In certain cases of mass tourism, the local people may begin questioning their right of ownership of their usual place of residence and the permanent, existential meaning of place. In opposition, the visitor, as the outsider, only appreciates the destination as a place of recreational and temporary significance (Kianicka et al., 2006). This discrepancy may result in cases of increased irritation (Doxey, 1975) usually manifesting themselves at later stages in the product life cycle of the destination, where social carrying capacity is far exceeded (Peeters et al., 2018). The locals grow resistant through feelings of resentment, disappointment, animosity, and hostility (Doğan, 2004). In cases including Barcelona, Mallorca, Trinidad and Tobago, Santorini, etc., visible protests against tourists and tourism are well documented (Milano et al., 2018; Peeters et al., 2018).

As noted above, blaming mass tourism categorically for overtourism would be misleading. Factors including the failure to plan, market, and coordinate tourism for the long term; educate visitors, establishments, and locals; and many more are at play here (Delgado, 2008). While effective zoning regulations may be useful in limiting tourist activity in open air recreation areas (Dowling, 1993), organizing tours and groups of visitors effectively should prevent overexposure of locals to visitors and cases of overtourism, where too much of a good thing turns sour. To top it off, losing the right of ownership usually associated by overtourism is usually exacerbated by the "hordes" or "occupying forces" of visitors' desire to "infiltrate" back stages and the resulting shrinkage of locals' breathing space (Delgado, 2008; Peeters et al., 2018). The desire to penetrate and actively observe back stages, however, is usually attributable to search of authenticity and special interest tourism, and here, the swarming of unorganized individual tourists is more detrimental to the sustainability of the destination than organized mass tourists.

Where special interest tourism has the absolute advantage over mass tourism is the ability to create a tourist experience that may be deeply personal, elevating, and transformative, therefore more memorable. Since the tourist is motivated to pursue activities directly related to a personal and specifically defined area of interest, this type of tourism offers much higher personal appeal and satisfaction, through the creation of memorable experiences (Pine & Gilmore, 1999). Special interest tourism usually requires the active participation of the visitor in the experience creation process (Sims, 2009). The special interest tourist actively performs to improve on their own personal area of interest and fulfills higher, cultural needs like self-actualization. These instances of creative tourism through cocreation, copresence, and coperformance relate to the individual within a small group of people sharing the same specialist area of interest on a deeper personal sense, elevating the sense of self, in contrast to the group in mass tourism moving together as a singular entity (Hamilton & Alexander, 2013). The creativity factor in special interest tourism usually implies active participation, creation of authentic experiences, and development of (self) potential and skill (Tan et al., 2013). Here, the visitor is no longer a leisurely spectator of a staged cultural appearance, but actively involving, creating, and performing (Richards & Wilson, 2006) in the momentary manifestation of common reality and a curator of authenticity (Cohen, 1988; Giovanardi et al., 2014).

As the special interest tourist delves into these engaging activities in a tourism setting, they effectively engage in the natural and cultural environment of the destination. The effects of this engagement are twofold. First, the visitor builds an effectual and increased awareness of self, and the new cultural center, and the place, and ultimately the presence of the self therein. This most likely leads to the appreciation of the new culture and a more favorable basis of positive cultural interaction (Thomas, 2010). Second, the increased awareness to environmental stimuli creates an elevated sense of place (Tuan, 1974), defined as the meaning, feeling, and emotion attributed to places (Stedman, 2003). Active engagement in the environment and the mutually beneficial cultural interaction forms a favorable basis for the conveyance of meaning. When factors including active involvement in the environment and the meaning and experience creation processes are considered, this heightened sense of place leads to permanent, personal, transformative... experiences associated with the destination (Kim & Fesenmaier, 2015), repeat and referral visits and competitive advantage. Sense of place implies increased awareness of the environment and its features that distinguish it from other places (i.e., competitors) (Tuan, 1980).

As a result, cases of special interest tourism are more likely to engage the visitor on a much deeper level, offering benefits of active participation, creative experiences, self-improvement, and a heightened sense of self and place through novel types of tourist attraction. These cases usually provide solid grounds for positive cultural interaction and transfer of meaning, contributing to peace. Special interest tourism is also perceived to imply tourism activities that are less intrusive to the natural and cultural environment of the destination. Through product differentiation, special interest tourism may help in tourism congestion and offer competitive advantage.

Limitations of Special Interest Tourism

The very nature of special interest tourism is its own limitation: scale. The notion of special interest inherently indicates smaller groups of individuals. While expenditure per person tends to be higher than in mass tourism, total income generated by such tours leads to doubts over their feasibility. Special interest tour planning requires travel intermediaries to plan attractions, activities, and destinations from scratch, which increases the costs and labor hours. Service providers must also keep up with changing trends and adapt to new environments, products, and emerging types of special interest tourism to create engaging offers for novel types of tourism product (Rittichainuwat, 2018).

Types of products associated with special interest are specialist, tailor-made, single item products, unsuitable for mass production, which greatly limit their commercial longevity. While a special interest product that offers supporting motivation to the general public may become appealing to a wider market, it will undoubtedly lose its niche identity. This fact also necessitates careful selection of the audience, channels, and method of the marketing communication (Rittichainuwat, 2018; Séraphin et al., 2019).

While cases of special interest tourism are often perceived to be less detrimental, and more sustainable for the destination, a special interest itself may not always be sustainable in the long run, as the demand shifts away from it. This further raises the questionability of its commercial rationale, considering the investment and commitment in the form of itinerary development, planning, and research. Service providers are also more dependent on local communities for the limited information instead of the wealth of experience and established commercial links available for cases of mass tourism. Even before such considerations, service providers and local governments alike need to define special interest tourism in terms of trip quality and quantity, travel purposes, and the economic and behavioral effects of special interest tourism. These should also clearly discourage unethical motivations as well as activities potentially dangerous for human or animal safety (Wen & Wu, 2020). The latter bears importance in adventure tourism, especially in situations of high risk and high attraction (Trauer, 2006).

Lastly, once the conveyance of meaning is considered, cases of elevated awareness and a keen search of meaning may lead to the separation of sense from reality. Such instances may create museification of the destination and the shrinification of the mundane (Ruy & Almeida, 2020). This negates the need for destinations to be alive.

Conclusion

This chapter has, critically, analyzed the notion of special interest tourism in an attempt to reach comparative benefits and limitations. Therefore, it is inevitable to compare and contrast it against what it offers an alternative to, namely mass tourism. It is however vital to note that this dichotomy may not always be accurate, but it serves the purpose.

It has been shown in the literature that, to pursue tourism activities based on special interest, the visitor needs to take extra steps since services for mass tourism are generally all too readily available. However, while the latter attempts to appeal to (virtually) everyone, it does so on a fundamentally basic level, the lowest common denominator. So, special interest tourism appeals to a singular niche market with a specifically defined interest but satisfies the visitor on a much, much higher level. This necessitates or ensures the active participation of the visitor in the experience creation process, who, in return, improves oneself in that defined interest and cocreates a self-improving/self-realizing/transformative tourism experience. Conversely, the service providers also should do their homework to facilitate this experience, which is tailor-made, novel, unsuitable for standardization, and therefore pushing the cost per capita.

Special interest may offer promises of alleviating threats including congestion and loss of tourist attraction, readily associated with mass tourism; it is not its replacement. Mass tourism is here to stay. Special interest tourism, however, will continue to offer alternatives on a smaller scale. Types of tourism product that generally appeal to special interest, such as mycotourism, recluse tourism, battlefield tourism, craft beer tourism, shipwreck tourism, suicide tourism, etc., have been rising to prominence; new ones are emerging, and it seems they will continue to multiply and diversify.

References

ARTN. (2020). *The guide to best practice destination management.* Knowledge Transfer Services Pty Ltd for the Australian Regional Tourism Network.

Ashworth, G., & Hartmann, R. (2005). *Horror and human tragedy revisited: The management of sites of atrocities for tourism.* Cognizant Communication Corporation.

Cohen, E. (1972). Toward a sociology of international tourism. *Social Research, 39*(1), 164–182. http://www.jstor.org/stable/40970087

Cohen, E. (1979a). Rethinking the sociology of tourism. *Annals of Tourism Research, 6*(1), 18–35.

Cohen, E. (1979b). A phenomenology of tourist experience. *Sociology, 13*(2), 179–201.

Cohen, E. (1988). Authenticity and commoditization in tourism. *Annals of Tourism Research, 15,* 371–386.

Crompton, J. L. (1979). Motivations for pleasure vacation. *Annals of Tourism Research, 6*(4), 408–424. https://doi.org/10.1016/0160-7383(79)90004-5

Dann, G. (1977). Anomie, ego-enhancement and tourism. *Annals of Tourism Research, 4,* 184–194. https://doi.org/10.1016/0160-7383(77)90037-8

Delgado, M. (2008). *Turistofobia.* El Pais. https://elpais.com/diario/2008/07/12/catalunya/1215824840_850215.html

Doğan, H. Z. (2004). *Turizmin Sosyo-Kültürel Temelleri (Socio-cultural foundations of tourism)* (2nd ed.). Detay Yayıncılık.

Dowling, R. (1993). An environmentally-based planning model for regional tourism development. *Journal of Sustainable Tourism, 1*(1), 17–37.

Doxey, G. (1975). A causation theory of visitor-resident irritants: Methodology and research inferences in the impact of tourism. In *Sixth annual conference proceedings of the travel research association.* San Diego.

Dumazedier, J. (1974). *Sociology of leisure.* Elsevier Scientific Publishing Company.

Eurostat. (1998). *Community methodology on tourism statistics.* European Commission.

Fischler, C. (1988). Food, self and identity. *Social Science Information*, *27*(2), 275–292. https://doi.org/10.1177/053901888027002005

Giovanardi, M., Lucarelli, A., & Decosta, P. L. (2014). Co-performing tourism places: The "Pink Night" festival. *Annals of Tourism Research*, *44*, 102–115.

Goeldner, C. R., & Ritchie, J. B. (2009). *Tourism, principles, practices, philosophies* (11th ed.). John Wiley & Sons.

Gray, H. P. (1970). *International travel-international trade*. Heath Lexington.

Hamilton, K., & Alexander, M. (2013). Organic community tourism: A cocreated approach. *Annals of Tourism Research*, *42*, 169–190. https://doi.org/10.1016/j.annals.2013.01.015

İçöz, O. (2005). *Turizm Ekonomisi (Tourism economy)* (3rd ed.). Turhan Kitabevi.

İçöz, O. (Ed.). (2007). *Genel Turizm – Turizmde Temel Kavramlar ve İlkeler (General tourism – Basic concepts and principles in tourism)*. Turhan Kitabevi.

Iso-ahola, S. (1982). Toward a social psychological theory of tourism motivation: A rejoinder. *Annals of Tourism Research*, *9*, 256–262. https://doi.org/10.1016/0160-7383(82)90049-4

Kianicka, S., Buchecker, M., Hunziker, M., & Müller-Böker, U. (2006). Locals' and tourists' sense of place: A case study of a Swiss alpine village. *Mountain Research and Development*, *26*, 55–63.

Kim, J. J., & Fesenmaier, D. R. (2015). Designing tourism places: Understanding the tourism experience through our senses. In *2015 TTRA annual conference Portland, Oregon: Tourism travel and research association: Advancing tourism research globally*.

Kruja, D., & Gjyrezi, A. (2011). The special interest tourism development and the small regions. *Turizam*, *15*(2), 77–89. https://doi.org/10.5937/Turizam1102077K

Lickorish, L., & Jenkins, C. L. (1999). *An introduction to tourism*. Butterworth-Heinemann.

MacCannell, D. (1973). Staged authenticity: Arrangements of social space in tourist settings. *American Journal of Sociology*, *79*(3), 589–603.

Maslow, A. H. (1943). A theory of human motivation. *Psychological Review*, *50*(4), 370–396. https://doi.org/10.1037/h0054346

Maslow, A. H. (1954). *Motivation and personality*. Harper & Row Publishers.

Milano, C., Cheer, J., & Novelli, M. (2018). Overtourism: A growing global problem. *The Conversation*. https://theconversation.com/overtourism-a-growing-global-problem-100029

Olalı, H. (1990). *Turizm Politikası ve Planlaması (Tourism policy and planning)*. İstanbul.

Olalı, H., & Timur, A. (1988). *Turizm Ekonomisi (Tourism economy)*. Ofis Ticaret Matbaacılık.

Peeters, P., Gössling, S., Klijs, J., Milano, C., Novelli, M., Dijkmans, C., Eijgelaar, E., Hartman, S., Heslinga, J., Isaac, R., Mitas, O., Moretti, S., Nawijn, J., Papp, B., & Postma, A. (2018). *Research for TRAN Committee – Overtourism: Impact and possible policy responses*. European Parliament, Policy Department for Structural and Cohesion Policies.

Pine, B., & Gilmore, J. (1999). *The experience economy – Work is theatre and every business a stage*. Harvard Business School Press.

Plog, S. C. (1974). Why destination areas rise and fall in popularity. *Cornell Hotel and Restaurant Administration Quarterly, 14*(4), 55–58. https://doi.org/10.1177/001088047401400409

Plog, S. (2001). Why destination areas rise and fall in popularity. *Cornell Hotel and Restaurant Administration Quarterly, 42*(3), 13–24.

Richards, G., & Wilson, J. (2006). Developing creativity in tourist experiences: A solution to the serial reproduction of culture? *Tourism Management, 27*, 1209–1223.

Rittichainuwat, B. N. (2018). *Special interest tourism* (3rd ed.). Cambridge Scholars Publishing.

Ruy, A. T., & Almeida, R. H. (2020). Territorial museification: Fundamentals of a concept. *City, History and Culture, 22.* https://doi.org/10.22296/2317-1529.rbeur.202026en

Selby, M. (2016). Editorial – Views from the editorial advisory board of the International Journal of Tourism Cities. *International Journal of Tourism Cities, 2*(4), 279. https://doi.org/10.1108/IJTC-10-2016-0041

Séraphin, H., Zaman, M., Olver, S., Bourliataux-Lajoinie, S., & Dosquet, F. (2019). Destination branding and overtourism. *Journal of Hospitality and Tourism Management, 38*, 1–4. https://doi.org/10.1016/j.jhtm.2018.11.003

Sims, R. (2009). Food, place and authenticity: Local food and the sustainable tourism experience. *Journal of Sustainable Tourism, 17*(3).

Stange, J., & Brown, D. (2011). *Tourism destination management – Achieving sustainable and competitive results. Sustainable tourism: International cooperation for development.* International Institute for Tourism Studies The George Washington University. https://www.usaid.gov/sites/default/files/documents/2151/DMOworkbook_130318.pdf

Stankey, G. H., McCool, S. F., & Stokes, G. L. (1984). Limits of acceptable change: A new framework for managing the Bob Marshall wilderness complex. *Western Wildlands, 10*(3), 33–37.

Stebbins, R. (1996). Cultural tourism as serious leisure. *Annals of Tourism Research, 23*, 948–950.

Stedman, R. C. (2003). Is it really just a social construction? The contribution of the physical environment to sense of place. *Society and Natural Resources, 16*(8), 671–685.

Steiner, C. J., & Reisinger, Y. (2006). Understanding existential authenticity. *Annals of Tourism Research, 33*(2), 299–318. https://doi.org/10.1016/j.annals.2005.08.002

Tan, S.-K., Kung, S.-F., & Luh, D.-B. (2013). A model of "Creative Experience" in creative tourism. *Annals of Tourism Research, 41*, 153–174. https://doi.org/10.1016/j.annals.2012.12.002

Thomas, A. (2010). The self, the other, the intercultural. In A. Thomas, E.-U. Kinast, & S. Schroll-Machl (Eds.), *Handbook of intercultural communication and cooperation volume 1: Basics and areas of application* (pp. 39–53). Vandenhoeck & Ruprecht GmbH & Co. KG. Translated by C. Weston-Horsmann.

Trauer, B. (2006). Conceptualizing special interest tourism-frameworks for analysis. *Tourism Management, 27*(2), 183–200. https://doi.org/10.1016/j.tourman.2004.10.004

Tuan, Y. (1974). *Topophilia: A study of environmental perception, attitudes and values.* Prentice-Hall.

Tuan, Y. (1980). Rootedness versus sense of place. *Landscape, 24*(1), 3–8.

UNWTO. (2010). *International recommendations for tourism statistics 2008*. United Nations Department of Economic and Social Affairs. ISBN 978-92-1-161521-0.

Weiler, B., & Hall, C. M. (1992). *Special interest tourism*. Wiley.

Wen, J., & Wu, M.-Y. (2020). How special is special interest tourism – And how special are special interest tourists? A perspective article in a Chinese context. *Current Issues in Tourism, 23*(16), 1968–1972. https://doi.org/10.1080/13683500.2020.1750575

Section 2

Battlefield Tourism Setting the Context

Introduction

Tourism and war seem antithetical at first glance. Tourism is often considered one of the world's salient industries in the contemporary age. The modern understanding of tourism requires travel away and return to a home. Therefore, no tourism movement will be available once society's habit of living around a home is established (Beech & Chadwick, 2006, p. 3).

The struggle for survival is more advantageous for the collective than the individual. Therefore, establishing a society and home may be the nature of human beings. However, as in society, war was also a common aspect of man. Numerous wars existed in the course of history. War for sovereignty, religion, culture, and other themes were common.

At the same time, wars in history have affected today's society. Present-day society is the cause of the current wars. This cycle may be a prominent feature of the man. Current developments confirm that there is no evidence that the cycle will end.

Although they contrast, the birth of modern tourism and modern warfare seems parallel. Social, political, economic, and technological aspects contribute to developing both phenomena. There is no doubt that the appearance of the state and its great armies enhanced the severity of the war. So, as the number of soldiers, weapons, and their impacts rise, it influences more people and societies. Historic bloody battlefields once had a chance to become tourist attractions with accompanying narratives. The growing number of tourists and their needs create requirements for different tourism forms. Battlefield tourism is among these different forms of tourism.

The following two chapters in this section dwell on the battlefield tourism phenomenon. The first chapter discusses the meaning and definition of battlefield tourism, and the second chapter discusses the historical background of battlefield tourism. In comparison, the first chapter tries to define battlefield tourism by investigating its components, and the second chapter investigates the historical background of the phenomenon.

References

Beech, J., & Chadwick, S. (2006). Introduction: The unique evolution of tourism as "business". In J. Beech & S. Chadwick (Eds.), *The business of tourism management* (pp. 3–18). Pearson.

Chapter 3

The Meaning and Definition of Battlefield Tourism: What Is Battlefield Tourism?

Onur Akbulut

Muğla Sıtkı Koçman University, Türkiye

> "Arma virumque cano"
>> opening line of Vergil's Aeneid (ca. BCE 17/1899, p. 1).

Abstract

War is one of the worst characteristics of human nature. Wars over territory, religion, and governance were and are always present through history. War and tourism seem dissonant at first glance. However, the post effects of war enable its components, such as battlefields and artefacts, to become tourist attractions. People share the impetus to visit war attractions such as battlefields, military museums, cemeteries, memorials, and other war-related sites. There is a supply for this type of tourism in exchange for the demand. This type of tourism is referred to in the literature as battlefield tourism. The meaning and definition of battlefield tourism are the main aim of this chapter. What is battlefield tourism? What are the components of battlefield tourism? How can battlefield tourism be defined? These are the primary questions this study tries to address.

Keywords: War and tourism; battlefield tourism; war tourism; war tourism attractions; warfare tourism; social memory

Introduction

War, Zhanzeng, Yuddh, Guerra, Harb, Savaş, Krieg, Bellum, etc., every nation and every society have a phrase describing men's everlasting phenomenon. From Acheulean Handaxes (1.7 mya) to Greek Hoplite Phalanx (700 BCE) and from Blitzkrieg (1939–1945) to Hiroshima and Nagasaki atomic bombs (1945), and

Battlefield Tourism, 35–74

Copyright © 2024 Onur Akbulut

Published under exclusive licence by Emerald Publishing Limited

doi:10.1108/978-1-83909-990-820241005

more recently from cyber warfare to armed land, sea, and air drones, the history of war and military tactics has been a practice of effective and deadly battlefield technology adaption, reinvention, and progression (Smithsonian Institution, 2011). According to the latest figures from Stockholm International Peace Research Institute's (SIPRI) (2023) Military Expenditure Database, the world's annual military spending is 2,240 billion dollars in 2022. This high military and arms spending record shows how serious the arms race has become in a 100 trillion dollar (GDP) (World Bank, 2023) world economy with a 2% ratio. Moreover, the 21st century will be the age of "weapons based on new principles," and these include: "directed energy weapons," "electromagnetic weapons," "nonlethal weapons," "geophysical weapons," "radiological weapons," and "genetic weapons" (Tsukanov, 2023, p. 23). No matter the world order, unipolar or multipolar, wars, and conflicts are extreme characteristics of human civilization. With these figures at hand, it is not wrong to say that the world is dangerous. This study tries to focus on facts instead of truths. However, war, as one of the central concepts of this section, is open to multiple truths.

In the law of the jungle, killing one another is a regular cause of the struggle for survival. Aristotle said that "art was the imitation of nature" (Blumenberg, 2000, p. 17). There were numerous expressions of this terrible, evil art of humanity, as seen in Sun Tzu's (ca. BCE 600/2005) The Art of War. There have been many wars and battles throughout human history, similar to the instances from now. The history of warfare includes battles, campaigns, conquests, and armed confrontations. Human history is full of wars. Conflicts over territory, religion, and governance escalated into wars and battles. Greek–Persian Wars (490–448 BCE), Peloponnesian War (431–404 BCE), Punic Wars (264–146 BCE), Roman Civil Wars (49–31 BCE), Byzantine–Seljuk Wars (1064–1076), the Crusades (1095–1272), Mongol Conquests (1206–1405), Hundred Years' War (1337–1453), Onin War (1467–1477), the Italian Wars (1494–1544), Wars of Japanese Unification (1560–1603), 80 Years' War (1568–1648), War of the Three Kingdoms (1642–1651), the 30 Years' War (1618–1648), the Great Northern War (1700–1721), the 7 Years' War (1756–1763), American Revolutionary War (1792–1802), the Napoleonic Wars (1803–1815), Crimean War (1853–1856), the Indian Mutiny (1857–1858), American Civil War (1861–1865), Franco–Prussian War (1870–1871), Taiping Rebellion (1850–1864), Boer Wars (1880–1902), Balkan Wars (1912–1913), World War I (1914–1918), Russian Civil War (1918–19121), Spanish Civil War (1936–1939), World War II (1939–1945), Chinese Civil War (1945–1949), Korean War (1950–1953), French Indochina War (1946–1954), Arab–Israel Wars (1948–1973), Vietnam War (1961–1975), Iran–Iraq War (1980–1988), Gulf Wars (1990–1991, 2003), Afghanistan War (2001–2021) are just some of the major wars in the historical timeline (Smithsonian Institution, 2011, p. 480).

At the time of writing, the Russia–Ukraine War, which escalated on February 24, 2022, has been ongoing for over a year. The Gaza–Israel conflict has the potential to turn into a wider regional war. Likewise, the dispute between China and Taiwan through "the One China" concept may become a large-scale war. Moreover, tensions on the Korean peninsula are intense. Present-day popular media outlets are full of analyses that examine current wars (as in Lendon's (2023) analysis of weapons in the Russia–Ukraine war). Modern trench warfare was ferociously taking place at a 1000 km long front line in the Donbass region of Russia and Ukraine, 109 years after the brutal trench battle on the Western Front. Jens Stoltenberg (2023), the secretary general of North Atlantic Treaty Organization (NATO), stated about the Russia–Ukraine War that "this is now a war of attrition, which is a battle of logistics. This is about, you know, getting the supplies, the ammunition, and the fuel to the frontline to the soldiers. The current rate of consumption compared to the current rate of production of ammunition is not sustainable. Therefore, we need to ramp up production." At the same time, Finland's accession to NATO was accepted by organization members as the 31st member, doubling the border of alliance with Russia (John, 2023). In response, Russia deployed tactical nuclear weapons to Belarus (Gregory, 2023). Kremlin spokesman Dimitri Peskov (2023) stressed Russia would do everything to ensure its security after Finland acceded to NATO. The recent developments in a short time frame signify how the phenomenon of war is still on the agenda. A small snapshot from major media outlets shows that war is always present for humankind.

As recent global events have shown, war has always been dirty. Objectives are simple to define, but results are more challenging to manage. Time and history are characterized by the periods before, during, and after conflicts, in which during war bad luck and bad generalship play essential roles (Chamberlain, 2001, p. 175; Smith, 1996). Indeed, "a battlefield where thousands died is not necessarily a good place, but it is often an important one" (Thompson, 2004, as cited in Stone, 2012, p. 1566).

At first glance, war and tourism seem incompatible. Nonetheless, wars induce "promotional, emotional, military and political tourism" (Smith, 1998, p. 202). Unsurprisingly, war has been a constant pattern throughout history, making it a distinctly human institution. It is noteworthy that war preparation uses many national resources, even in the poorest nations. Despite the agony it causes, it still happens. What continues to attract tourists and draw them to the numerous battlefield sites is the inevitable nature of conflict and the desire that such an institution never existed (Prideaux, 2007, p. 26).

Total war has been the norm since the turn of the 20th century. More military and civilian people are now directly impacted by armed conflict than ever before (Watson, 2001, p. 181). "Shall not be repeated" is written on the prominent memorial at the Hiroshima site of the first atomic explosion (Nishino, 2017, p. 444). Similarly, the Terrorhaza in Budapest lives "to research, document, educate and ensure remembrance of this Holocaust" (Williams, 2008, p. 131 as cited in Wight, 2009, p. 131). In addition, many site owners contend that such sites assist in preventing future atrocities by increasing knowledge of past horrors among present and future generations (Schofield, 2003). Battlefield tourism may educate people about the "realities of war" and is valid for civilian and military audiences (Melvin, 2005, p. 75). Alternatively, will there be a transformation from a dark heritage to a touristic commodity due to current wars, similar to Podoshen and Hunt's (2011, p. 1336) observation of the former death camp Auschwitz as the "Industry of Auschwitz" or "Auschwitz-land"

(Stone, 2009, p. 58)? Is education the primary purpose of battlefield tourism? Or is it about the commodities and their consumption? Or entertainment? Or education? Or edutainment? Due to its intense and heavy background, there is no doubt that the interrelations between war and tourism are an essential study area. Moreover, the new millennium will undoubtedly involve tourism and war (Smith, 1998, p. 220).

The Vietnam War Memorial in Washington as well as historical battlefields like ancient Troy, Culloden, Waterloo, Gettysburg, Western Front, Gallipoli, Pearl Harbor, and Omaha Beach are visited by tourists (Hall et al., 2011, pp. 419–420; Stone, 2009, p. 56). The battle altered the topography of the areas it was fought over and gave tourists a new selection of attractions to see (Lloyd, 1998, p. 95). Many battlefields, cemeteries, prisons, and other wartime artefacts will eventually be saved, restored, redeveloped, or sometimes neglected and allowed to deteriorate (Smith, 2007, p. 103). The heritage is "homogenized" by "global popularity" (Lowenthal, 1998, p. 23).

History and heritage tourism are an important part of the tourism. The "martyrdom" and "heroic" sacrifice are the essential elements of "collective heritage" (Lowenthal, 1998, p. 77). War is one of the most famous historical tourism resources. It is possible to turn tales of military heroes, battlefields, fortifications, weaponry, and many other details, events, and deeds into tourist attractions (Kostiainen, 2001, p. 1074). Visitors have been drawn to areas connected with death and destruction, conflict, weaponry, and artefacts related to war, bravery, and glory for thousands of years (Baldwin & Sharpley, 2009; Dewar, 2008, p. 1046; Kang et al., 2012).

The rapidly expanding subsector of the tourism industry is battlefield tourism (Hall et al., 2011, p. 420; Prideaux, 2007, p. 17). Travelers were drawn to the battlefields by a mostly "imaginary" landscape, and these specific locations attract people because of their associations, not the sites (Lloyd, 1998, p. 112). Many visit battlefields to commemorate important dates and events (Hall et al., 2010, p. 246). Given how profoundly ingrained conflict is in human behavior, war-related tourist attractions may rank as one of the top tourism subcategories (Smith, 1996). Research has shown that various people and the functions currently connected with them have made battlefields, memorials, and commemorations essential destinations for many tourists (Winter, 2018, p. 212).

Tourism studies are not "integrated"; they combine a variety of academic viewpoints from different academic fields, including politics, ecology, sociology, architecture, psychology, physics, and more. Additionally, with its massive infrastructure, tourism is a global phenomenon that impacts society, culture, politics, and, most crucially, the economy (Gyr, 2010, p. 1). Similarly, war is a recurring aspect of human society connected to numerous academic fields. The relationship between humanity and violence is also "complex and paradoxical." War is the topic that garners the most attention and interest since peace and love are the perfect terms to achieve consensus on it (Malesevic, 2010, p. 2).

Leiper's (1990) tourism system serves as the backdrop for this study. This chapter will address a holistic understanding of battlefield tourism, specifically focused on tourism system theory. This section aims to review and define the battlefield tourism phenomenon. The work in this section began as early as the author became interested in battlefield tourism. From the start, the main focus here is to provide an understanding of battlefield tourism.

All arts and sciences must consider the whole rather than developing in a "fragmentary way." "All appertains to a single subject is a part of the area of investigation" (Aristotle, ca. 350 BCE/1999, p. 80). Following Aristotle's way of investigation, the meaning and definition of battlefield tourism are the primary tasks of this study. What is battlefield tourism? What are the components of battlefield tourism? How can battlefield tourism be defined? These are some questions that this chapter tries to answer. This is also crucial because one of the investigation's topics is tourism, and the other is war (and warfare).

Some Basic Concepts

Despite its horrors, Smith (1996, p. 248) writes that "the memorabilia of war, such as battlefields, cemeteries, monuments, museums, armaments, and historical re-enactments, probably constitute the largest single category of tourist attractions in the world." War is a crucial driving force behind tourism. Battlefield tourism and its heritage are a prized "tourism commodity" (Butler & Suntikul, 2013). The tourism experiences of war tourism attractions include monuments, cemeteries, museums, battlefields, tunnels, and memorials in the context of Vietnam War (Upton et al., 2018, p. 200). These tourism experiences are shared by many other battlefields. Therefore, some fundamental concepts must be considered before diving into battlefield tourism.

War

The dictionary.com (2023) defines war as "a conflict carried on by force of arms, as between nations or between parties within a nation; warfare, as by land, sea, or air." War could be categorized on many levels, such as urban against rural, religious against secular, center against periphery, and generational conflicts (Smith, 2007, p. 100). One crucial aspect of war is that it is primarily a collective effort with individual support. War is fundamental to the development of humanity. Humans have lived in groupings since the prehistoric eras; the order of villages, towns, societies, and nations has developed. Many theories are available regarding the interrelations between the state and war (Malesevic, 2010). In this process, war is always present. Marx's theory of social evolution proposes a five-stage model (primitive communism-slave society-feudalism-capitalism-communism) that transition was achieved through conflict and violence (Black, 2002, p. 71). All of these illuminating approaches underline the importance of war in world history. Although the investigation of the reasons for war is beyond the scope of this study, some basic arguments are considered. An excellent place to start is with Herodotus and Freud's classic instances of war. First to illustrate, the "historian of war" Herodotus offered the following famous exchange between Croesus, the wealthy King of Lydia, and Solon, writer, Athens statesman, legislator, and poet who was one of the seven sages of Greece (Dewald, 2011, pp. 53–54):

King Croesus:	"So, Solon, who is the happiest man in the world?" (King Croesus's expectation for a polite response may be "Why you are clearly, Croesus the magnificent!").
Solon:	"Tellus the Athenian. When you asked me about men and their affairs, you put your question to someone aware of how utterly jealous the divine is and how it is likely to confound us. Anyone who lives for a long time is bound to see and endure many things he would rather avoid. I place the limit of a man's life at seventy years. No two days bring events that are the same. Tellus was the lucky man because he was from a community on the right track. He had children and saw them grow up to be fine and upstanding, and all of them to have children who survived. And throughout his life, he was well off. But that is not all: Tellus also received a glorious death in battle at an advanced age, repulsing Eleusinian aggression against his city, so he received public honors where he fell in death."

War tourism, or battlefield tourism as it is widely referred to, is the topic of this book, and it needs a detailed examination. Furthermore, war plays an essential role in social memory because it contains some of the most challenging moments a society has faced throughout history. Therefore, before focusing on the phenomenon, it is vital to explore the causes of why human groups go to war and murder one another, as well as whether there is a connection between human nature and the causes of war. The second to illustrate is Freud's Why War? Letter to Einstein (Freud, 1932, pp. 1–7):

You begin with the relations between Might and Right, and this is assuredly the proper starting-point for our enquiry. But, for the term might, I would substitute a tougher and more telling word: violence. In right and violence we have today an obvious antinomy. It is easy to prove that one has evolved from the other...

Conflicts of interest between man and man are resolved, in principle, by recourse to violence. It is the same in the animal kingdom, from which man cannot claim exclusion; nevertheless men are also prone to conflicts of opinion, touching, on occasion, the loftiest peaks of abstract thought, which seem to call for settlement by quite another method. This refinement is, however, a late development.

To start with, brute force was the factor which, in small communities, decided points of ownership and the question of which man's will was to prevail. Very soon physical force was implemented, then replaced, by the use of various adjuncts; he proved the victor whose weapon was the better, or handled the more skilfully.

Now, for the first time, with the coming of weapons, superior brains began to oust brute force, but the object of the conflict remained the same: one party was to be constrained, by the injury done him or impairment of his strength, to retract a claim or a refusal. This end is most effectively gained when the opponent is definitively put out of action in other words, is killed.

This procedure has two advantages; the enemy cannot renew hostilities, and, secondly, his fate deters others from following his example. Moreover, the slaughter of a foe gratifies an instinctive craving a point to which we shall revert hereafter. However, another consideration may be set off against this will to kill: the possibility of using an enemy for servile tasks if his spirit be broken and his life spared. Here violence finds an outlet not in slaughter but in subjugation. Hence springs the practice of giving quarter; but the victor, having from now on to reckon with the craving for revenge that rankles in his victim, forfeits to some extent his personal security.

From violence to law

[...] We know that in the course of evolution this state of things was modified, a path was traced that led away from violence to law. But what was this path? Surely it issued from a single verity; that the superiority of one strong man can be overborne by an alliance of many weaklings, that l'union fait la force. Brute force is overcome by union, the allied might of scattered units makes good its right against the isolated giant.

Thus we may define "right" (i.e. law) as the might of a community. Yet it, too, is nothing else than violence, quick to attack whatever individual stands in its path, and it employs the selfsame methods, follows like ends, with but one difference; it is the communal, not individual, violence that has its way.

A distinctively human institution, war frequently defies reason but is invariably marked by paradox. The brutality and carnage of battle are frequently necessary for peace and harmony, with the ultimate sacrifice of the few necessary for the comfort and prosperity of the many (Prideaux, 2007, p. 17). As can be seen from the famous ancient dialogue above, Tellus was the luckiest man in the world because he fought for his city and died heroically defending his city. Therefore, he was the luckiest man; he might die, but his family, community, and the town would live. This story has some similarities with the ideas of Freud. The organization of human society as first cities and then nations occurred with might and right. Tellus was the luckiest man because his community would live and his community's right and might exist, although he lost his life while defending his city.

War plays a central role in the earliest literature, such as epic poems, Ergenekon (Turkish Mythology), Illiad and Odyssey (Greek Mythology), and Aeneid (Roman Mythology). The narrative of the war between good and evil was also a common theme among the religious texts. The Iliad and Odyssey, for instance, are frequently taught as historical works, complete with the knowledge that much of their substance may only partially be validated historically (Gordon, 2018, p. 96). However, the early narratives still play an essential role in the meaning of battles that occurred a 1,000 years ago. The ancient battlefields, such as Troy, Roman battlefields in Europe, and numerous sites in Japan, China, India, and elsewhere continue to attract visitors (Prideaux, 2007, p. 20).

If war is, in reality, at least partially a theatrical production or classical drama, this is hardly a 19th-century invention. How do the simulacra and virtualities of the 21st century vary from the romantic sagas and representations of past eras? Homer's Iliad and Odyssey instantly come to mind (Gordon, 2018, p. 95). The fact that these ancient epic poems also served as the first religious writings is exciting to notice. The epic history and poetry of Homer, Vergil, Tacitus, Caesar, and Livy, all of which praised battle, served as the foundation for the Grand Tour's structural itineraries, and as a result, the Grand Tour was somewhat influenced by war (Seaton, 1999, p. 132).

The tradition of interpreting wars mythically is a common understanding in the more recent era. According to Lloyd (1998, p. 89), it was said that World War I's Unknown Warrior was a "successor to Aeneas and Arthur" and was also known as the "Unknown Arthur." The Unknown Warrior occupies a more significant place at Westminster Abbey than the high-ranking commanders of World War I (Lowenthal, 1998, p. 81). Iles (2006, p. 162) pointed out that although World War I had been fought long before, the battlefields of the Western Front still hold a "Homeric" potential for tourism; nevertheless, to understand the battlefields, notable decoding is required. Therefore, war played an essential role in the lives and survival of collectivities. It also influences the establishment of society and culture. Likewise, wars are the primary attribute in social life, whose main feature is collective rather than individual. The most prominent feature of war is that it is "dangerous," "bloody," and "deadly." Therefore, all belligerents depend on the faction they serve together (Ryan, 2007a, p. 217). According to postmodern understanding, a more complicated and rewarding multidimensional view of war has replaced military history's broad but constrained "meta-narratives" (Miles, 2017, pp. 443–444).

For Aristotle (ca. 350 BCE/1999), man is a "zoon politikon." Moreover, "Man is in his actions and practice, as well as in his fictions, essentially a storytelling animal" (MacIntyre, 1981, p. 201). Therefore, the battlefield sites were colonized with the conflicts of nations, the collapse of mighty civilizations, the stories of fallen martyrs, and victory and defeat (Seaton, 1999, p. 132).

Battlefield

A battlefield is described as "a place where battle is fought" and "an area of conflict and disagreement" in the Britannica Dictionary (2023). A battlefield is defined as "the area of land over which a battle was fought, and significant related activities occurred" by the Historic Scotland Inventory of Historic Battlefields. A conflict between primarily or exclusively military troops with the intention of using fatal force against an opposing army is referred to as a battle (as cited in Miles, 2012, p. 59; Proos & Hattingh, 2019, p. 4). Not every war takes place on a field. The urban environment of Modern War is frequently distinguishing. One could assert that calling the numerous conflicts that have taken place "battle-fields" is a fair descriptor (Piekarz, 2007, p. 29).

The military prioritizes conflict; a "battle" is defined by its characteristics, such as its location, length of time, and scale (Dupuy, 1987 as cited in Winter, 2016, p. 243). For instance, the responsibility of legally choosing the names of the major conflicts was assigned to the British Battles Nomenclature Committee, which was founded in 1920. The official recognition of a conflict leads to its designation, naming, and location being honored by inclusion on monuments, use of regimental colors, and citation at ceremonies (Winter, 2016, p. 243). For Chronis (2005, p. 389), Gettysburg's historic battlefield may be defined as a storyscape. Storyscapes are commercial settings where the interplay between producers and customers shapes, negotiates, and transforms narratives. Battlefield preservation is known to significantly impact local economic development (Johnson & Sullivan, 1993).

Another example is the designation of historic Scottish battlefields. According to the Historic Environment of Scotland (2019, p. 7): "To be included on the inventory, a battlefield must be of national importance. To decide if a site is of national importance, we assess its: – associations with historical events or figures of national significance – physical remains or archaeological potential (or both), and – the wider battlefield landscape around where the battle took place and the interest and evidence in it. This may include vantage points, lines of sight, earthworks, camps, or burials. Also, a battlefield can only be included on the inventory if the area of the battle can be defined, with confidence, on a modern map." This designation process can be regarded as the authorization of authenticity (see MacCannell, 1976; Urry & Larsen, 2022, p. 11). Recent technological developments contribute to the investigations of conflict (or battlefield) archaeology. For instance, "drone mounted light detection and ranging (LIDAR)" and "very high-resolution simultaneous localisation and mapping (SLAM)" methods used for survey in the World War II battlefield of Bulge (Stichelbaut et al., 2023).

Because most people live on land, where most wars have been fought, most military battlefield tours and staff rides focus on land warfare at the tactical level

(Melvin, 2005, p. 75). For instance, the battlefield of Waterloo was traversed by civilian armies of visitors and antique collectors. Even though the war made Cape St. Vincent, Cape Trafalgar, and Aboukir Bay well-known, the effects of naval combat were swiftly swept away by the water (Sellars, 2005, p. 680).

Modern warfare has transformed due to new technologies that have changed the setting and nature of war. Historically, a geographical location where opposing troops clashed on land or in the sea served as a metaphor for the battlefield. The locations of wars expanded in the 20th century to include both the sea and the air (Prideaux, 2007, p. 20). Consequently, the battlefield becomes free of geography and is instead constrained by the geography of the enemy's location outside any given entity known as a state or country (Ryan, 2007b, p. 4).

The "battleless" battlefield, which in some ways accomplishes nearly the same result as a physical battle but without the damage that reflects the typical battlefield concept (for example, the Cold War), is one facet of war that is rarely explored. The "battleless" battlefield contains essential components like missile silos, military fortifications, military barracks, and tools that might be utilized to wage war. The concept of war has had to be expanded and redefined due to modern combat (Prideaux, 2007, pp. 20–21). Similarly, Ryan argues (2007c, p. 251), with time, the traditional concept of the battlefield starts to become questionable with an increasingly new type of warfare with new belligerents (for instance, the war against terrorism, drug wars, etc.).

Memorials and Cemeteries

Within the context of World War I, memorials were typically designed and built by people who had experienced the horror of war, bringing together personal, familial, and selected recollections (Clarke & Eastgate, 2011, p. 33). It is vital to consider the factors that led to the myth of the martyrs and the sanctification of battlegrounds; after the war, people needed to come to terms with their loss because it had been so severely affected by the conflict (Kavrecic, 2017, p. 148). The society enshrined its memories of the deceased in monuments to the missing and national cemeteries for "unknown soldiers," where they were most obviously expressed (Winter, 2015, p. 17).

Battles on the Western Front during the World War I's 1914–1918 campaign were fought over a 700 km trench line that extended from the Belgian coast across northern France to the Swiss border. Along these battle lines, several countries, people, and military organizations created memorials in the shape of cemeteries, stone monuments, and museums. In order to memorialize the conflict, events, including memorial walks, artistic exhibitions, community gatherings, re-enactments, and both modest and opulent official remembrance services, are held regularly each year. Many of the battlefields offer attractive surroundings and leisure activities like consuming food and wine in addition to the war memorials (Winter, 2012, p. 248). After World War I, there were several contexts for remembering the war, including memorials, rituals, and popular publications. Additionally, European and British society and culture were more resolute in their engagement with the war's memories (Lloyd, 1998, p. 3). When a nation chooses to commemorate the war by building and maintaining certain memorials and cemeteries, it does so to further its objectives (Clarke & Eastgate, 2011, p. 35).

American Civil War battlefields are another example. For instance, the terrain is another means of articulating the Gettysburg imagination on the Gettysburg battlefield. Through monuments, museums, structures, and artefacts, it is materially performed. The national park is dotted with about 1400 monuments and memorials, 400 cannons, and 400 carriages. These tangible reminders of the past serve more purposes than only serving as a memory of the past. Given that they are situated where soldiers stood throughout the battle, they are also topographical markers. The numerous artefacts shown in museums and maintained in private collections serve as additional physical witnesses to the battle (Chronis, 2012, p. 1805). As another example, in a study conducted in Turkiye, Akbulut and Ekin (2018, p. 407) found 140 monuments related to the wars of the Turkish nation in a historical timeline. Piekarz mentions (2007, p. 37) that "monuments" and, more recently, "facilities and centers of interpretation" assist in preventing the "memory slippage." As illustrated above, there were numerous memorials erected on other battlefields all around the world.

One of the main effects of war is the death of the soldiers. There is hardly any battlefield or war site that does not have a cemetery for the fallen. The industrial warfare of World War I resulted in severe losses for the combatants' soldiers. Due to the placement of national armies in specific sectors along the trench lines, military cemeteries, memorials, visitor centers, and museums were constructed to designate these areas as the distinct geographic locations where their soldiers had fought (Winter, 2018, p. 214). The British Commonwealth policy after 1915 was to have standard graves with headstones for all identified fallen soldiers. The standard graves do not show the difference between "rank," "social class," or "religion," and this same uniformity provides an "auratic poignancy" (Seaton, 2009, p. 88; Winter, 2018, p. 214). Instead of being trained soldiers, most were average citizens who had either volunteered or been drafted into the military. Everyone would be recognized equally after death regardless of their prewar social background or position (Winter, 2015, p. 17).

The construction of prominent monuments and other memorials, such as cemeteries, further commemorated battlegrounds and drew many pilgrims and tourists (Winter, 2016, p. 242). After World War I, cleaning up battlefields, establishing cemeteries, and resuming agriculture with the "peaceful and sanitized view of the war" were the main memorialization processes (Winter, 2009, p. 614). Like World War I, many other wars, like the American Civil War, have cemeteries for memorialization.

War Museums and Artefacts

Monuments, artefacts, and museum exhibits also serve to commemorate and remember wars. In specialist national museums or designated sections of national museums, nations frequently recall the war and its participants. Specialized National War Museums honor the memory of war in several countries, including Australia, the United Kingdom, South Korea, and others (Prideaux, 2007, p. 22). For instance, after the end of prolonged trench warfare, 10 million people died in World War I, and double that number suffered physical and mental injuries. Later, war museums were created to interpret stories, serve as repositories for artefacts and other wartime evidence, and honor those who had served (Winter, 2018, p. 211). New technologies like interactive museums such as In Flanders Fields Museum in Ieper (Ypres), Belgium, and digital investments related to the social memory of war (Winter, 2009) are changing the nature of battlefield tourism.

War objects can range from "small," like a bullet, to "intermediate," like a tank, to "large," like a whole battlefield. All share that they result from human effort rather than a natural process. Thus, the Western Front of World War I is just as much an artefact as a portable war souvenir, a V2 rocket from the World War II, the symbolic landscape of war memorials, or the "Cross" formed by the World Trade Center's remaining structural components (Saunders, 2000, as cited in Zhang & Crang, 2016, p. 424).

Social Memory

Social memory is the reconstruction of the past in the present context through the selection and articulation of information (Coser, 1992, p. 34). War memories endure for generations, but individual and violent patterns in crime and terrorism make this impossible. For instance, the meaning of "Trojan horse" has not changed (Smith, 1998, p. 205). According to Winter (2009, p. 618), social memories are changing according to the needs of generations, and therefore, new memorials for wars are built close to older ones.

Walter (2009, p. 46) argues that memory can include first generation (people individually experienced the event), second generation (relatives or friends of the individually experienced people), third generation, and later (memory becomes history for this generation). World War I altered the connections between personal and world history in ways that had never been witnessed before; "family history collided with world history" (J. Winter, 2006, p. 179). The battlefields are darker because first- and second-generation memories of the war are still fresh (Walter, 2009). Even though the war was highly personal and familial for many people, society shared these memories (Winter, 2016, p. 244).

As Stone (2012) observes, memories of those who have been murdered or of groups of the collective dead who pass away in tragedies can haunt society. For instance, the mass death and the construction of "memorials" and "cemeteries" on the central Western Front as the main front of the war support the creation of social memory within the context of belligerents. However, the central perspective for the social memory was Victor's account (Winter, 2009, pp. 609–610). In order to convey collective memory, national ideals, sorrow, and hopes of European society that the war so severely marked, war tourism also developed into a cultural and political movement (Capuzzo, 2020, p. 36).

More recently, the articulation of social memory has been extended through new mediums. The internet and computer use (smartphones, iPads, etc.) extended the information available to the public related to World War I. Moreover, social memory is an essential need for the new generation, and education and information contribute to social memory (Winter, 2009, p. 619). One method of passing down the memory of this event to future generations is by promoting and making tourist-friendly locations where World War I occurred (Capuzzo, 2020, p. 55). For Capuzzo (2020, p. 52), World War I battlefield tourism may provide an opportunity to contribute to the European identity. However, it is ironic that World War I and the World War II started in Europe.

Pilgrimage, Commemoration, and Remembrance

The 19th century has witnessed a change in commemoration. It changes from elite to popular and personal to collective (Lowenthal, 1998, p. 81). During that period, military cemeteries and battlefields became revered as sacred sites, sanctified by the fallen soldiers (Gatewood & Cameron, 2004, p. 193). Lowenthal (1998, p. 93) observes that "sacrifice sacralizes loss." People can engage with significant events in human history by visiting battlefields. Some visitors consider battlefields sacred places; therefore, battlefield tourism may serve the same purpose as a pilgrimage (Gatewood & Cameron, 2004, p. 194; Kuo et al., 2016, p. 106).

Visitors to battlefield memorials are more driven by a desire to honor and commemorate the fallen than by a curiosity about death (Brown, 2014). For instance, the Australian and New Zealand Army Corps (ANZAC) Day pilgrimage is not religious but a "secular pilgrimage" of national identity in which the nationhood myths are of utmost importance. Such pilgrimage is vital for domestic and international travel (Hall, 2002, p. 84). When literature is examined, pilgrimage and secular pilgrimage are common themes, and research is mainly focused on World War I battlefields.

World history is full of numerous wars; nonetheless, hardly any are chosen for remembrance. This election may be because the battlefields cause the memory of death, destruction, disgrace, anger, and despair (Gatewood & Cameron, 2004, p. 193). Winter (2009) states that each generation's war memories are articulated worldwide by creating memorials to honor and remember the death. Finding a suitable language and instrument to remember and commemorate horrifying historical events is the primary goal of displaying a nation's war history in museums, through memorials, and even in tourist attractions (Leopold, 2007, p. 49).

The disastrous battles of 1916, the massive numbers of dead, and their burial in individual rather than mass graves changed the nature of war remembrance and, subsequently, battlefield visitation (Winter, 2012, p. 248). The Western Front is both a landscape of remembering and historical resonance. The thousands of military cemeteries and memorials strewn throughout the fields and villages cannot fail to impress upon first-time visitors who may know nothing about the war's events or the fact that they are passing through a terrain marked by mass death. The sheer quantity and variety of monuments and memorials demonstrate how unusual the war was (Iles, 2008, p. 146). For Winter (2011a), combining national and family history with acts of remembrance is a crucial element of "national identity" within the scope of World War I battlefield tourism.

Following World War I, the surviving felt compelled to pay respect to, commemorate, and visit the graves of their heroes. Numerous tributes are still left at cemeteries and memorials 90 years after the war's end, including "wreaths, photos, silk poppies, field flowers, small flags, and messages in visitor books" (Winter, 2009, p. 612). The remembrance of World War I (1914–1918) in Europe gave rise to a distinctive type of war heritage tourism, aided by the introduction of many projects to celebrate the Centenary of the War's start (Tizzoni, 2016, p. 85). In the United Kingdom, the British government believes Western Front battlefield visits are the best approach to educating young people about the World War I's centenary (Pennel, 2018, p. 84). Tourism is one of the fundamental forces helping to remember World War I and reinvigorate family and national memories (Winter, 2012, p. 261). The battlefield tours teach the British experience of World War I to ensure the "next generation" has commemoration and remembrance activities (Pennel, 2018, p. 94). While remembrance remains a priority for battlefield tourists, education (rather than just the presentation of historical artefacts) has become more critical, and leisure experiences are regarded as an essential part of visits (Hall et al., 2010; Hyde & Harman, 2011; Miles, 2014).

There may be a war plan or not. Nonetheless, celebrations of victories, remembrance, and commemorations are planned (Getz, 2007, p. 108). The tourist industry, media, and private and public organizations support and organize the "global industry concerned with the commemoration of war" (McKenna, 2014, p. 151), for instance, during ANZAC Day, visitors to the battlefields where ANZAC forces fought for commemoration events (Hall et al., 2010, p. 246). History written by winners' heritage belongs to the defeated (Lowenthal, 1998, p. 96).

Thanatourism / Dark Tourism

Thanatourism refers to the combination of death and travel and is a subset of the more significant phenomena known as dark tourism (Upton et al., 2018, p. 198). The umbrella term for tourism associated with "death, atrocity, tragedy, or crime" is dark tourism. The late twentieth century was the origin of this form of tourism. In contrast, thanatourism is a type of tourism with "the motive of specific desire for encounters with death." The two concepts are closely linked and reviewed (Light, 2017, p. 277). "Thanatourism" (Seaton, 1996, 1999) and "dark tourism" (Foley & Lennon, 1996) have received increasing attention from researchers in recent years (Cohen, 2010, p. 193; Upton et al., 2018, p. 198). According to Stone (2012, p. 1565), in Western secular society, "death is sequestered behind medical and professional facades, yet extraordinary death is recreated for popular consumption; dark tourism mediates a potential social filter between life and death." Dark tourism contains the presentation or production (supply) and consumption (demand) of "real or commodified" sites of death and disaster (Foley & Lennon, 1996, p. 198).

In the context of battlefield tourism, thanatourism/dark tourism, as the related concepts, must be considered (Winter, 2012, p. 252). Dark tourism encompasses "tourist" identity or "heritage," tourism to battlefields and memorials that affected one's country or where one's relatives fought, and populations affected by significant tragedies; memorials may be "sites of memory" (Cohen, 2010, p. 203). The study of thanatourism/dark tourism strongly focuses on battlefield tourism. It focuses on well-known battlefields, cemeteries, and war attractions like Waterloo, Red Cliff, and Normandy (Chen & Tsai, 2019, p. 82). This approach takes battlefield tourism under the umbrella of thanatourism/dark tourism.

As Stone argues (2012, p. 1568), although battlefield tourism attractions are diverse, they are a "subset" of dark tourism sites. Is battlefield tourism a subset of dark tourism? For instance, the books *Battlefield Tourism* (Ryan, 2007d) and *Tourism and War* (Butler & Suntikul, 2013) avoid dark tourism or thanatourism as explanatory frameworks (Light, 2017, p. 279). According to the research of Miles (2014), "thanatopsis (interest upon death)" is a rare characteristic of battlefield visitors in British battlefields. Furthermore, visitors prefer to view the sites as heritage. However, for some authors, battlefield tourism attractions, though diverse, are a subset of tourist sites associated with death and suffering, and close links exist between war and tourism, particularly thanatourism, which concerns a desire to experience sites associated with death (Sharpley, 2009, p. 10; Stone, 2006; Winter, 2011b, p. 463).

Dark tourism sites can be categorized into shades of light and darkness, and battlefields belong to the dark end of the spectrum (Stone, 2006). However, for Baldwin and Sharpley (2009, p. 190), although battlefields are arguably one of the most visited thanatourist sites, few visitors to battlefields would happily regard themselves as "dark tourists" or "thanatourists." Different motivations exist among different visitors to the same site. Hence, distinct "shades of darkness" are available for the consumer behavior of the tourist (Sharpley, 2009, p. 17).

According to Sharpley's (2009, p. 12) "categorization of dark tourism," battlefields are among the "fields of fatality; areas/land commemorating death, fear, fame, or infamy" category. As for Seaton (1996, pp. 240–242), thanatourism or dark travel (Sharpley, 2009, p. 15) has five diverse tourism activities. Battlefield tourism may be included in "travel to see the sites of mass or individual deaths after they have occurred," "travel to internment sites of, and memorials to, the dead," "travel to view the material evidence or symbolic representations of death, in locations unconnected with their occurrence," and "travel for re-enactments or simulation of death."

There is a relationship between visits to Auschwitz, World War I battlefields, Culloden, etc., and interactions with their representations in media (Walter, 2009, p. 44). As Foley and Lenon noted (1996, p. 198), dark tourism is "positioned at the crossroads of" the history of brutal events and their representation in media. Whether brutal or not, these dark tourism destinations' "commercialization" and "exploitation" are crucial to understanding this area. Nevertheless, one crucial aspect is that the supply and demand of dark tourism create apparent "moral commentary," asking whether it is right to gain profit from death and suffering and validate the experience (Stone, 2009, pp. 59–60).

War and Tourism

In his bestseller book "Man's Search for Meaning," Holocaust survivor and Austrian psychiatrist Frankl (2009) wrote about his experiences in concentration camps. He witnessed what atrocities men can do to men. Prisoners lost their self-confidence as they fought for survival because of the imminent threat of death, hunger, and never-ending insults. Nevertheless, in these horrific conditions, Frankl found that he was free. Regardless of the horrors, he found he could determine how to think and react. As the subject of this book, tourism seems to have nothing to do with Frankl's unspeakable experiences; however, in his experiences as one of the victims of war, Frankl's experiences summarize what man can do to man. From Holocaust to Nagasaki and Hiroshima, the anteced-ences of wars are horrific.

Tourism is central to the cultural output and the evolutionary processes of culture (Chronis, 2005, p. 400). There is a common saying that "travel cultivates" (Reisen bildet), since it "broadens the horizon" or "the mind" (de Guevara, 2016, p. 63). At first glance, tourism looks contradictory to war. However, on the contrary, tourism's origins seem connected with the war (see Smith's (1998) ethnographic study for war and tourism relations in the American context). The assumption of the cessation of tourism during the war (Gordon, 1998, p. 616) greatly contrasts battlefield tourism when considering the inter-relationship between war and tourism.

The tourism industry's search for novel attractions and interest in visiting battlefields created a new type of tourism, "battlefield tourism" (Prideaux, 2007, p. 17). One of the elements of the economy of knowledge of a nation is battlefield heritage; the tourism experience includes that heritage as social constructions with ideologies. The "myths" of battlefield history (or, instead of history, heritage) with commemorative events place it to the attention of audiences (Graham, 2007 as cited in Wight, 2007, p. 117; Wight, 2007, p. 117).

Piekarz (2007, p. 155) categorizes war zones as "hot" and "cold." For him, regarding the passage of the timeline, battlefield tourism attractions have become "cold" while hostilities finish, the landscape recovers, and people return to normal. In contrast, "conflict zones" can be defined as "hot." The cliché of Wehrmacht soldiers carrying cameras and acting like naive tourists in Paris during the World War II (Shirer, 1941, p. 413 as cited in Gordon, 1998, p. 621) is an excellent example of wartime and/or hot battlefield tourism. Another example was the Spanish Civil War battlefield tourism, for it was an organization spon-sored by a hostile force during the war. Moreover, the tour combines battlefield and recreational tourism (Holguin, 2005, p. 1400).

A historic battlefield of 100 years ago can attract visitors. For instance, the site for the Battle of Naseby, which took place in 1645, attracted 10,000 visitors in 2008 (Evans, 2014, p. 17). Moreover, battlefield tourism, "hot" or "cold," as Zhang argues (2010, p. 401), has the potential to foster peace between enemies of the past and present.

Early Examples

The creation of "leisure facilities" by the Roman Empire provided its citizens with tourism opportunities. Likewise, the gladiator games and the Colosseum construction were created for tourism (Page, 2007, p. 30). Similarly, the evolution of pilgrimage in the Middle Ages became an international movement during the Crusades. "Patterns of consumption," "ideas about health," and "notions of aesthetics" stimulated modern tourism, which emerged after the middle of the eighteenth century (Zuelow, 2016, p. 9). Moreover, around 1840, mass travel, eagerness for travel, and the development of photography as a "tourist gaze" evolved into the main component of Western style modernity (Urry & Larsen, 2022, p. 14). The appearance of the tourist gaze was not unexpected during that period. However, the "Industrial Revolution," changed society's structure. This revolution may be the precedence of some significant developments in tourism. The dichotomy between tradition and the modern reflected the changing nature of tourism from elite pursuit to the movement of the masses. Although tourism has existed for centuries, it has turned into an "accessible product" for the "consumer-led leisure society" (Page, 2007, p. 29).

Dark tourism supply and demand have grown parallel to tourism development (Sharpley, 2009). During the French Revolutionary Wars, people visiting the Rhineland wrote about the war nearby (Gordon, 1998, p. 616). The rise of the economic wealth of the American and European bourgeois classes and the development of the transportation and tourism industry during the Belle Epoque contributed to tourism growth (Martinez, 2020, p. 207). In the years 1860–1914, tourism experienced a surge in expansion. Tourism patterns were nonetheless described as a "linear progression" in the range of travel for "pleasure." This development "shades" the battlefield tourist component of pilgrimage. Although it was uncommon for these excursions to be referred to as pilgrimages, battlefields like Waterloo were among the sites that drew many visitors before 1914 (Lloyd, 1998, p. 13). Battlefield tourism related to the Battle of Waterloo (1815), the American Civil War (1861–1865), and the Boer Wars (1880–1902) were one of the first examples of modern tourism consciousness. These battlefields served as attractions for developing the tourism industry. The Battlefield of Waterloo gained worldwide tourism status in Europe, received public attention during the war, and was often considered educational. Today, it is Belgium's second most crucial tourism attraction (Lloyd, 1998, pp. 19–20; Seaton, 1999, p. 130). The Battle of Waterloo in 1815 was the first "mega-attraction" and had a prominent place in "tourism generation" with the partnership between "warfare" and "sightseeing" (Holguin, 2005, p. 1402; Seaton, 1999, p. 132).

The individual nature of battlefield tourism requires freedom to visit cemeteries, bunkers, trenches, and other battlefield artefacts, and automobility as a hallmark puts this into practice (Akerman, 2016, p. 164). Thomas Cook also sold tourist packages, including "battlefield excursions" (Kavrecic, 2017, p. 144). Waterloo was amongst Europe's prominent battlefield tourism attractions; the visits there by coaches and, alternatively, trains were later added to automobiles by the beginning of the 21st century (Seaton, 1999).

Leisure purposes were at the forefront during the 19th century within tourism development. The wealthy tourists visited health, beach, and climate resorts to consume the tourist supply. At these sites, visitors could enjoy leisure time and were not troubled by fatal incidents (Kavrecic, 2017, p. 143). The mass casualties of World War I were a watershed moment in history, as the significant belligerents England, Germany, and France lost 4 million soldiers. All families and Europe's cultural history were impacted by World War I's tragically high death toll (Winter, 2011b). The mass destruction of World War I gave rise to a new market for the tourism industry: battlefield tourism. Nevertheless, it was regarded as "morally inappropriate" to profit off death and suffering. As a result, a more respectable mode of travel was established in connection with commemorative activities and memorial visits (Kavrecic, 2017, p. 143). After World War I, there was a growing number of pilgrims and battlefield tourists to the battlefields of the war. The nationalist tone of battlefield guides originated for commercial purposes came into use for battlefield tourists and pilgrims. Moreover, the famous Michelin guides signified the birth of cartography and tourism centered on automobiles, prioritizing independent exploration of the countryside and national patriotism with education (Akerman, 2016, p. 159).

"The war is relentless: it puts the alternative in a ruthless relief: either to perish or catch up with the advanced countries and outdistance them, too, in economic matter" (Lenin, 1917). The technological breakthroughs by the belligerents to win the World War II resulted in an international tourism movement after the war with freedom and utilizing air transport (Smith, 1998, p. 2). The linkage of tourism origin regions with leisure time and recreation and destination regions with attractions (Leiper, 1990; Pearce, 1989) contribute to the growth of international tourism.

Following Smith's (1998, p. 208) argument, the World Wars may justify the European and American-style mass tourism. In the 1970s and 1980s, as the European tourism industry matured, it began to diversify into specialized niche markets (Richards, 1996, p. 13). Moreover, there is an emergence of "alternative tourism (the pursuit of unusual destinations, experiences, and activities)" (Wight, 2009, p. 133). A new sort of tourist has emerged due to the new information and communicational channels, the increase in affluence and free time, the awareness of individual requirements, and its effects on changes in lifestyle and values (Gretzel et al., 2006, p. 9). Until recently, battlefield tourism was an international trend that was quickly developing (Hall et al., 2011, p. 420). Battlefield tourism is also a niche market within modern tourism's scope.

Conventional marketing knowledge distinguishes between production and consumption. The supply (production) side of tourism (the phases of the tourism product as production, promotion, etc.) and the demand (consumption) side of tourism (demand, motivation, experience, etc.) should be investigated more. However, a collaborative, constructive approach to production and consumption sites with stories attracts people who want to gaze at them; moreover, places associated with death, destruction, and war receive increased visitation (Chronis, 2005, p. 389; Chronis, 2008, p. 6). The end effect of this dialectic between the creation and consumption of the "experience" of battlefield tourism is frequently the safest, most carefully chosen, and sanitized history being offered to tourists (Wight, 2007, p. 111).

The following section is structured around two approaches (see a threefold example in dark tourism for Virgili et al., 2018): a demand-led understanding of battlefield tourism and a supply-led understanding of battlefield tourism.

Demand-led Understanding of Battlefield Tourism

Visitors to battlegrounds actively consume historical events and create meaning from various sources, including the government, ancestors, and families (Clark & McAuley, 2016). Demand for dark places is not just mere "voyeuristic sightseeing"; visitors to those places are "more critical and questioning" (Light, 2017, p. 283). Battlefield visits are "expressions of a particular hobby or passionate interest" (Seaton, 2000). Many various types of visitors are drawn to battlefields, from the simply curious who seek a new kind of holiday to historians, military enthusiasts, and people who wish to research their family history. Tens of thousands of schoolchildren from Britain also visit World War I battlefields due to National Curriculum requirements (Iles, 2008, p. 139).

Visitors to battlefields are engaged consumers of historical events and creators of meaning drawn from a variety of sources, including the government, ancestors, and families (Clark & McAuley, 2016, p. 1103). Tourism focused on recapturing the "meaning" of the war rather than just the sights that might be seen. Tourists were frequently drawn to battlefields not because they had a specific sight in mind but because the locations' names had emotional resonance (Lloyd, 1998, p. 112).

The battlefield tourism demand for World War I battlefields after the war ended was not created by marketing activities but by "curiosity, patriotism and, most importantly, loss" (Akerman, 2016, p. 160). Battlefields not only attracted "civilian audiences," they also attracted "military audiences" with the terms "battlefield tour," "staff ride," "staff tour," "staff reisen," "terrain walk," and "tactical exercise without troops" (TEWT) (Melvin, 2005, p. 66).

Visits to battlefields can take many forms, and to provide visitors with satisfying and meaningful experiences, it is essential to adequately identify the motivations for their visit (Winter, 2011a, p. 165). Depending on the expectations and attitudes of the tourists, a journey to war-related sites could take many different forms and be experienced in various ways. They might also have varied interpretations of the meanings of the sites they visit. Tourism, which is related to wars and conflicts, has expanded significantly during the past century (Kokkranikal et al., 2016, p. 2). Warfare as the "almost inexhaustible source of potential carnage" has long motivated tourism (Tunbridge & Ashworth, 1996, p. 94). Various factors impact tourists, and they visit battlefields for various reasons, regardless of the primary factor that pushes or pulls them to do so (Swarbrooke & Horner, 2007). The question of how to present war to tourists through a "multisensory experience" without making it "too real" is noteworthy (Schwenkel, 2006, p. 9).

For some authors, battlefield tourists are not thanatourists, nor are they motivated by thanatouristic reasons instead; they are visiting a site associated with death (Slade, 2003, p. 781). Pilgrimage (Hannaford, 2001; Hyde & Harman, 2011), commemoration (Hall et al., 2011), desire to connect with history and/or interest in history (Bigley et al., 2010; Kang et al., 2012; Kokkranikal et al., 2016; Winter, 2009), knowledge seeking (Henderson, 2000, p. 270), familial connections (Dunkley et al., 2011), and national identity (Cheal & Griffin, 2013) are just some of the motives identified in the literature. As Iles (2006, p. 176) puts forward, the tourist on the battlefield asks the question, "What am I trying to understand here?" instead of "What am I looking at." "Interpretation" and "images" design with the "cultural significance" of the battlefields are the decisive elements of the visitor experience (Ryan, 2007b, p. 10).

Battlefield tourism is an essential study area because it defines people's courage to face history from the shades of war (Lee, 2016, p. 697). Le and Pearce (2011, p. 461) made a distinction for the Vietnam War battlefield visitors as "Battlefield Visitors for a Day" and "Battlefield Visitors to Vietnam." Ryan and Cave (2007, p. 184) investigate battlefield tourism from the perspective of "serious leisure."

Pilgrim/Tourist Dichotomy

There are various reasons why people wish to visit battlefields, some of which may or may not involve pilgrimage (Hall et al., 2018, p. 716). Before World War I, the pilgrimage notion for battlefield tourism was expressed less in battlefields such as Waterloo (Lloyd, 1998, p. 13).

The connection between World War I and pilgrimage results from numerous factors. The carnage and horror of the industrial warfare war led to alleged sightings of "supernatural beings" on the battlefields. One of the most famous is the Angels of Mons, who were thought to have saved the British forces from total annihilation in August 1914 (Winter, 2011a, p. 165). Because the British government decided against sending the dead back to their home nations and instead had them buried in cemeteries established by the Commonwealth War Graves Commission, the traditional practice of grave visitation by citizens of Britain and her allies could only be carried out after an exhausting journey. In the years immediately following the war, many people traveled together. They were called pilgrims (Lloyd, 1998). Although visitors had previously been visiting the battlefields, World War I's widespread casualties and the burial of deceased soldiers (sometimes on battlefields outside their home countries) transformed the nature of remembrance and battlefield visits (Winter, 2012). "Unwanted feelings" toward tourists on the battlefield resulted from the grieving and searching for relatives and comrades. The nations who participated in World War I have a long-standing custom of visiting battlefields and the graves of family members, countrymen, and women. This tradition includes numerous remembrance gestures that help keep the memory of the war alive. While pilgrimage has traditionally been the primary reason for travel, today's tourists increasingly emphasize tourism (Winter, 2011b, p. 475). Following World War I of 1914–1918, pilgrimage/tourism to the battlefields was sometimes divided into two categories: those who came to mourn and commemorate (pilgrimage) and those who came for pleasure (tourist) (Digance, 2003; Lloyd, 1998; Mosse, 1990; Walter, 1993; Winter, 2011a, p. 164; Winter, 2011b, p. 463).

The tension between "sacred and profane" for "pilgrim/tourist" is coined by some authors as the "trivialization of war experience" (Scates, 2001, p. 198). The prime reason for memorials was commemoration and remembrance; although they were designed for that purpose, their tourist use was adopted (Russell, 1980 as cited in Winter, 2009, p. 616). For Baldwin and Sharpley (2009, p. 195), compared to a pilgrimage, tourists to the battlefield search for an understanding of "what" and "why." Secular and maybe non secular pilgrimage to the birthplaces of a nation primarily found in that country's borders (Hall, 2002, p. 86). For instance, the Battle of Manzikert commemorations in eastern Turkiye is an excellent example of this type of visit. Nevertheless, for other nations like Australia and New Zealand, the birthplace of nationhood is in Gallipoli (Hall, 2002, p. 86). While pilgrims tend to have a direct connection to the battlefield, tourists visit these sites for (special) interest (Winter, 2009).

Supply-led Understanding of Battlefield Tourism

War and its events and sites are important attractions. Historic wars such as the Napoleonic Wars, the American Civil War, World War I, and the World War II, and more recent conflicts and wars serve as tourist attractions (Henderson, 2000, p. 269). Not all battles constitute the supply for battlefield tourism. Some battlefields have visitor centers and signage, while others do not. Some battlefields were remembered, others were only recalled (Mclean et al., 2007, p. 225), and some were forgotten. The rise of the nation-state of the nineteenth century is believed to have created the restorations of battlefields as a subset of commemoration events (Gatewood & Cameron, 2004, p. 193). It is common for European cities to include their historic military buildings, like castles and walls, as tourist attractions in their tour itineraries. Moreover, 20th-century war attractions such as Menin Gate in Belgium and American Air Force Cemetery near Cambridge have become tourist attractions. Using military sites as a tourist attraction is not an "urban phenomenon" (Beech, 2000, p. 29). Battlefields are now sought as tourist attractions by visitors ranging from ex-combatants to scuba divers. On one level, they are outstanding examples of the war disaster turned into peace-time profit. On the other hand, they are memorials to battlefield action and human suffering. Many authors have noted that nostalgia has long been a potent factor in tourism (Cooper, 2007, p. 73).

The battlefields, memorials, and museums are established, retained, restored, adjusted, or promoted for public interest as representations of "death and tragedy" (with a focus on touristic consumption). The interpretations of these sites focused on commercial profit from tourism and conveying political messages (Wight, 2009, p. 147). According to Cohen (2010), these types of sites can be categorized as primary (actual site of the event), secondary (museums and memorials of the event in another location), and "in populu" ("located at population and/or spiritual centers of the victimized people, irrespective of the geographical distance from the events") sites.

Ground Zero in New York, Robben Island Prison in South Africa, and even Auschwitz Concentration Camp all share the characteristics of being associated with death and suffering while being popular tourist attractions (Virgili et al., 2018, p. 61). L'Arc de Triomphe, Gettysburg Cemetery, the Nazi death camps, and Hiroshima are just some sites (Smith, 1998, p. 205). Tourism helps to transform war-related sites (Nagasaki, Hiroshima, Nazi death camps as the most extreme examples) into peace-time profit attractions (Cooper, 2006, p. 213). According to critics, in the Vietnam War context, the failure to effectively convey the atrocities of the war years and the suffering of the soldiers on both sides and in the locals have turned warfare into a game of hide and seek in a rural and sanitized setting (Henderson, 2000, p. 277).

According to Clarke and Eastgate (2011, p. 35) the management of cultural assets (cultural capital) can be both tangible (battlefields, artefacts, and sites) and intangible (commemoration, remembrance, cultural memory, collective memory, and remembrance). Tourists may become interested in a location if wars are prominent. As Weaver (2000) noted, war-related events can contribute to the development of a destination in ways that would not have otherwise happened. In the historical battlefield context, tourists, however, observe a landscape that visually shows little evidence of the War's actions today. The warfare and its impact on terrain vanished long before and were replaced by framing and/or urban development (Iles, 2008, p. 139).

Each year, hundreds of thousands of people visit old battlefields. Like other destinations, they need management (Ryan, 2007b, p. 13). For World War I battlefields, the new edition battlefield guide books with the history of the War, battlefields, and cemeteries may be an antecedent for the growing demand for battlefield tourism information (Akerman, 2016, p. 161). The supply of this kind of tourism grew as the demand did. "Entrance fees," "souvenirs," "tourist guides," and "guide books" also cover the battlefield tourism supply (Seaton, 1999, p. 137). The introduction of this type of tourism supply, if local people are employed, may seem less "crass" (Seaton, 2009, p. 87). It is advantageous to draw domestic and international visitors to the historic battlefields (Chen & Tsai, 2019, p. 96). For Foulk (2016, p. 1), the "economy of history" drives history and historical monuments, especially in the tourism sector. For instance, in France, the history of two World Wars ensures the visitors a standalone destination or attraction during their visit. Moreover, battlefield tourism provides more jobs and visitors to the less-visited parts of northern France.

Supply of battlefield tourism primarily focuses on education and commemoration, emphasizing memory and/or history. Pilgrimages are believed to be visits to battlefields, emphasizing their "sacredness" spiritually (Butler & Suntikul, 2013; Virgili et al., 2018, p. 63; Winter, 2009). There are advantages to forging deeper ties between the military and civil society. The army continues to be a small and distant part of most people's lives in a world where "experiences" of military violence are easily accessible to young people through social media, movies, and video games, potentially making deployment without proper care and attention more accessible (Pennel, 2018, p. 90). Along with the benefits of war tourism, historians and heritage managers are concerned about the contradictory features of memory and the challenges of integrating divergent national histories into a standard tourism supply (Tizzoni, 2016, p. 88). Therefore, battlefield tourism may have a lifecycle as the other destinations. Battlefield destination life cycle suggests "five-fold typology:" "the heroic phase," "remembrance of the fallen," "lest we forget," "when we were young," and "reliving the past" (Smith, 1996 as cited in Ryan, 2007b, p. 8; Weaver, 2000).

Although there may be numerous reasons and cause-and-effect relations in the nature of war, a simple cause-and-effect relation for war may be defined as the cause (offensive-defensive nature) and the effect (take-give territory) (see Fig. 3.1). Survival on the battlefield requires solidarity. This deadly collective cause-effect relation results in the birth of historic or actual battlefields, which may evolve into battlefield tourism attractions.

The creation of "sites of memory" (lieux de memoire concept of Pierre Nora) with parks and monuments was pertinent for affirming "national identity" (Kavrecic, 2017, p. 142). The victories in battles (or vice-versa) contribute to the national identity and heritage. Heritage celebrates victory (success, conquest, supremacy) and consecrates loss (defeat, misery, degradation). Victors leave behind a variety of legacies. Defeat can be just as powerful a legacy as winning;

DEFENSIVE/TAKE TERRITORY	OFFENSIVE/TAKE TERRITORY
DEFENSIVE/GIVE TERRITORY	OFFENSIVE/GIVE TERRITORY

Fig. 3.1.   A Simple Cause-And-Effect Relation for War. *Source:* Author's own work.

suffering creates enduring ties (Lowenthal, 1998, p. 86). New tourist attractions can be created through military, political, or memorial heritage (Rodriguez, 2020, p. 7). Therefore, battlefields with solid bonds to history, myths, heritage, narrative, and interpretation may become authentic attractions with "sight sacralization" (see MacCannell, 1976). The tourist visiting these battlefields may align them with the "tourist gaze" (Urry & Larsen, 2022) or "sensuous performances" (Iles, 2006).

Interpretation

It is easier to become aware of a battlefield with the fallen soldiers and remains of the war on the battlefield. The plain terrains of the battlefields transform into "culturally meaningful landscapes." War monuments, statues, war machines of that period as physical artefacts and brochures, guidebooks, signs, plaques, and tour guides as verbal texts help this transformation (Gatewood & Cameron, 2004, p. 193). Battlefields depend on a passionate and dense interpretation (Clarke & Eastgate, 2011, p. 34). The interpretation of war can be regarded as "hot." "Hot" defines profound interpretation. Events that touch on visitors' "values, beliefs, relationships, interests, or memories" are referred to as being "hot," and these events "excite a degree of emotional arousal that needs to be recognized and addressed in interpretation" (Uzzell & Ballantyne, 1998, p. 152).

The "three keys" of history are the past as a historical narrative, the experience of the participants, and the subsequent myth, how events are later used to suit particular purposes (Roberts, 2002, p. 91). Much of the histography of war is afflicted by a paradox. On the one hand, the writing of the history of wars tends to be shaped by the fact of victory, focusing mainly on the victors and paying attention to the vanquished only in order to explain their defeat. However, this approach is different in the case of genocide (Beech, 2009, p. 222; Smith, 2001, p. 1129). For Lowenthal (1998, p. 10), history and heritage are different, and heritage is "bad history." Heritage was "bogus history," as many historic sites gave a sanitized narrative of history that prioritized nostalgia and assurance (Hewison, 1987, p. 144).

War and battlefield sites support the argument that reformulating von Clausewitz's (1832/1989) famous quote interpretation is the continuation of war by other means (as cited in Packer et al., 2019, p. 114). Government manipulation of the portrayal and interpretation of contested places, particularly war attractions, is not uncommon (Upton et al., 2018, p. 199). For Frost (2007, p. 187), battlefields are not just military conflicts but also "ethnic, social, and political" conflicts. Using war attractions for tourism instead or as places of remembrance generally "provokes opposition" ethically (Beech, 2000, p. 29). Tunbridge and Ashworth (1996) coined the term "dissonant heritage" in the understanding of heritage. War with its participants and heritage is open to heritage dissonance (for dissonant heritage, see Tunbridge & Ashworth, 1996).

Battles with victories of war are an essential part of the "nation-building narrative," often with epic myths. Tourism development contributes to developing a narrative with economic aims and politics of memory. American Civil War, the commune of Paris in May 1871, and World War I supported "battlefield tourism" as a genre of the tourism sector (Rodriguez, 2020, p. 9).

Battlefields and their historical associations are subject to "cooling" over time. With time, "cooling" is interpreted and reinterpreted (Ryan, 2007e, p. 121). The strategies managers use of "battlefield" tourist attractions in commoditizing such locations and the means of interpretation used, such as media, signage, and simulation, are crucial (Wight, 2007, p. 112).

One element of interpretation is battlefield guides. The battlefield guides were around for a time. Their first emergence was in the Battle of Waterloo. After that, the American Civil War and World War I developed their content (Akerman, 2016, p. 160). For instance, Michelin produced about 1,000 maps and 4,500 photographs of World War I battlefields between 1917 and 1921 (Rodriguez, 2020, pp. 13–16). On the battlefield guides, interpretation of war's horrors comes one after another with the appreciation for architecture and landscape (Akerman, 2016, p. 166).

Re-Enactment

Re-enactment of battles is an attempt to replicate the look of a specific historical war or battle in an original manner by using the replicas of uniforms, weapons, and equipment of the re-enacted war or battle. Battlefield re-enactments amongst the Seaton's (1996) "thanatourism typology." A new concept of battlefield tourism has emerged that incorporates both the "real" and, increasingly, the "play" due to the tourist industry's desire for new attractions. The "real" is the actual site of the conflict. A new type of battle known as "play" entails re-enacting previous battles and, more recently, creating battle situations based on alternate histories. Alternative history develops a different understanding of the past by using the "what if" factor of how events might have played out differently than they did (Prideaux, 2007, p. 23). There is a clear contrast between the severity of war, the bloody mess that is war, and the "playing at war" that is engaged in staging battles for amusement and financial benefit. Is this a case of the sacrifices of earlier generations being turned into a commodity (Ryan & Cave, 2007, p. 183)?

The interest in battlefield re-enactment becomes a significant attraction in some countries. The United States (Civil War Battlefield re-enactments), New Zealand, and Australia are among the some of them (Prideaux, 2007, p. 23). The Sealed Knot Society is Europe's biggest re-enactment society, focusing on English Civil War battles (1642–1651) (Sharpley & Stone, 2009, p. 111). There are also some other re-enactment events available in the European context and, more recently, in Turkiye with the commemoration event of the Battle of Manzikert (1074).

Numerous battlefields across the world may become a subject of battlefield tourism. However, academic research from various disciplines primarily focused on the American Civil War (Chronis, 2005, 2008, 2012; Gatewood & Cameron, 2004; Giordano & Nolan, 2007; Hanink & Stutts, 2002; Johnson & Sullivan, 1993;

Melstrom, 2014; Mitas et al., 2012; Sellars, 2005; Wahl et al., 2020), World War I (Ahmad & Hertzog, 2020; Akerman, 2016; Bornarel et al., 2020; Cakar, 2018; Clark & McAuley, 2016; Clarke & Eastgate, 2011; Das & George, 2018; Dunkley et al., 2011; Fathi, 2014; Gordon, 2018; Hall, 2002, 2005; Hall et al., 2010, 2011, 2018; Hyde & Harman, 2011; Iles, 2006, 2008; Kavrecic, 2017; Lloyd, 1998; Lockstone-Binney et al., 2013; MacCarthy & Rigney, 2020; McKenna, 2014; Miles, 2017; Okumus et al., 2022; Packer et al., 2019; Pennel, 2018; Seaton, 2000; Slade, 2003; Tizzoni, 2016; Virgili et al., 2018; Winter, 2009, 2011a, 2011b, 2012, 2015, 2016, 2018; Yirik et al., 2016), the Spanish Civil War (Brown & Ibarra, 2018; Holguin, 2005; Smith, 2007; Sospedra-Roca et al., 2023), the World War II (Cooper, 2006; Cooper, 2007; Gibson et al., 2022; Gordon, 1998; Jefrey et al., 2021; McKinnon, 2017; Nishino, 2017; Panakera, 2007; Siegenthaler, 2002), the Kinmen War (Chen et al., 2011; Chen & Tsai, 2019; Hsu, 2022; Kuo et al., 2016; Lee, 2016; Zhang, 2010; Zhang & Crang, 2016), and the Vietnam War (Henderson, 2000; Le & Pearce, 2011; Madigan & West, 2023; Quang et al., 2023; Schwenkel, 2006; Upton et al., 2018).

The American Civil War

Through the 19th century, the most extensive and broad historic preservation endeavor in the United States was the attempt to preserve the first five Civil War military parks (Sellars, 2005, p. 27). Unquestionably, the American Civil War is one of the most captivating national narratives for the American nation. Battlefield visits are one of this popularity's most apparent manifestations (Chronis, 2008, p. 13). Battlefield tourism advanced in North America in the second half of the 19th century with industry, including guides, maps, and organized tours to the American Civil War battlefields (Akerman, 2016, p. 160).

It should come as no surprise that many battlegrounds have been maintained as parks to honor the individuals and events they represent. Many important Civil War battlefields are still preserved today, and the war is commemorated through memorials and parks. Tourists follow the path of belligerents by visiting and seeing the battlefields. Interpretation, maps, and signs are marking major battlefield events for tourists. The major events were determined using narrative accounts, contemporary maps, and occasionally, long after the incident, participant memories (Giordano & Nolan, 2007, p. 69). Late military parks of the Civil War had many monuments (Sellars, 2005, p. 31).

American Civil War commemoration and monuments elevated ordinary soldiers above famed commanders (Lowenthal, 1998, p. 81). For example, in the case of "American origin and nationhood," the Gettysburg is one of commonly recognized historic battlefield of the American Civil War and also the best examples of commemoration in the United States. It became a "passage between past and present" (Chronis, 2005, pp. 397–398; Giordano & Nolan, 2007, p. 69; Sellars, 2005, p. 25). The Battle of Gettysburg and the Gettysburg Battlefield have different histories. The history of the Battle of Gettysburg is military history; nevertheless, the history of Gettysburg Battlefields is commemorative history focused on "perpetuating and strengthening the national remembrance of Gettysburg" (Sellars, 2005, p. 25). Most Americans view Gettysburg as an imaginative site rather than a real place. For many, the national vision that predominates is centered on the ideas of patriotism and unity that this and other civil war battlefields generate (Chronis, 2012, p. 1797).

World War I

A single debate has long dominated the cultural historiography of World War I: Did the war usher in the modern era, or did it affirm the resilience of the traditional world (Vance, 2000, p. 123)? The Western Front stretched in a long line of trenches, fortified settlements, bunkers, and strongpoints from the North Sea to the Swiss Border. New concepts of death and the cruelty of contemporary industrialized warfare were developed for more than four years of violent attritional warfare. Six million soldiers died on this Front, another 14 million were wounded, and 300,000 missing fallen never found (Miles, 2017, p. 441). World War I and the advancement of national tourist agencies improved battlefield tourism into a mass venture. The mass losses of human life impacted all Europeans, and this ensured the visitation of battlefields such as Verdun and the Somme (Holguin, 2005, pp. 1402–1403).

In contrast to being a destination for refinement and enjoyment, the tourists saw the Western Front battlefields as a singular entity based on "emotion, earthiness, and respect" (Clarke & Eastgate, 2011, p. 39). Education has become necessary as a component of the services offered to visitors along the Western Front as the temporal distance between the current generation and the battle widens. Museums and visitor centers of Ieper, Tyne Cot, Thiepval, and Peronne use advanced technologies to provide information to visitors (Winter, 2011a, p. 173). In the field of battlefield tourist motivations, some authors argue that mass death and "industrial warfare" are some of the origins of pilgrimage after World War I; however, there is a tendency of change between pilgrims to tourists on the battlefields of World War I over time (Winter, 2011b).

Many tourists joined the trips to view the battles during and after World War I. The tourists include veterans, families of the fallen, and widows (Kokkranikal et al., 2016, p. 2). Graphic media, including drawings, photographs, maps, war maps, illustrated magazines, and new aerial military images, detailed the war experience for civilians during World War I (Akerman, 2016, pp. 160–161). The cemeteries on the Western Front and the sheer number of deaths there were the main reason the battlefield tourist understood the true nature and magnitude of World War I (Dunkley et al., 2011).

Thousands of tourists visit the battlefields, military cemeteries, and memorials in the Somme and Ypres Salient regions of the old Front Lines every year as tourism in these areas of the Front Lines continues to develop (Iles, 2008, pp. 138–139). Even today, visits to World War I battlefields are frequent and even on the rise (Kavrecic, 2017, p. 144).

Another prominent battlefield tourism site, Gallipoli or Canakkale (more often used as a general name for the Turkish part), has earned the reputation as the birthplace of the young nations of Australia, New Zealand, and Turkiye Many people think of Gallipoli as a sacred place with special national significance for these nations (Hall et al., 2018, p. 716). Gallipoli is the main part of the Anzac story and is regarded as an essential part of the national identity of Australians. Although Gallipoli is found in a different country, they represented as a crucial national heritage site (Packer et al., 2019, pp. 105–107).

The Spanish Civil War and The World War II

During the period of World War II, a sizable portion of the tourism industry was devoted to battlefield tourism, backed by several devoted tour operators and supported by national or local tourism organizations eager to "cash in" on the history of warfare and battle (Baldwin & Sharpley, 2009, p. 188). The combination of "war propaganda" and traditional tourism is a feature of that Spanish Civil War battlefield tourism differed from the battlefield tourism in other countries (Holguin, 2005, p. 1414). The Franco regime's "War Routes" battlefield tourism promotional campaign was a strategic movement during the war (Rodriguez, 2020, p. 17).

The Holocaust heritage attractions are one of the "most extreme and unpleasant" parts of the twentieth century. The National Socialism (Nazi) period of the first half of the 20th century contains a "Heritage That Hurts" (Beech, 2000, p. 30) with the atrocities committed in that period. The eastern European Holocaust sites are presently regarded as dark tourism attractions.

Several significant locations in the modern tourism geography of war and peace may be found in the World War II's Pacific Theater. The World War II and its attractions in the Pacific within the geography of war and peace today attract visitors ranging from veterans to scuba divers. The battlefields of Malaysia, Saipan, Tinian, Okinawa, the Northern Marianas, and other Pacific Islands attract veterans and young people as battlefield tourists from both sides of the war (Cooper, 2006, p. 213).

Battlefield tourism literature mainly focuses on tourism on historic battlefields; however, some studies, like Gordon (1998), investigate the influence of the tourist values of Germans on their political and military decision-making during the World War II. Therefore, battlefield tourism should have an extensive evaluation. The tourist movement during wartime remains an undiscovered area. However, some studies illustrate the actual wartime tourism (Gordon, 1998, p. 617).

The Kinmen War and The Vietnam War

In the context of the Kinmen War, once the military, fortifications of the island almost immediately became tourist attractions and started to serve tourists (Zhang, 2010, p. 401). The island's scenery, coasts, mountains, and battlefields receive

450,000 tourists annually. The islands' main tourist attractions and resources are historical artefacts and battlefield remnants (Chen et al., 2011, p. 247).

Vietnam is another important battlefield tourism destination with a history of jungle warfare, tunnels, Vietcongs, and booby traps. For some foreign tourists, visiting the shooting range and firing a Soviet AK-47 on the Chu Chi tunnel tour is the quintessential virtual guerilla experience (Schwenkel, 2006, p. 16). For instance, education, entertainment, and propaganda, as in The Chi Chu Tunnels in Vietnam, could be more apparent to visitors (Henderson, 2000, p. 277). Vietnam and its management of battlefield tourism is an exciting area of investigation. As a country with numerous wars, entertaining tourists by showing the dark side of a war-motivated community may assist in gaining income and show the might and endurance of the community.

Conclusion: The Definition of Battlefield Tourism

There are some definitions of "battlefield tourism," "war tourism," "war tourism attractions," and "warfare tourism." War zones, historical battlefields, war memorials, cemeteries, and war museums are war tourism attractions (Moeller, 2005, p. 6; Timothy, 2013). According to Dunkley et al. (2011, p. 860), "warfare tourism" is a particular category of thanatourism that includes visiting war memorials and museums and having "war experiences." Battle re-enactments and, the specific area of interest here, battlefield tours and warfare tourism is a significant niche market. "Battlefield tourism" refers to the emergence of cultural attractions and regional specialties near historic battlegrounds and travel to these locations and/or monuments (Das & George, 2018, p. 321; Ryan, 2007d; Smith, 1996; Van der Merwe, 2014, p. 123; Winter, 2012).

Battlefield tourism is a particular form of warfare tourism, which falls under dark tourism or thanatourism (Dunkley et al., 2011, p. 860). According to Baldwin and Sharpley (2009), battlefield tourism is paying respect to and remembering the dead while emphasizing spiritual and emotional experiences. For Misztal (2003, pp. 130–131), battlefields are places of cultural memory, and in battlefields, "memory becomes institutionalized through cultural means, such as commemorative rituals, memorials, and museums." Many of the insights into battlefield/war tourism, including travel to World War I sites, come from three related fields of tourism research: secular pilgrimages, collective memory, and cultural or heritage tourism (and within these, the subfield of thanatourism or dark tourism) (Das & George, 2018, p. 320).

A comprehensive definition of this form of tourism within the context of this book may have two concepts. The first is warfare tourism as an umbrella term, and the second is battlefield tourism as a particular type of warfare tourism.

Warfare tourism: A form of tourism where tourists (military and/or civilian audiences) visit historical or active battlefields, war zones, military installations, parades, exhibitions, bases, cemeteries, memorials, monuments, museums, artefacts, visitor centers, commemoration events, re-enactments, and thematic trails associated with warfare with a focus on special interest and/or mere sightseeing.

Battlefield tourism: A particular type of warfare tourism where tourists (military and/or civilian audiences) visit historic battlefields, their visitor centers, cemeteries, memorials, monuments, museums, artefacts, commemoration events, re-enactments, thematic trails, and attractions related to the battlefields such as trenches, fortifications, charge points, etc., with a focus on special interest and/or mere sightseeing.

References

Ahmad, R., & Hertzog, A. (2020). Itineraries of the Great War and the rise of the local on the Western Front: Memory, commemoration and the shifting regimes of remembrance tourism. *Memory Studies, 13*(6), 1166–1182. https://doi.org/10.1177/1750698018784117

Akbulut, O., & Ekin, Y. (2018). Kültürel miras turizmi olarak savaş alanları turizmi: Türkiye'de yer alan savaş anıtlarının coğrafi bilgi sistemleri analizi. *Hitit Üniversitesi Sosyal Bilimler Enstitüsü Dergisi, 11*(1), 395–420. https://doi.org/10.17218/hititsosbil.397914

Akerman, J. R. (2016). Mapping, battlefield guidebooks, and remembering the Great War. *History of Military Cartography, Lecture Notes in Geoinformation and Cartography.* https://doi.org/10.1007/978-3-319-25244-5_7

Aristotle. (1999). *Politics* (B. Jowett, Trans.). Batoche Books.

Baldwin, F., & Sharpley, R. (2009). Battlefield tourism: Bringing organised violence back to life. In R. Sharpley & P. R. Stone (Eds.), *The darker side of travel the theory and practice of dark tourism* (pp. 186–206). Channel View Publications.

Beech, J. (2000). The enigma of holocaust sites as tourist attractions – The case of Buchenwald. *Managing Leisure, 5*(1), 29–41. https://doi.org/10.1080/1360671 00375722

Beech, J. (2009). Genocide tourism. In R. Sharpley & P. Stone (Eds.), *The darker side of travel: The theory & practice of dark tourism* (pp. 207–223). Channel View Publications.

Bigley, J. D., Lee, C.-K., Chon, J., & Yoon, Y. (2010). Motivations for war-related tourism: A case of DMZ visitors in Korea. *Tourism Geographies, 12*(3), 371–394. https://doi.org/10.1080/14616688.2010.494687

Black, J. (2002). *Review of the book the paths of history* (Vol. 71). The Historical Association.

Blumenberg, H. (2000). "Imitation of nature": Toward a prehistory of the idea of the creative being. *The End of Nature, 12*(1), 17–54.

Bornarel, F., Delacour, H., Liarte, S., & Virgili, S. (2020). Exploring travellers' experiences when visiting Verdun battlefield: A TripAdvisor case study. *Current Issues in Tourism, 6*, 824–841. https://doi.org/10.1080/13683500.2020.1751593

Britinnica/Dictionary.com. (2023). *The definition of battlefield.* https://www.britannica.com/dictionary/battlefield

Brown, L. (2014). Memorials to the victims of Nazism. The impact on tourists in Berlin. *Journal of Tourism and Cultural Change, 13*(3), 244–260.

Brown, L., & Ibarra, K. A. (2018). Commemoration and the expression of political identity. *Tourism Management, 68*, 79–88. https://doi.org/10.1016/j.tourman.2018.03.002

Butler, R., & Suntikul, W. (2013). *Tourism and war*. Routledge.

Cakar, K. (2018). Experiences of visitors to Gallipoli, a nostalgia-themed dark tourism destination: An insight from TripAdvisor. *International Journal of Tourism Studies, 4*(1), 98–109. https://doi.org/10.1108/IJTC-03-2017-0018

Capuzzo, E. (2020). War tourism in Italy (1919–1939). In C. Pellejero & M. Luque (Eds.), *Inter and post-war tourism in Western Europe, 1919–1960* (pp. 35–63). Palgrave Studies in Economic History.

Chamberlain, M. E. (2001). Review of the book. Death or glory: The legacy of the Crimean War. *The International History Review*, 175–176.

Cheal, F., & Griffin, T. (2013). Pilgrims and patriots: Australian tourist experiences at Gallipoli. *International Journal of Culture, Tourism and Hospitality Research, 7*(3), 227–241.

Chen, C. M., Chen, S. H., & Lee, H. T. (2011). The destination competitiveness of Kinmen's tourism industry: Exploring the interrelationships between tourist perceptions, service performance, customer satisfaction and sustainable tourism. *Journal of Sustainable Tourism, 19*(2), 247–264. https://doi.org/10.1080/09669582.2010.517315

Chen, C.-M., & Tsai, T.-H. (2019). Tourist motivations in relation to a battlefield: A case study of Kinmen. *Tourism Geographies, 21*(1), 78–101. https://doi.org/10.1080/14616688.2017.1385094

Chronis, A. (2005). Constructing heritage at the Gettysburg storyscape. *Annals of Tourism Research, 32*(2), 386–406. https://doi.org/10.1016/j.annals.2004.07.009

Chronis, A. (2008). Co-constructing the narrative experience: Staging and consuming the American Civil War at Gettysburg. *Journal of Marketing Management, 24*(1–2), 5–27. https://doi.org/10.1362/026725708X273894

Chronis, A. (2012). Between place and story: Gettysburg as tourism imaginary. *Annals of Tourism Research, 39*(4), 1797–1816. https://doi.org/10.1016/j.annals.2012.05.028

Clark, P., & McAuley, A. (2016). The Fromelles Interment 2010: Dominant narrative and reflexive thanatourism. *Currrent Issues in Tourism, 19*(11), 1103–1119.

Clarke, P., & Eastgate, A. (2011). Cultural capital, life course perspectives and western front battlefield tours. *Journal of Tourism and Cultural Change, 9*(1), 31–44.

Cohen, E. H. (2010). Educational dark tourism at an in populo site The Holocaust Museum in Jerusalem. *Annals of Tourism Research, 38*(1), 193–209. https://doi.org/10.1016/j.annals.2010.08.003

Cooper, M. (2006). The Pacific War battlefields: Tourist attractions of war memorials? *International Journal of Tourism Research, 8*, 213–222. https://doi.org/10.1002/jtr.566

Cooper, M. (2007). Post-colonial representations of Japanese military heritage: Political and social aspects of battlefield tourism in the Pacific and East Asia. In C. Ryan (Ed.), *Battlefield tourism: History, place and interpretation* (pp. 73–86). Elsevier.

Coser, L. A. (1992). *On collective memory*. University of Chicago Press.

Das, M., & George, E. W. (2018). American and Canadian perspectives on the First World War: Similarities and differences between neighbours. *Journal of Heritage Tourism, 13*(4), 320–338.

de Guevara, B. B. (2016). Journeys to the limits of first-hand knowledge: Politicians' on-site visits in zones of conflict and intervention. *Journal of Intervention and Statebuilding, 10*(1), 56–76. https://doi.org/10.1080/17502977.2015.1137394

Dewald, C. (2011). Happiness in Herodutus. *Symbolae Osloenses Norwegian Journal of Greek and Latin Studies, 85*(1), 52–73. https://doi.org/10.1080/00397679.2011.631357

Dewar, K. (2008). Review of the book Battlefield tourism: History, place and interpretation. *Tourism Management, 29,* 1046–1047.

Dictonary.com. (2023). The definition of war. https://www.dictionary.com/browse/war

Digance, J. (2003). Pilgrimage at contested sites. *Annals of Tourism Research, 30,* 143–159.

Dunkley, R., Morgan, N., & Westwood, S. (2011). Visiting the trenches: Exploring meanings and motivations in battlefield tourism. *Tourism Management, 32,* 860–868.

Dupuy, T. N. (1987). *Understanding war: History and theory of conflict.* Paragon House Publishers.

Evans, M. M. (2014). Presenting Naseby. *Arms & Armour, 11*(1), 17–32. https://doi.org/10.1179/1741612414Z.00000000029

Fathi, R. (2014). Connecting spirits: The commemorative patterns of an Australian school group in Northern France. *Journal of Australian Studies, 38*(3), 345–359.

Foley, M., & Lennon, J. J. (1996). JFK and dark tourism: A fascination with assassination. *International Journal of Heritage Studies, 2*(4), 198–211. https://doi.org/10.1080/13527259608722175

Foulk, D. (2016). The impact of the "economy of history": The example of battlefield tourism in France. *Mondus du Tourisme, 12,* 1–21. https://doi.org/10.4000/tourisme.1338

Frankl, E. V. (2009). *İnsanın anlam arayışı.* Okuyan Us Yayınları (Original work published 1947).

Freud, S. (1932). *Why war? A letter from Freud to Einstein.* https://en.unesco.org/courier/marzo-1993/why-war-letter-freud-einstein

Frost, W. (2007). Refighting the Eureka Stockade: Managing a dissonant battlefield. In C. Ryan (Ed.), *Battlefield tourism: History, place and interpretation* (pp. 187–194). Elsevier.

Gatewood, J. B., & Cameron, C. M. (2004). Battlefield pilgrims at Gettysburg National Military Park. *Ethnology, 43*(3), 193–216.

Getz, D. (2007). *Event studies: Theory, research and policy for planned events.* Elsevier.

Gibson, D., Yai, E., & Pratt, S. (2022). Journeying into the past to discover the potential for WWII dark tourism in the Solomon Islands. *Current Issues in Tourism, 25*(14), 2285–2302. https://doi.org/10.1080/13683500.2021.1957787

Giordano, A., & Nolan, T. (2007). Civil war maps of the battle of Stones River: History and the modern landscape. *The Cartographic Journal, 44*(1), 55–70. https://doi.org/10.1179/000870407X173850

Gordon, B. M. (1998). Warfare and tourism Paris in World War II. *Annals of Tourism Research, 25*(3), 616–638.

Gordon, B. M. (2018). The Musée de la Grande Guerre du Pays de Meaux – A simulacrum of the 1914–1918 war? *Journal of Tourism and Cultural Change, 17*(1), 85–99. https://doi.org/10.1080/14766825.2019.1560914

Graham, E. T. (2007). The danger of Durkheim: Ambiguity in the theory of social effervescence. *Religion, 37*, 26–38.

Gregory, J. (2023, March 26). Putin: Russia to station nuclear weapons in Belarus. https://www.bbc.com/news/world-europe-65077687

Gretzel, U., Fesenmaier, D. R., & O'Leary, J. T. (2006). The transformation of consumer behavior. In D. Buhalis & C. Costa (Eds.), *Tourism business frontiers consumers, products and industry* (pp. 9–18). Elsevier.

Gyr, U. (2010). The history of tourism: Structures on the path to modernity. In *European history online (EGO)*. Institute of European History (IEG). http://www.ieg-ego.eu/gyru-2010-en

Hall, C. M. (2002). ANZAC day and secular pilgrimage. *Tourism Recreation Research, 27*(2), 83–87. https://doi.org/10.1080/02508281.2002.11081224

Hall, D. (2005). The modern model of the battlefield tour and staff ride post-1815 Prussian and German traditions. *Defence Studies, 5*, 37–47. https://doi.org/10.1080/14702430500096848

Hall, J., Basarin, V. J., & Lockstone-Binney, L. (2010). An empirical analysis of attendance at a commemorative event: Anzac Day at Gallipoli. *International Journal of Hospitality Management, 29*, 245–253. https://doi.org/10.1016/j.ijhm.2009.10.012

Hall, J., Basarin, V. J. A., & Lockstone-Binney, L. (2011). Pre- and posttrip factors influencing the visitor experience at a battlefield commemorative event: Gallipoli, a case study. *Tourism Analysis, 16*(4), 419–429. https://doi.org/10.3727/108354211X13149079788891

Hall, J., Basarin, V. J., Lockstone-Binney, L., & Yusuf, A. (2018). Spiritual values and motives of secular pilgrims. *International Journal of Consumer Studies, 42*, 715–723. https://doi.org/10.1111/ijcs.12436

Hanink, D. M., & Stutts, M. (2002). Spatial demand for national battlefield parks. *Annals of Tourism Research, 29*(3), 707–719.

Hannaford, J. A. (2001). *Two Australian pilgrimages.* Australian Catholic University.

Henderson, J. C. (2000). War as a tourist attraction: The case of Vieatnam. *International Journal of Tourism Research, 2*, 269–280.

Hewison, R. (1987). *The heritage industry: Britain in a climate of decline.* Methuen.

Historic Environment Scotland. (2019). Scotland's inventory of historic battlefields. https://www.historicenvironment.scot/archives-and-research/publications/publication/?publicationId=c59262de-b652-4e68-b88d-a5fe008ff1c8

Holguin, S. (2005). "National Spain invites you": Battlefield tourism during the Spanish Civil War. *The American Historical Review*, 1399–1426.

Hsu, P.-H. (2022). Lodging as a catalyst for historical landscape preservation: A case study of Kinmen National Park, Taiwan. *Journal of Chin Tourism Research, 18*(2), 433–452. https://doi.org/10.1080/19388160.2020.1829231

Hyde, K. F., & Harman, S. (2011). Motives for a secular pilgrimage to the Gallipoli battlefields. *Tourism Management, 32*, 1343–1351. https://doi.org/10.1016/j.tourman.2011.01.008

Iles, J. (2006). Recalling the ghosts of war: Performing tourism on the battlefields of the Western Front. *Text and Performance Quarterly, 26*(2), 162–180. https://doi.org/10.1080/10462930500519374

Iles, J. (2008). Encounters in the fields – Tourism to the battlefields of the Western Front. *Journal of Tourism and Cultural Change, 6*(2), 138–154.

Jefrey, B., Mckinnon, J. F., & Tilburg, H. V. (2021). Underwater cultural heritage in the Pacific: Themes and future directions. *International Journal of Asia Pacific*, *17*(2), 135–168. https://doi.org/10.21315/ijaps2021.17.2.6

John, T. (2023, April 4). *Finland joins NATO, doubling military alliance's border with Russia in a blow for Putin*. CNN. https://edition.cnn.com/2023/04/04/europe/finland-joins-nato-intl/index.html

Johnson, D. G., & Sullivan, J. (1993). Economic impacts of civil war battlefield preservation: An ex-ante evaluation. *Journal of Travel Research*, *32*(1), 21–29.

Kang, E.-J., Scott, N., Lee, T. J., & Ballantyne, R. (2012). Benefits of visiting a "Dark tourism" site: The case of the Jeju April 3rd Peace Park, Korea. *Tourism Management*, *33*(2), 257–265. https://doi.org/10.1016/j.tourman.2011.03.004

Kavrecic, P. (2017). "Sacro Pellegrinaggio" visits to World War I memorials on the Soča/Isonzo Front in the interwar period. *Etnološka Tribina*, *47*, 141–160.

Kokkranikal, J., Yang, Y. S., Powell, R., & Booth, E. (2016). Motivations in battlefield tourism: The case of "1916 Easter Rising Rebellion", Dublin Springer proceedings in business and economics. In V. Katsoni & A. Stratigea (Eds.), *Tourism and culture in the age of innovation* (1st ed., pp. 321–330). Springer.

Kostiainen, A. (2001). Review of the book Battlefield tourism: Pilgrimage and the commemoration of the Great War in Britain, Australia and Canada, 1919–1939. *Publications in Review*, 1074–1076.

Kuo, N.-T., Chang, K.-C., Cheng, Y.-S., & Lin, J.-C. (2016). Effects of tour guide interpretation and tourist satisfaction on destination loyalty in Taiwan's Kinmen battlefield tourism: Perceived playfulness and perceived flow as moderators. *Journal of Travel & Tourism Marketing*, *33*(1), 103–122. https://doi.org/10.1080/10548408.2015.1008670

Le, D.-T. T., & Pearce, D. G. (2011). Segmenting visitors to battlefield sites: International visitors to the former demilitarized zone in Vietnam. *Journal of Travel & Tourism Marketing*, *28*(4), 451–463. https://doi.org/10.1080/10548408.2011.571583

Lee, Y.-L. (2016). The relationships amongst emotional experience, cognition, and behavioural intention in battlefield tourism. *Asia Pacific Journal of Tourism Research*, *21*(6), 697–715. https://doi.org/10.1080/10941665.2015.1068195

Leiper, N. (1990). Tourist attraction systems. *Annals of Tourism Research*, *17*(3), 367–384. https://doi.org/10.1016/0160-7383(90)90004-B

Lendon, B. (2023, February 25). Three weapons that changed the course of Ukraine's war with Russia. https://edition.cnn.com/2023/02/25/europe/ukraine-war-three-key-weapons-intl-hnk/index.html

Lenin, V. I. (1917). *The impending catasthrope and how to combat it: Workers of all countries unite*. Literary Licensing LLC.

Leopold, T. (2007). A proposed code of conduct for war heritage sites. In C. Ryan (Ed.), *Battlefield tourism: History, place and interpretation* (pp. 49–58). Elsevier.

Light, D. (2017). Progress in dark tourism and thanatourism research: An uneasy relationship with heritage tourism. *Tourism Management*, *61*, 275–301. https://doi.org/10.1016/j.tourman.2017.01.011

Lloyd, D. W. (1998). *Battlefield tourism pilgrimage and the commemoration of the great war in Britain, Australia and Canada, 1919–1939*. Berg.

Lockstone-Binney, L., Hall, J., & Atay, L. (2013). Exploring the conceptual boundaries of diaspora and battlefield tourism: Australians' travel to the Gallipoli battlefield, Turkey, as a case study. *Tourism Analysis*, *28*, 297–311. https://doi.org/10.3727/108354213X13673398610736

Lowenthal, D. (1998). *The heritage crusade and the spoils of history.* Cambridge University Press.

MacCannell, D. (1976). *The tourist: A new theory of the leisure class.* Schoken Books.

MacCarthy, M., & Rigney, K. N. H. (2020). Commemorative insights: The best of life, in death. *Journal of Heritage Tourism, 16*(4), 395–411. https://doi.org/10.1080/1743873X.2020.1840572

MacIntyre, A. (1981). *After virtue: A study in moral theory.* University of Notre Dame Press.

Madigan, T., & West, B. (2023). Western tourism at Cu Chi and the memory of war in Vietnam: Dialogical effects of the carnivalesque. *Thesis Eleven, 174*(1), 118–134. https://doi.org/10.1177/07255136221147954

Malesevic, S. (2010). *The sociology of war and violence.* Cambridge University Press.

Martinez, C. P. (2020). Conclusion. In C. Pellejero & M. Luque (Eds.), *Inter and post-war tourism in Western Europe, 1919-1960* (pp. 35–63). Palgrave Studies in Economic History.

McKenna, M. (2014). Keeping in step: The Anzac "resurgence" and "military heritage" in Australia and New Zealand. In S. Sumartojo & B. Wellings (Eds.), *Nation, memory and Great War commemoration: Mobilizing the past in Europe, Australia and New Zealand* (pp. 151–167). Peter Lang.

McKinnon, J. F. (2017). Memorialization, graffiti and artifact movement: A case study of cultural impacts on WWII underwater cultural heritage in the commonwealth of the Northern Mariana Islands. *Journal of Maritime Archaeology, 10,* 11–27. https://doi.org/10.1007/s11457-015-9133-4

Mclean, F., Garden, M.-C., & Urquhart. (2007). Romanticising tragedy: Culloden battle site in Scotland. In C. Ryan (Ed.), *Battlefield tourism: History, place and interpretation* (pp. 221–234). Elsevier.

Melstrom, R. T. (2014). Valuing historic battlefields: An application of the travel cost method to three American Civil War battlefields. *Journal of Cultural Economics, 38,* 223–236. https://doi.org/10.1007/s10824-013-9209-7

Melvin, R. A. M. S. (2005). VI. Contemporary battlefield tours and staff rides: A military practitioner's view. *Defence Studies, 5*(1), 59–80. https://doi.org/10.1080/14702430500097218

Miles, S. (2012). *Battlefield tourism: Meanings and interpretations.* http://theses.gla.ac.uk/3547/1/2012milesphd22.pdf

Miles, S. (2014). Battlefield sites as dark tourism attractions: An analysis of experience. *Journal of Heritage Tourism, 9*(2), 134–147.

Miles, S. (2017). Remembrance trails of the Great War on the Western Front: Routes of heritage and memory. *Journal of Heritage Tourism, 12*(5), 441–451.

Misztal, B. (2003). *Theories of social remembering.* Open University Press.

Mitas, O., Yarnal, C., & Chick, G. (2012). Jokes build community: Mature tourists' positive emotions. *Annals of Tourism Research, 39*(4), 1884–1905. https://doi.org/10.1016/j.annals.2012.05.003

Moeller, M. (2005). *Battlefield tourism in South Africa with special reference to Isandlwana and Rorke's Drift KwaZulu-Natal.* Dissertation, University of Pretoria.

Mosse, G. L. (1990). *Fallen soldiers: Reshaping the memory of World Wars.* Oxford University Press.

Nishino, R. (2017). From memory making to money making? Japanese travel writers' impressions of cross-cultural interaction in the southwestern Pacific islands battle sites, 1962–2007. *Pacific Historical Review, 86*(3), 443–471. https://doi.org/10.1525/phr.2017.86.3.443

Okumus, F., Zeliha, E., & Koseoglu, M. A. (2022). How did the battlefield at Gallipoli become a tourist site? Epic tourism. *Tourism Analysis, 27*(2), 219–232. https://doi.org/10.3727/108354222X16449628077720

Packer, J., Ballantyne, R., & Uzzell, D. (2019). Interpreting war heritage: Impacts of Anzac museum and battlefield visits on Australians' understanding of national identity. *Annals of Tourism Research, 76*, 105–116. https://doi.org/10.1016/j.annals.2019.03.012

Page, S. J. (2007). *Tourism management* (2nd ed.). Butterworth-Heinemann.

Panakera, C. (2007). World War II and tourism development in Solomon Islands. In C. Ryan (Ed.), *Battlefield tourism: History, place and interpretation* (pp. 125–142). Elsevier.

Pearce, D. (1989). *Tourism development.* Pearson Education.

Pennel, C. (2018). Taught to remember? British youth and First World War centenary battlefield tours. *Cultural Trends, 27*(2), 83–98.

Peskov, D. (2023, April 5). *Russia to do everything for its security after Finland's accession to NATO, says Kremlin.* https://tass.com/politics/1599705?utm_source=google.com&utm_medium=organic&utm_campaign=google.com&utm_referrer=google.com

Piekarz, M. (2007). Hot war tourism: The live battlefield and the ultimate adventure holiday. In C. Ryan (Ed.), *Battlefield tourism: History, place and interpretation* (pp. 153–172). Elsevier.

Podoshen, J. S., & Hunt, J. M. (2011). Equity restoration, the Holocaust and tourism of sacred sites. *Tourism Management, 32*, 1332–1342. https://doi.org/10.1016/j.tourman.2011.01.007

Prideaux, B. (2007). Echoes of war: Battlefield tourism. In C. Ryan (Ed.), *Battlefield tourism: History, place and interpretation* (pp. 17–28). Elsevier.

Proos, E., & Hattingh, J. (2019). Advancing heritage tourism in the central Karoo: The South African War Battlefields Route. *Development Southern Africa*, 1–16. https://doi.org/10.1080/0376835X.2019.1698409

Quang, T. D., Vo, N. M. D., Nguyen, H. V., Nguyen, Q. X. T., Ting, H., & Vo-Thann, T. (2023). Understanding tourists' experiences at war heritage sites in Ho Chi Minh city, Vietnam: A netnographic analysis of TripAdvisor reviews. *Leisure Studies*, 1–20. https://doi.org/10.1080/02614367.2023.2249252

Richards, G. (1996). *Cultural tourism in Europe.* CAB International.

Roberts, J. A. G. (2002). *History in three keys: The boxers as event, experience, and myth* (Vol. 91). The Historical Association.

Rodriguez, M. C. (2020). Battlefield tourism, from one (post) war to the other, France–Spain. Touring from the Great War to the Spanish Civil War. In C. Pellejero & M. Luque (Eds.), *Inter and post-war tourism in Western Europe, 1919-1960* (pp. 7–34). Palgrave Studies in Economic History.

Russell, W. (1980). *We will remember them: The story of the shrine of remembrance.* Dominion Press and Trustees.

Ryan, C. (2007a). Yorktown and Patriot's Point, Charleston, South Carolina: Interpretation and personal perspectives. In C. Ryan (Ed.), *Battlefield tourism: History, place and interpretation* (pp. 211–219). Elsevier.

Ryan, C. (2007b). Acts of resource management introduction. In C. Ryan (Ed.), *Battlefield tourism: History, place and interpretation* (pp. 1–10). Elsevier.

Ryan, C. (2007c). Synthesis and antithesis. In C. Ryan (Ed.), *Battlefield tourism: History, place and interpretation* (pp. 249–254). Elsevier.

Ryan, C. (2007d). *Battlefield tourism: History, place and interpretation.* Elsevier.

Ryan, C. (2007e). Acts of discovery and re-discovery introduction. In C. Ryan (Ed.), *Battlefield tourism: History, place and interpretation* (pp. 121–124). Elsevier.

Ryan, C., & Cave, J. (2007). Cambridge armistice day celebrations: Making a carnival of war and the reality of play. In C. Ryan (Ed.), *Battlefield tourism: History, place and interpretation* (pp. 177–186). Elsevier.

Saunders, N. J. (2000). Bodies of metal, shells of memory: Trench art and the Great War recycled. *Journal of Material Culture, 5,* 43–67.

Scates, B. (2001). Review of the book Battlefield tourism: Pilgrimage and the commemoration of the Great War in Britain, Australia and Canada, 1919–1939. *The International History Review,* 197–198.

Schofield, J. (2003). Monuments and the memories of war: Motivations for preserving military sites in England. In C. M. Beck, W. G. Johnson, J. Schofield, & M. J. Schofield (Eds.), *Material culture: The archaeology of twentieth-century conflict,* (Vol. 44, pp. 143–158). Routledge.

Schwenkel, C. (2006). Recombinant history: Transnational practices of memory and knowledge production in contemporary Vietnam. *Cultural Anthropology, 21*(1), 3–30.

Seaton, A. V. (1996). Guided by the dark: From thanatopsis to thanatourism. *International Journal of Heritage Studies, 2*(4), 234–244.

Seaton, A. V. (1999). War and thanatouriam: Waterloo 1815–1914. *Annals of Tourism Research, 26*(1), 130–158.

Seaton, A. V. (2000). "Another weekend away looking for dead bodies ...": Battlefield tourism on the Somme and in Flanders. *Tourism Recreation Research, 25*(3), 63–77.

Seaton, T. (2009). Purposeful otherness: Approaches to the management of thanatourism. In R. Sharpley & P. R.Stone (Eds.), *The darker side of travel the theory and practice of dark tourism* (pp. 75–108). Channel View Publications.

Sellars, J. (2005). Zero ground: Mapping maritime commemoration in the age of Nelson. *European Romantic Review, 26*(6), 679–698. https://doi.org/10.1080/10509585.2015.1092082

Sharpley, R. (2009). Shedding light on dark tourism: An introduction. In R. Sharpley & P. R.Stone (Eds.), *The darker side of travel the theory and practice of dark tourism* (pp. 3–22). Channel View Publications.

Sharpley, R., & Stone, P. R. (2009). (Re)presenting the macabre: Interpretation, kitschifi cation and authenticity. In R. Sharpley & P. R.Stone (Eds.), *The darker side of travel the theory and practice of dark tourism* (pp. 109–128). Channel View Publications.

Shirer, W. L. (1941). *Berlin diary, the Journal of a Foreign Correspondent 1934.* Alfred A. Knopf.

Siegenthaler, P. (2002). Hiroshima and Nagasaki in Japanese guidebooks. *Annals of Tourism Research, 29*(4), 1111–1137.

Slade, P. (2003). Gallipoli thanatourism the meaning of ANZAC. *Annals of Tourism Research, 30*(4), 779–794. https://doi.org/10.1016/S0160-7383(03)00025-2

Smith, V. L. (1996). War and its tourist attractions. In A. Pizam & Y. Mansfeld (Eds.), *Tourism, crime and international security issues* (pp. 247–264). Wiley.

Smith, V. L. (1998). War and tourism an American ethnography. *Annals of Tourism Research, 25*(1), 202–227.

Smith, R. (2001). Review of the book The Vietnam War. *The International History Review*, 229–231.

Smith, H. (2007). Seventy years of waiting: A turning point for interpreting the Spanish Civil War? In C. Ryan (Ed.), *Battlefield tourism: History, place and interpretation* (pp. 99–110). Elsevier.

Smithsonian Institution. (2011). *The timelines of history the ultimate visual guide to the events that shaped the world.* Dorling Kinddersley.

Sospedra-Roca, R., Hernandez-Cordona, F. X., Boj-Cullel, I., & Iniquez, D. (2023). Virtual approach to a battlefield: Fatarella Ridge 1938. Spanish Civil War. *Cogent Arts & Humanities, 10*(1), 1–23. https://doi.org/10.1080/23311983.2023.2172807

Stichelbaut, B., Cpucke, D., Passmore, D. G., Winkel, J. V., & Mulder, G. D. (2023). LiDAR and conflict archaeology: The Battle of the Bulge (1944–1945). *Antiquity, 97*(394), 945–963. https://doi.org/10.15184/aqy.2023.95

Stockholm International Peace Research Institute (SIPRI). (2023, September 23). https://www.sipri.org/publications/2023/sipri-fact-sheets/trends-world-military-expenditure-2022

Stone, P. R. (2006). A dark tourism spectrum: Towards a typology of death and macabre related tourist sites, attractions and exhibitions. *Tourism, 54*(2), 145–160.

Stone, P. R. (2009). Dark tourism: Morality and new moral spaces. In R. Sharpley & P. R.Stone (Eds.), *The darker side of travel the theory and practice of dark tourism* (pp. 56–74). Channel View Publications.

Stone, P. R. (2012). Dark tourism and significant other death towards a model of mortality mediation. *Annals of Tourism Research, 39*(3), 1565–1587. https://doi.org/10.1016/j.annals.2012.04.007

Stoltenberg, J. (2023, March 8). *Doorstep statement ahead of the meeting of the Foreign Affairs Council of the European Union with Defence Ministers.* https://www.nato.int/cps/en/natohq/opinions_212479.htm

Swarbrooke, J., & Horner, S. (2007). *Consumer behaviour in tourism* (2nd ed.). Butterworth-Heinemann.

Thompson, C. (2004). *The 25 essential World War II sites: European theater: The ultimate traveler's guide to battlefields, monuments, and museums.* Greenline Historical Travel.

Timothy, D. J. (2013). Tourism, war, and political instability: Territorial and religious perspectives. In R. Butler & W. Suntikul (Eds.), *Tourism and war* (pp. 12–25). Routledge.

Tizzoni, E. (2016). The touristification of Great War heritage in the Province of Trento between European history and local identity. *Alma Tourism Special Issue, 5*, 84–104.

Tsukanov, I. (2023, September 17). What does Putin mean by weapons based on "New Physical Principles"? *Sputnik.* https://sputnikglobe.com/20230912/what-does-putin-mean-by-weapons-based-on-new-physical-principles-1113316548.html

Tunbridge, J., & Ashworth, G. (1996). *Dissonant heritage: The management of the past as a resource in conflict.* Wiley.

Tzu, S. (2005). *The art of war* (S. B. Griffith, Trans.). Oxford University Press.

Upton, A., Schänzel, H., & Lück, M. (2018). Reflections of battlefield tourist experiences associated with Vietnam War sites: An analysis of travel blogs. *Journal of Heritage Tourism, 13*(3), 197–210. https://doi.org/10.1080/1743873X.2017.1282491

Urry, J., & Larsen, J. (2022). *Turist Bakışı 3.0* (Y. Ekin & O. Akbulut, Trans.). Nobel Yayıncılık. (Original work published 2011).

Uzzell, D., & Ballantyne, R. (1998). Heritage that hurts: Interpretation in a postmodern world. In D. Uzzell & R. Ballantyne (Eds.), *Contemporary issues in heritage and environmental interpretation* (pp. 152–171). The Stationary Office.

Van der Merwe, C. D. (2014). Battlefields tourism: The status of heritage tourism in Dundee, South Africa. *Bulletin of Geography. Socio-Economic Series, 26*(26), 121–139.

Vance, J. F. (2000). Review of the book Battlefield tourism: Pilgrimage and the commemoration of the Great War in Britain, Australia and Canada, 1919–1939. *Social History*, 123–125.

Vergil, P. M. (1899). *The Aeneid of Vergil* (A. A. Maclardy, Trans.). Hinds & Noble.

Virgili, S., Delacour, H., Bornarel, F., & Liarte, S. (2018). "From the Flames to the Light": 100 years of the commodification of the dark tourist site around the Verdun battlefield. *Annals of Tourism Research, 68*, 61–72.

Wahl, J., Lee, S., & Jamal, T. (2020). Indigenous heritage tourism development in a post-COVID world: Towards social justice at Little Bighorn Battlefield National Monument, USA. *Sustainability, 12*(22), 1–23. https://doi.org/10.3390/su12229484

Walter, T. (1993). War grave pilgrimage. In I. Reader & T. Walter (Eds.), *Pilgrimage in popular culture* (pp. 63–89). Macmillan.

Walter, T. (2009). Dark tourism: Mediating between the dead and the living. In R. Sharpley & P. R.Stone (Eds.), *The darker side of travel the theory and practice of dark tourism* (pp. 39–55). Channel View Publications.

Watson, J. S. K. (2001). Review of the book women and war in the twentieth century: Enlisted with or without consent. *The International History Review*, 181–182.

Weaver, D. B. (2000). The exploratory war distorted destination life cycle. *International Journal of Tourism Research, 2*, 151–161.

Wight, C. (2007). The legerdemain in the rhetoric of battlefield museums: Historical pluralism and cryptic parti pris. In C. Ryan (Ed.), *Battlefield tourism: History, place and interpretation* (pp. 111–120). Elsevier.

Wight, C. (2009). Contested national tragedies: An ethical dimension. In R. Sharpley & P. R.Stone (Eds.), *The darker side of travel the theory and practice of dark tourism* (pp. 129–144). Channel View Publications.

Williams, P. (2008). *The afterlife of Communist Statuary: Hungary's Szoborpark and Lithuania's Grutas Park*. University of St. Andrews, Forum for Modern Language Studies.

Winter, J. (2006). *Remembering war the Great War between memory and history in the twentieth century*. Yale University Press.

Winter, C. (2009). Tourism, social memory, and the Great War. *Annals of Tourism Research, 36*(4), 555–776.

Winter, C. (2011a). Battlefield visitor motivations: Explorations in the Great War town of Ieper, Belgium. *International Journal of Tourism Research, 13*, 164–176.

Winter, C. (2011b). First World War Cemeteries: Insights from visitor books and France by the commonwealth war graves commission following the First World War of 1914–1918. *Tourism Geographies, 13*(3), 462–479.

Winter, C. (2012). Commemoration of the Great War on the Somme: Exploring personal connections. *Journal of Tourism and Cultural Change, 10*(3), 248–263. https://doi.org/10.1080/14766825.2012.694450

Winter, C. (2015). Ritual, remembrance and war: Social memory at Tyne Cot. *Annals of Tourism Research, 54*, 16–29.

Winter, C. (2016). Social memory and battle names: Exploring links between travel, memory and the media. *Tourism and Hospitality Research, 16*(3), 242–253.

Winter, C. (2018). The multiple roles of battlefield war museums: A study at Fromelles and Passchendaele. *Journal of Heritage Tourism, 13*(3), 211–223.

World Bank. (2023, October 3). https://data.worldbank.org/indicator/NY.GDP.MKTP.CD

Yirik, S., Seyitoglu, F., & Cakar, K. (2016). From the white darkness to dark tourism: The case of Sarikamish. *International Journal of Culture, Tourism and Hospitality Research, 10*(3), 245–260. https://doi.org/10.1108/IJCTHR-06-2015-0064

Zhang, J. J. (2010). Of Kaoliang, bullets and knives: Local entrepreneurs and the battlefield tourism enterprise in Kinmen (Quemoy), Taiwan. *Tourism Geographies, 12*(3), 395–411. https://doi.org/10.1080/14616688.2010.494685

Zhang, J. J., & Crang, M. (2016). Making material memories: Kinmen's bridging objects and fractured places between China and Taiwan. *Cultural Geographies, 23*(3), 421–439. https://doi.org/10.1177/1474474015591488

Zuelow, E. G. E. (2016). *A history of modern tourism.* Palgrave.

Chapter 4

Historical Background of Battlefield Tourism

Pınar Işıldar

Dokuz Eylül University, Türkiye

Abstract

From ancient times, people have been drawn to the sites of past battles to pay their respects, learn about history, and gain a deeper understanding of the sacrifices made by those who fought. Today, battlefield tourism is a popular way for people to connect with the past and honor those who served their countries. Battlefield tourism is a significant component of war tourism and is not a new phenomenon (Smith, 1996). Even before the concepts of dark tourism or thanatourism emerged, studies were mostly carried out within the scope of heritage tourism at battlefields and war-related sites. However, with the increasing interest in the macabre and morbid aspects of history, dark tourism has gained popularity as a distinct form of tourism, encompassing sites related to death, tragedy, and disaster.

The debate about how to interpret war or how battlefield tourism relates to death is not new, and many studies on battlefield tourism compare and contrast various aspects of travel, whether they are dreary, educational, or enjoyable. To examine battlefield tourism from a historical perspective, firstly conceptually, it is necessary to consider how it has been perceived from the past to the present and what structures are involved. This section aims to examine the tourism of the battlefields from a historical perspective. In this context, at the first stage, its development in the literature was examined from a conceptual point of view, and then the turning points where tourism activities started were discussed.

Keywords: Battlefield tourism; war tourism; war tourism history; dark tourism; thanatourism

Battlefield Tourism, 75–97

Copyright © 2024 by Emerald Publishing Limited

All rights of reproduction in any form reserved

doi:10.1108/978-1-83909-990-820241006

Introduction

Visits to battlefields are as old as human history. Journeys to historic battlefields have been an intrinsic part of the human narrative since time immemorial. Throughout the ages, individuals have been curious about the places where past conflicts occurred, not only to pay homage but also to understand their history and gain awareness of the sacrifices of the warriors and heroes who were once on the front lines. Today, it has become a widely adopted tool for individuals to establish a tangible connection to bygone eras and to recognize those who served their nation. Nowadays, these places have become more popular, battlefield tourism has emerged, and its impact has become stronger. As societal contexts have evolved, so too has the nature of this death-related travel. Death-related travel has been a distinct form of tourism for centuries, for various reasons such as understanding death, commemoration, pilgrimage, curiosity, and adventure. However, as tourism participation has increased, there has been a rise in both the supply and demand for dark tourism, especially since the mid-1900s. This has led to a growing demand for dark tourism in various sociocultural contexts (Smith, 1998).

Battlefield tourism is a significant component of war tourism and is not a new phenomenon. Battlefield tourism is rooted of war tourism, a phenomenon that has been explored well before the advent of terms like dark tourism or thanatourism (Smith, 1996). Early studies, which were mainly in the field of heritage tourism, were evaluated within war tourism by focusing on battlefields and war-related areas. However, as social interests increasingly turned toward the bleak and morbid aspects of history, the concept of dark tourism began to emerge and a different form of travel emerged, covering places associated with death, tragedy, and disaster. These developments have led to many studies on whether battlefield tourism converges among tourism types. Its conceptual structure was shaped by the research carried out. While some researchers see it as an essential part of dark tourism, others have argued that battlefield tourism lacks "dark" interest and should be considered outside of travel that focuses on the dark side of death.

While battlefield tourism is undeniably linked to the somber aspect of death, it uniquely strives for enlightenment and upliftment rather than dwelling solely on the darkness of the past. Contrary to expectations, the resurgence of battlefield tourism a century after wars has not taken a "dark" turn. Nowadays, a sizable number of people travel to battlefields as part of a postwar pilgrimage out of respect, peace, and remembrance. An examination of the motivations driving participation in tours of battlefield tourism reveals that people travel to these sites to witness what they consider sacred ground, to pay homage to those who sacrificed their lives, and to establish an emotional connection with the past (Baldwin & Sharpley, 2009; Dunkley et al., 2011).

Touristic attractions related to the war are among the tourist destinations that attract a lot of attention worldwide. Although visiting these destinations is often considered an example of "dark" motivation and interest, different perspectives have emerged in ongoing discussions from past to present. The interpretation of war and the complexity of the relationship between battlefield tourism and the concepts of darkness and death are not a new debate. Many studies explore the multifaceted nature of war tourism-related travel experiences and examine whether these trips are dark, serve an educational purpose, or are entertaining. To understand the history of battlefield tourism, it is necessary to understand how it evolved by examining its conceptual development and revealing the turning points that encouraged the initiation of activities in this type of tourism.

Various studies on war tourism have been carried out throughout the historical process. Although visiting war zones is often considered an example of "dark" motivation, different sources of motivation have been shown to emerge over time. Many studies explore the nature of travel experiences in battlefield tourism and examine whether these trips are death-related, serve an educational purpose, or are enjoyable. To comprehend the historical development of battlefield tourism, it is necessary to examine its conceptual evolution and examine the turning points that encouraged the initiation of battlefield tourism activities. This chapter attempts to explore the historical journey of battlefield tourism by shedding light on its conceptual structure and examining in historical order the turning points that spurred its beginning. The conceptual development of battlefield tourism has been evaluated within the scope of dark/thanatourism, focusing on conceptual evolution within the scope of early and 21st-century approaches. Then, the categories, chronological order, and history of battlefield tourism were shed light on with examples from past to present.

Conceptual Development: The Battlefield Tourism Is Part of the "Dark/Thanatourism"

Early Period on Dark/Thanatourism Approaches

Dark/thanatourism, which has been studied academically for the last 30 years, is still being discussed, and its past is being questioned. In the early 1990s, some academics became interested in the growing connection between tourism and locations where people suffer or die.

The literature shows that dark tourism studies are approached from two angles: supply and demand. In studies on the demand perspective, the focus was on the travel motivations of people participating in dark tourism. Studies that consider the supply part have made classifications by dividing dark tourism into certain activity branches. The supply perspective focuses on the providers of dark tourism, such as tour operators and museums, while the demand perspective examines the motivations and behaviors of tourists who seek out these types of experiences. Both perspectives are important in understanding the phenomenon of dark tourism.

Rojek (1993, p. 136) examined the rising tourist interest in celebrity cemeteries and other locations associated with their deaths and dubbed these locations "black spots." He looked at this trend through the lens of postmodernism because of the blurring of lines between what is real and what is made up (spectacle). Later, Rojek (1997) came up with the term "sensation sights," which were places where violent deaths happened. He said that these places were social spaces where people could reaffirm their own and society's identities after events that changed daily routines.

Dark tourism and thanatourism theories were first put forth by Foley and Lennon (1996) and Seaton (1996). Dark tourism was defined by Foley and Lennon (1996) and thanatourism by Seaton (1996). Foley and Lennon (1996, p. 198) defined "dark" or "tragic" tourism as "the presentation and consumption (by visitors) of real death and disaster sites that have been commercialized." Through sites connected to the death of President Kennedy, they looked at the problems with representing and interpreting places associated with death in their study. While emphasizing spectacle and reproduction, they claimed to argue that dark tourism is a postmodern phenomenon, in line with Rojek's theory.

When they were first conceptualized, dark tourism and thanatourism had significant differences (Hartmann, 2014; Seaton, 2009b). Foley and Lennon (1996) concentrated on the "supply" aspect of dark tourism and sites that are how places of death or suffering are represented or interpreted (about commodification, ethics, and appropriateness). Seaton (1996), on the other hand, took a behavioral approach to thanatourism and concentrated on why people choose to travel to locations that are connected to death. The foundation of Foley and Lennon's (1996) arguments was the presumption that any location connected to death is inherently dark. However, Seaton (1996) wasn't as concerned with how these locations presented themselves to visitors; he focused on the motivations of tourists. Frequently, these distinctions are disregarded. Despite these distinctions, numerous researchers have tended to conflate dark tourism and thanatourism.

Seaton (1996) says that the main motivation source in dark tourism is death, and it comes from the thanatopsis tradition. He states that "dark tourism," whose main motivation is death, is the travel dimension of thanatopsis, and he renamed it "thanatourism." Seaton (1996, p. 240) defined thanatourism as "travel to a location wholly or partially motivated by the desire for actual or symbolic encounters with death, particularly but not exclusively violent death." According to this definition in thanatourism, the only reason to travel is a fascination with death itself, no matter who is doing the traveling. Early, this approach to dark tourism envisioned it as a motivational category for travelers motivated by confronting death. According to Seaton (1996), "thanatourism" includes travel that is solely inspired by a fascination with death and visiting places connected with death that the visitors are familiar with and value, regardless of who passed away. According to Seaton, thanatourism is only about death, it has a smaller scope than dark tourism. However, as time went on, he saw that thanatourism was not a fixed form and that its intensity changed according to whether or not death was the visitor's main goal or if it coexisted with other reasons. Therefore, Seaton also distinguished five categories of thanatourism that entail different interactions between the traveler and death or the afterlife.

While describing dark or thanatourism, Seaton (1996, p. 240) made a behavioral definition according to the traveler's motives rather than an attempt to determine the characteristics of the travel destination. Seaton defines thanatourism as a "morbid fascination with death" and says that its prevalence makes it a taste we all share to a certain degree. According to Seaton (1996, pp. 240–242), "thanatourism" comprises five distinct travel activities. First, individuals have traveled to observe public re-enactments of deaths. This is the most extreme and morally reprehensible form of thanatourism in modern societies, though it was prevalent previously, through gladiatorial fights to the death, and in Britain, public hangings and political executions were permitted until 1868. Today, although it is seen as the most extreme and morally reprehensible form of thanatourism, there are still some individuals who rush to plane crashes, ferry sinkings, and terrorist attacks to witness death. The second aspect of thanatourism is a visitation to the sites of individual or collective deaths that have already occurred. This is the most prevalent type of thanatourism, which comprises a vast array of tourist activities. Travels to locations where mass (Auschwitz, Culloden, the Colosseum of Rome, and Lockerbie) or individual deaths have occurred (such as where Kennedy was assassinated in Dallas, the room in the Tower of London where the Princes were killed, or the road where James Dean crashed). Visits to cemeteries and memorials of the dead are a third characteristic of thanatourism. This form of thanatourism entails visits to cemeteries, catacombs, war memorials, mausoleums, and similar locations. Famous cemeteries, memorials, and mass war memorials of national or international cultural significance are extremely popular travel destinations. These types of visits provide a way for people to connect with the past, feel a sense of reverence and appreciation for those who have come before them, and honor those who have lost their lives in conflicts or other tragedies. The fourth is to go to places that have nothing to do with the deaths to see physical evidence of them or symbols of them. This type of thanatourism focuses on synthetic fields that exhibit evidence of the deceased. It includes museums displaying murder weapons, victims' clothing, and other artifacts. For instance, the Museum of the Revolution in Cuba displays the blood-stained, lead-filled clothing of the revolution's heroes as well as the instruments of torture they authorized. Madame Tussauds also features wax statues of notorious killers. Through such exhibitions, thanatourism attempts to immortalize the dead and keep alive a sense of their legacy. Lastly, thanatourism includes traveling to watch or take part in a death simulation or reenactment. For example, during Easter, re-enactments centered on religious themes like the crucifixion and resurrection of Jesus are arranged. People interested in these activities travel to observe these presentations. In addition, today, people travel to see war reenactments put on by members of communities devoted to specific wars. And there are trips to tourist events where murder stories from famous novels or reality are reenacted and people come together to solve the murder. People are getting more and more interested in these thanatourism events, which give them a fun way to celebrate history and interact with it.

Due to the wide range of experiences and reactions related to dark tourism, it's hard to find a single motivation that applies to everyone. According to some research, tourists who travel to locations associated with death have motives other than encountering and witnessing death. During Australian and New Zealand tourist trips to the Dardanelles, for instance, motivations such as history, national pride, and pilgrimage were prominent. Similarly, some battlefields (the Dardanelles Strait, which was significant to the Turks during World War I (WWI), was referred to as impassable) are visited by those who view them not as sites of death but as sites where national identity is strengthened (Cheal & Griffin, 2013; Slade, 2003). Such visits can be seen as a way to honor those who died in the conflict while also allowing visitors to gain a better understanding of the history and culture of the area. In addition, Lennon and Foley (1996) claim that death is not the only motivation for dark tourism; many other pleasures and entertainment activities are also entering the dark tourism field. Their study found that dark tourists who visit death-related sites seek three types of experiences: "remembering, educating, and entertaining" (Lennon ve Foley, 1996, p. 195). In this context, dark tourism also includes activities such as riding ghost trains in theme parks for entertainment, dining in a horror-themed restaurant, visiting cemeteries, attending a memorial concert of famous singers to remember and commemorate them, or singing songs at the top of monuments erected in their honor, or organizing educational family trips to historical areas related to death (some people visit sites associated with tragedies such as the 9/11 Memorial Museum in New York City). Even in certain cases, the "dark" aspects weren't clear to visitors of the sites they initially visited. They were often surprised to discover the hidden history of the places they had seen (Seaton, 2009a, 2009b).

The perspective of Lennon and Foley (1996) on dark tourism is evaluated as a result of postmodernism, where experiencing death as a "Western phenomenon" is met with demands such as education and entertainment, besides gloomy places. Lennon and Foley suggest that visitors to "dark" sites seek three distinct types of experiences: "remembering, entertainment, education" (Lennon & Foley, 1996, p. 195).

However, Seaton (1996, 2009a) has convincingly shown that there is a long history of links between travel and death and is rooted in recognized "thanatopsis." Also, there are many examples of tourists being interested in death before the 20th century (Bowman & Pezzullo, 2010; Casbeard & Booth, 2012; Casella & Fennelly, 2016; Coughlin, 2014; Gibson, 2006; Johnston, 2013; Murphy, 2015; Schaffer, 2016; Seaton, 1999, 2009a). For example, the catacombs in Paris have been a popular tourist attraction since the late 18th century, the Tower of London has been known for its public executions since the Middle Ages, and the same way Waterloo War in 1815 and trips to battlefields. These historical examples suggest that the fascination with death and dark tourism is not a recent phenomenon.

As a result, although we accept that dark tourism is not a new phenomenon of the 20th century and is shaped by thanatourism, it seems to have differentiated and diversified over time. Especially with the diversification of studies, it has been observed that it cannot be limited to a single definition and that there are different motivation sources. Today, there is a dark tourism concept that diversifies with the existence of tourists with different motivations apart from encountering death and the existence of touristic places that arouse different emotions.

Dark/Thanatourism in the 21st Century Approaches

Over time, dark tourists and dark tourism approaches, whose main motivations are to travel to meet real or symbolic death, have begun to change. As a result of the modern world, the definition of "dark tourism" has changed over time. It used to mean sad, death-themed, or directly related to death travels from the Middle Ages. It now also includes visits to sites connected to death for a variety of reasons, such as remembrance, pride, entertainment, or education. In recent decades, it has frequently been asserted that tourists' interest has increased in going to places where there is death and suffering as a result of postmodernism. Also, it has been said (Blom, 2000; Dann & Potter, 2001; Korstanje & George, 2015; Lenon & Foley, 2000; Sharpley, 2009; Stone, 2006) that dark tourism has its roots in postmodernism, and that this type of tourism is based on the main ideas of postmodernism.

Lennon and Foley (2000, p. 11) conceptualized "dark tourism" as a twentieth-century phenomenon based on postmodernity. They identified it as a part of cultural tourism, rather than heritage tourism. They claimed that "anxiety and doubt" challenge the certainty and optimism of the modern world and are brought by dark tourism as a result of postmodernism. So, they said that dark tourism was the living memory of death, disaster, or an atrocity act. They concentrated on the presentation and explanation of death sites to visitors, emphasizing the ethical dilemmas that arise and examining the implications for management. They noticed a significant change in how the tourism industry views death and the deceased, with death becoming more and more commodified and commercialized. Lennon and Foley's (2000) study has been a seminal and foundational study in the literature of dark tourism. However, it has faced criticism for its inadequate theoretical exploration of the phenomenon, selection of case studies, and its assertion that dark tourism is confined to occurrences within recent memory and living memory (Ashworth & Isaac, 2015; Carrigan, 2014; Casbeard & Booth, 2012; Stone, 2011).

Modernism is characterized by enhanced urbanization, widespread literacy, widespread improved work environments, health care, and greater mobility (MacCannell, 1999, pp. 43–44). According to McCannell (1999), modern tourists desire to know what is authentic. The main desire of modern tourists is to observe what is happening in the locations they go to, behind the scenes. However, since tourists' desires are to seek originality, creating or presenting absolute originality has ultimately been difficult. By creating authenticity, different experiential attempts result in the creation of fake and fabricated (pseudo) activities. As a result, there was a development in the way of thinking, and a new era called postmodernism began. Postmodernity has features such as the convergence of time and space thanks to developing technology, the creation of the desired space and the desired feeling, and the importance given to education. Postmodernism also questions the concept of a singular, objective truth and underscores the importance of individual perspectives and experiences in shaping reality. It has had a notable impact on a variety of fields, including art, literature, architecture, philosophy, and more.

Postmodernity is characterized by the production and consumption of educational elements (such as museums) for commercial purposes via tourism. There have been numerous instances of conflict or tragedy in the past. According to Lennon and Foley (2000), however, these events and locations can only be included in dark tourism if they are educational, produced differently, and used commercially. Also, Lennon and Foley (2000, p. 12) make two assumptions regarding dark tourism. First assumption, for it to be confirmed, it was initially thought that it had to be restricted to memories of people who were still alive. The second assumption was that historical occurrences that took place long ago (outside of living memory) were ineligible as dark tourism. As per Lennon and Foley, dark tourism is a byproduct of late modernity and postmodernity; thus, its history is relatively brief. This perspective has shaped Lennon's subsequent work, primarily focusing on the challenges associated with representing significant human tragedies of the mid-20th century, such as Holocaust sites, within the realm of tourism. In this approach, which is seen as the result of the modern world, it can be seen that "dark tourism" has become more popular by putting on display some of the worst humanitarian disasters of the 20th century for tourists to see, especially in areas where there have been genocides. This has been started as a way to both commemorate and educate visitors on the atrocities of the past, to ensure that history does not repeat itself.

One of the ways that dark tourism differs from the way thanatourism views death was demonstrated in the literature by Stone (2011). Based on earlier definitions of thanatourism, he expanded dark tourism. He proposed that dark tourism is a more individualistic, emotion-driven, and motivational approach than thanatourism's memento mori exhibits, which focus on human skulls and death. Dark tourism, according to Stone, travels more to understand important people's deaths, commemorate events, and understand or learn lessons than to reflect on death, which modern society rejects (Stone, 2011). Stone's proposed distinction between dark tourism and thanatourism's memento mori exhibits illuminates a key difference in motivations for visiting sites associated with death. While thanatourism centers on the macabre and shocking representation of death, dark tourism is framed around a desire for deeper understanding and connection with historical tragedies or significant events.

Another method of investigating dark tourism has involved supply. It is seen that more studies examine dark tourism in terms of supply. Dann (1998) presented one of the first classifications of dark tourism supply, as five primary groups of place and activity: "Themed Thanatos, Houses of Horror, Tours of Torment, Fields of Fatality, and Perilous Places." These were separated into subcategories, such as "Terror Towns," "Death Dungeons," "Heinous Hotels," etc. (Dann, 1998, as cited in Stone, 2006, p. 148). This typology has been used in many studies and has been expanded in subsequent research, providing a useful framework for describing a variety of dark tourism experiences. However, some scholars have criticized this typology for simplifying the complex motivations and interests behind dark tourism.

The creation of the ghastly past was influenced by more than just consumer preferences, media sway, and supplier-sponsored promotional ploys. Also, it was shaped by the larger political and cultural environment (Seaton, 1999). Despite being an emotionally intense and politically charged heritage product, the main draw of dark tourism is thought to be its supply potential – simple to market but difficult to interpret (Shackley, 2001). For instance, historical events committed by "dark history sites" (such as the Galleries of Justice in England), which are viewed as guardians of the truth and frequently have a commercial orientation, can appear to be romanticized and simplified. Entertainment and commodification have the power to trivialize and deauthenticate the supply of dark tours intended for mass consumption (such as the creepy tours at the London Dungeon in the United Kingdom). In other words, the serious historical and cultural heritage that must be preserved can take on a different hue as entertainment. A transition is provided from the brutal aspect of death to a different experience. "Dark shift" is a common term used to describe this. This change, which evolves from the dark side of death to a completely enjoyable experience, can make history and culture more accessible and interesting to a wider audience. This can enable the past to be experienced, remembered, and appreciated by a wide audience, from children to the elderly. However, what needs to be taken into consideration is to ensure that these places, whose seriousness has decreased and turned into entertainment, do not lose or distort their importance, such as heritage sites and artifacts (Stone, 2006).

The universal term "dark" applied to tourism is considered too broad, as dark tourism products are intricate, nuanced, and diverse in design and purpose. It doesn't adequately convey the multifaceted layers present in the supply of dark tourism. In particular, a perceived "dark" shift between products also made classification difficult. To explain the various shades and degrees of dark tourism through distinguishable product characteristics, features, and perceptions, analyses were conducted (Stone, 2006, p. 150).

Miles (2002) supports the approach of a perceived darkness shift between products and acknowledges that there exists a paradigm in tourism that can be characterized as a "darker/lighter tourism paradigm." According to Miles, there is a significant distinction between locations that are associated with death and suffering and locations that are connected to death and suffering. In this case, it reveals the approach of "dark" tourism and "darker" tourism. Miles (2002) suggests that there is a distinction between "dark" tourism and "darker" tourism. According to Miles, World War II (WWII) concentration and death camps, like Auschwitz-Birkenau, are potentially "darker" compared to places like the US Holocaust Memorial Museum in Washington, DC. The key distinction lies in the fact that Auschwitz-Birkenau is the real site of death, whereas the US Holocaust Memorial Museum serves as a commemorative association. Miles argues that destinations in dark tourism should facilitate empathy between the visitor and the historical victim or the represented experience. According to Miles (2002), the spatial connection in the design of dark tourism products design enhances this empathy. He also contends that the temporal dimension of dark sites will increase visitors' empathy and be crucial to how the product is viewed, created, and ultimately consumed. As per Miles, tragic events that have taken place more recently and remain vivid in the memories of survivors or witnesses are potentially considered "darker" compared to those that occurred in the distant past. Hence, events categorized as "darker" are those with a more recent timeframe, allowing validation by the living and evoking a heightened sense of empathy. This suggests that the emotional impact of a dark event is heightened when it is recent and can be confirmed by others. Therefore, the term "darker" may refer to events that are more emotionally intense and easier to relate to. Consequently, Miles (2002) suggests that the design of dark tourism products should consider both spatial and temporal elements. This approach can help create a more meaningful and memorable experience for tourists, which can ultimately impact their perception and consumption of the product.

Similarly, to Mile's (2002) study, according to Sharpley (2005), various degrees or "shades" of dark tourism can be identified, determined by differing levels of purpose concerning both the demand and supply aspects of dark tourism. Based on the extent of the tourist's fascination with death, and how much effort is put into creating an attraction or exhibition to capitalize on that fascination or interest, certain locations and experiences may appear "paler" or "darker." According to Sharpley, the darkest forms of tourism occur in places where the desire for experiences related to death is intentionally met. For example, a historical cemetery may be considered a paler site as it primarily appeals to those interested in history and architecture, while a haunted house attraction or the sites of murder may be considered a darker experience as they cater to those seeking thrills and scares. However, the line between paler and darker sites can be blurred and subjective.

Stone (2006) has formulated a conceptual framework: "spectrum." Considering the potential for certain sites to offer a more intense or darker product and experience, Stone has developed a theoretical framework to identify various types of "dark suppliers" based on the characteristics and perceptions of the product. His idea of the "spectrum" considers potential levels of darkness, that is, the degree to which a dark tourism product is perceived to be "macabre" (Stone, 2006, p. 152). Stone transformed the spectrum into a color-coded inventory of dark tourism destinations, ranging from "lightest to darkest." This concept is important in understanding the motivations of dark tourism consumers, as it helps to explain why some people are drawn to experiences that others may find unsettling or disturbing. By acknowledging the spectrum of darkness, researchers and industry experts can better customize their offerings to satisfy various categories of dark tourists' needs and desires.

According to Stone (2006), a product can be characterized "darkest" or "lightest" product, which can be identified by design elements such as whether a product adheres to a commercial or educational ethic or whether a more extreme level of political influence and ideology is discernible in the intent behind and interpretation of the intended use (Stone, 2006, p. 152). This approach can be useful in identifying and categorizing products based on their dominant design features, which can aid in market research and product development. However, it is important to note that these typologies are not fixed and may change over time as products evolve and new design features emerge. Stone (2006) presented in his study a typological basis for the supply of dark tourism with "Seven Dark Suppliers." The spectrum had seven different categories, each with a different name, similar to Dann's typology: "Dark Exhibitions, Dark Dungeons, Dark Fun Factories, Dark Conflict Sites," "Dark Shrines, Dark Camps of Genocide, Dark Resting Places" (Stone, 2006, p. 152).

Examining supply-side aspects of dark tourism reveals that, similar to the diverse motivations of tourists who demand the same services, those who provide dark tourism services express that they do so for reasons other than death encounters. In the same way that many dark tourists in various regions deny that death is their primary motivation for visiting, many organizations dispute the characterization of their work as "dark." For instance, Seaton and Stone (2012) put forth that Toni and Valma Holt, the owners of the United Kingdom's first battlefield tourism company, rejected the term "dark" as a definition of the tours they organized on the battlefields of WWII and referred to their clients as respectful pilgrims (Seaton & Stone, 2012, as cited in Seaton, 2018). Similarly, The Association of Important Cemeteries in Europe's director rejected the notion that is a "dark" industry, when initiatives are taken to expand the significance of cemeteries in the neighborhood as a tool for teaching history and environmental awareness to young people. The director believes that cemeteries are important for preserving cultural heritage sites and teaching educational elements (Seaton, 2010). In another study, Friedrich (2016) showed that tourism planners vehemently disagreed with the description of their work as "dark" of tourism activities in Rwanda, which featured a public display of civil war artifacts and human bones. They saw their work as promoting peace by exposing the human suffering that both sides of the conflict had brought about. The tourism planners argued that the exhibition was a way to educate visitors about the country's history and honor the victims of the war. They believed that by acknowledging the past, they could contribute to building a more peaceful future for Rwanda.

As mentioned earlier, the initial definition of thanatourism, or dark tourism, referred to tourism driven by a quest for a real or symbolic engagement with death (Seaton, 1996). This definition is considered controversial on both the demand and supply sides. Even today, the difficulty remains in agreeing on a valid perspective on what is referred to as "dark tourism." It has been seen that academics' definitions and the opinions of people who work in the field don't match up. This mismatch can be attributed to various factors, such as differences in perspectives, motivational factors, and experiences. Traveling to places of death, which we refer to as darkness today, is seen as educational, instructive, or entertaining, apart from being seen as an actual encounter with death. In addition, the places that academics attribute as darkness are changing from the past to the present, and as a result of some events that occurred at different times and out of mind, they change shape with the perspective of the modern world. Especially in the 21st century, the number of such locations that producers and editors found and offered information about significantly increased when the press and then the broadcast media developed.

As a result, death is seldom cited as the primary motivation for tourists (Biran & Hyde, 2013). Furthermore, crucially, dark tourism does not entail the experience of 'real' death for anyone except those physically present during a passing. In essence, encounters in dark tourism do not involve real death; instead, they serve as symbolic commemorations of death and the departed. The presented recollections of death form a semiotic construct orchestrated and managed by the living. Therefore, it can be asserted that contemporary dark tourism entails an engagement with the memory of death rather than direct encounters with actual death. "Dark tourism/ thanatourism comprises encounters through travel with the engineered and orchestrated remembrance of mortality and fatality." From this point, dark tourism consists of three structures: "the represented dead, whether they are victims of mortality or fatality," "the engineers and orchestrators of representations about them," and "the tourists who encounter the represented dead." Therefore, dark tourism experiences range from the less serious, such as riding a horror train or dining in a Dracula restaurant, to the more serious ones, like visiting a battlefield, war museum, or national military shrine (Seaton, 2018, p. 14).

Battlefield Tourism

For as long as travel has been possible, individuals have journeyed to places linked with death. Although the reasons for travel are different, such as understanding death, commemoration, pilgrimage, curiosity, and adventure, death-related travel associated with death has consistently constituted a unique category of tourism, albeit evolving within changing sociocultural contexts. Nevertheless, with the rise in overall tourism engagement, especially from the mid-twentieth century onward, there has been a concurrent increase in both the demand for and provision of dark tourism. For instance, it is probable that tourist destinations related to wars represent the most extensive category of attractions globally (Smith, 1998). Dark tourism encompasses the vast majority of tourism to sites of death, and it is commonly considered that visiting war sites is also another illustration of "dark" motivation and interest.

Three levels of "battlefield tourism" are described in the literature. The first are tours to places where past wars took place (Gettysburg, Gallipoli Peninsula), the second are tours to places where there is social upheaval and security problems, but no real sense of adventure (in Mexico, drug cartel neighborhoods), and the third are tours to places where active conflicts are experienced and the security threat is the highest (regions with intense conflicts such as Iraq and Syria) (Bigley et al., 2010; Bowman & Pezzullo, 2010; Lisle, 2016; Prideaux, 2007; Smith, 1998).

Battlefield tourism focuses to some extent on the dark side of death; on the contrary, it aims for enlightenment and uplift. Considering the events held to commemorate the wars and losses and the commemorative trips made to these places some time after the wars, battlefield tourism does not seem so "dark". Currently, many individuals visit battlefields as part of a postwar pilgrimage motivated by respect, peace, and remembrance. Particularly, when we examine the motivations for participating in first-level tours of battlefield tourism, we can see that people travel to see places they consider sacred, to remember those who died there and to form an emotional bond with them (Baldwin & Sharpley, 2009; Dunkley et al., 2011). These visitors come from all over the world. The experience and the encounter at these locations is often emotional and thought-provoking, resulting in an enhanced comprehension of the repercussions of war on both individuals and society at large.

At the third level, the effort to make sense of both the security risk and the relationship between death and life is at the highest level. So, it's clear that there's a special interest goal in the background of trips to active or passive battlefields, whether it's the first level or the third level (Dunkley et al., 2011). This goal depends on the motivation for self-actualization. There is a desire for self-fulfillment through enlightenment and learning in both cases, whether it stems from a sense of death, a desire for adventure, or a desire to remember or go on a pilgrimage. Battlefield tourism presents the motivations of self-actualization and being a tourist in a somewhat sadomasochistic way by focusing on past or present pain.

According to Seaton (1999), after Waterloo, battlefield tours started. Jewish Holocaust tourism, which started after WWII and has increased significantly since then, is another significant battlefield tour (Winstone, 2010). Lennon and Foley (1999) also state that the WWII genocide museums have an important place in battlefield tourism.

According to some studies, battlefield tourism lacks "dark" interest and is considered outside of travel that focuses on the dark side of death. According to Bowman and Pezzullo (2010), the concept of dark tourism has not received adequate criticism, which may be why, as of now, the connection there is still a disconnect between dark tourism and battlefields. Also, the categorization of all war-related tourism as "dark tourism" may be erroneous (Butler & Suntikul, 2013). For example, Seaton (2000, p. 72) said that people placed wreaths with the words "honor, sacrifice, and love" on small tribute cards at the Menin Gate memorial in Ypres. In his study of three battlefields, Miles (2014, p. 114) also found that visitors did not have a predominant thanatoptic motive for visiting battlefields. Another study found that the majority of visitors to battlefield sites did not view these areas as particularly "dark" (Thi Le & Pearce, 2011). However, some argue that battlefield tourism can provide a unique opportunity for visitors to learn about the realities of war and its impact on individuals and societies. It can also serve as a way to honor and remember those who fought and died in these conflicts (Seaton, 1999, 2000).

According to Slade (2003, p. 782), Gallipoli, the WWI battleground where Australia and New Zealand suffered heavy losses is where both countries' psychological and cultural origins can be found. In contemporary times, visitors to the region partake in a type of nonreligious pilgrimage to the site. Chronis (2005) also demonstrates how service providers can symbolically transform and utilize battlefields like Gettysburg, the scene of one of the bloodiest battles of the American Civil War. He also discovered that both locals and foreigners sought to strengthen the cultural values of patriotism and unity within the nation.

Travel to active battlefields is said to have become popular after the 2000s, and the demand is still growing (Bryant, 2009; Kamin, 2014; Vonow, 2017). Some studies conducted on this type of battlefield have found that tourists visit with different motives than the dark side of the war. For example, a tourist from Japan went to Syria only to share a photo on social media indicating that he was on the battlefield (Somaiya, 2013). In another study, it was observed that a Swedish father and his son were influenced by the war game "Call of Duty" and went to this region to witness the conflicts in Palestine on site (Rundquist, 2014).

Chronology of Battlefield Tourism

Wars have occurred throughout history and continue in the 21st century. Humanity's first appearance on the stage of history is revealed by the wars fought for survival and their explanations. Throughout history, wars have been fought for various reasons such as homeland, power, resources, and ideology. Today, despite efforts to promote peace and diplomacy, wars do not end due to the complex nature of human society. Even though humanity condemns war, it continues to exist as a reality of the world.

Wars have occurred for various reasons throughout history, affected people's lives, and even changed the fate of all humanity from time to time. Especially the two great world wars that took place in the 20th century affected very large masses and changed the order of the world. Nowadays, millions of people are interested in the places where many important wars took place, especially these two recent great wars. As a result of the movement toward the battlefields, which first started with commemoration ceremonies, an important tourism product known as "Battlefield Tourism" emerged. Commemoration rituals performed with respect and pride after wars seem to be a tradition that continues from past to present, just like rituals to commemorate the dead. These rituals remind us of the sacrifices made by those who fought for their country and help keep their memories alive for future generations. They also provide an opportunity for people to come together and honor the bravery and bravery of those who serve. The appeal of battlefields begins at this point in history.

The appeal of battlefields has a long history, especially as a focal point for commemoration. For well over a 1000 years, people have visited battlefields, military cemeteries, memorials, and other places connected to conflict. Significant battles have been memorialized and commemorated in various forms throughout the course of history. Although there are no detailed notes on his visits to battlefields in classical times, it is known that in 334 BCE, Alexander the Great halted his campaign in Asia to pay homage to those killed in the Trojan War and to see the Tomb of Achilles (Baldwin & Sharpley, 2009; Miles, 2012). This suggests that even in ancient times, there was a recognition of the importance of honoring the fallen soldiers and paying respect to their sacrifices. Also, it is known that in classical times, monuments to gods, heroes, and the dead were built on battlefields. The memorials to the dead that were usually built at battlefield sites would have been the main attraction for visitors. For example, prominent battle memorials such as Battle Abbey and the Bayeux Tapestry, dating back to the late 11th century and commemorating the Battle of Hastings in 1066, Simonides' epigram dedicated to the Spartans at the Battle of Thermopylae in 480 BCE, and the Lion Mound completed in 1826 at Waterloo are widely recognized and regularly visited battle memorials (Baldwin & Sharpley, 2009). These memorials not only served as a way to honor the fallen but also helped to create a sense of collective memory and identity among the living. They were also used as sites for rituals and ceremonies that reinforced social norms and values.

The battlefields of the Middle Ages are mostly forgotten. The war itself and the victory were more important than the place where the war was fought. There isn't much evidence that people visited or commemorated battlefields during the Middle Ages, also known as the Dark Ages. This can be attributed to the fact that in the Middle Ages wars were fought not for victory but for survival and power. Moreover, since the majority of the population was illiterate and therefore unable to record historical events, the wars were forgotten and not commemorated. At that time, wars were often described and commemorated in churches or in hymns.

Many wars have occurred from the past to the present, and battlefields arouse people's curiosity. When evaluating the history of battlefield tourism, one should not forget that it originated from the foundations of dark tourism. It is a fact that the proximity of the spatial and temporal dimensions of dark tourism also applies to battlefield tourism. Bringing war zones into tourism and producing them as touristic products is possible by remembering these places, visiting them, being educational, symbolizing them, and using them commercially. In addition, the temporal proximity of the event is also important in dark tourism. That is, events should be such that people can remember them, doubt their consequences, feel anxiety, feel pride, and strengthen the sense of unity. In this context, if the wars that took place in Antiquity or the Middle Ages do not reinforce feelings and states such as pride and gratitude, do not create a sense of unity, are not educational, or do not lead to situations such as learning lessons from the past, they should not be evaluated within the scope of battlefield tourism (Lennon & Foley, 2000). On the other hand, if a modern-day battlefield or conflict site can evoke such emotions and contribute to the understanding of history and its consequences, it can be considered a part of battlefield tourism. The aim of battlefield tourism extends beyond mere site visits; it includes acquiring knowledge and insights into historical events. Therefore, battlefield tourism focuses on establishing a connection between visitors and the historical events that took place in the region and goes beyond factual narration and provides deeper meanings.

Military conflicts and warfare occurring from the early 1900s up to the present day have increased significantly over the past century, reflecting the growth of tourism more generally. WWI, in particular, represented a crucial juncture in the evolution of battlefield tourism. There are indications that systematic journeys to battlefield sites commenced in the latter part of the 19th century, with the Battle of Waterloo standing out as a notable illustration (Seaton, 1999). However, battlefield tourism became popular after WWI (Lloyd, 1998). Since that time, there has been a significant increase in the popularity of tourism related to war, in the point "war memorabilia and related products." Smith (1996, p. 248) says that "battlefields are probably the single largest group of tourist attractions in the world." The effects of war are so ingrained in human thought and memory that "despite the horrors and destruction (and also because of them), the memorabilia of warfare and allied products, probably constitute the largest single category of tourist attractions in the world" (Smith, 1996, p. 248). Last 20 years, visiting battlefields has also been the fastest-growing tourism phenomenon (Hall et al., 2010). It first started with the visits of veterans and their families to places that meant something to them. After WWII, with the important developments in air travel, many soldiers wanted to return to the areas they fought to call their fellow soldiers sons.

The earliest conclusive proof of individuals touring a battlefield can be traced back to the Waterloo War in 1815. This war site later evolved into a popular tourist destination during the nineteenth century. Seaton (1999, p. 136) identifies three groups of tourists for Waterloo: "those who witnessed the actual battle on June 18, 1815; those who visited the site in its immediate aftermath (journalists, relatives of the dead and injured, and government officials); and 'recreational tourists' who continue to visit the site in large numbers to this day." In 1815, even as the Battle of Waterloo was in progress, spectators were drawn to the war to watch (Seaton, 1996). From the 1850s onward, the tour operators provided frequent trips to Brussels and Waterloo for the second group, and a local tourism industry sprang up to meet their needs. In 1854, the first tour to Waterloo was conducted (Lloyd, 1998). Thomas Cook organized his first tour to Waterloo in 1856. According to Seaton (1999, p. 139), the Battle of Waterloo gave rise to a new and popular form of battlefield tourism. Waterloo in Belgium, for nearly two centuries, has remained the most favored tourist destination in the country. Seaton (1996, p. 151) emphasizes that all British visitors take values such as greatness, virtue, and heroism from their visit to Waterloo.

Following the Battle of Waterloo, the Gettysburg Battle emerged as one of the initial sites where the concept of battlefield tourism was assessed. During the American Civil War's Battle of Bull Run in 1861, the inaugural major conflict for the United States, numerous local residents attended as spectator (Piekarz, 2007). The initial major clash of the American Civil War, known as the First Battle of Bull Run or First Manassas, occurred on July 21, 1861, near Manassas in Virginia. This engagement marked the first extensive battle of the Civil War. Another pivotal battle, the Battle of Gettysburg, unfolded from July 1 to 3, 1863, close to Gettysburg, Pennsylvania, and is widely regarded as the turning point of the conflict. With 4,500 soldiers losing their lives, commemorative ceremonies for these fallen individuals began in 1863. Although the establishment of National Battlefield Parks was legally sanctioned in 1890, they swiftly gained popularity as tourist attractions. Presently, Gettysburg, the site of the deadliest encounter in the American Civil War, draws over 3 million visitors annually (Chronis, 2005; Hanink & Stutts, 2002).

In the Boer wars, which began in 11,880 and stretched into the 1915s, Thomas Cook began conducting tours of the battlefields. Before the conclusion of hostilities in 1902, Thomas Cook organized trips for clients to visit the South African battlefields of the Boer War. Due to their interference with the fighting, the High Commissioner had to forbid the tourists from entering (Lloyd, 1998). Thomas Cook continued to offer tours to the battlefields after the war ended, which helped to establish battlefield tourism as a popular niche market.

After the end of WWI, the major battlefields started to see a lot of tourists. Tourists began to visit the WWI battlefields and memorials starting in the 1920s (Seaton, 2000). With a rise in the number of people wanting to visit graves or locations where their loved ones perished, WWI marked a turning point in the development of battlefield tourism (Baldwin & Sharpley, 2009). People either took trips offered by for-profit tour companies or joined pilgrimages set up by a variety of nonprofit organizations, like the Salvation Army. With the aid of tour companies, 60,000 people visited the Western Front battlefields in 1919, and this trend persisted for the following 20 years (Seaton, 2000, p. 63). In 1928, the British Legion set up a pilgrimage to Belgium and France. More than 11,000 people went, making it the biggest trip of its kind to the battlefields of WWI (Baldwin & Sharpley, 2009). The Menin Gate Memorial (Menin Gate Memorial to the Missing), one of the most important monuments of World War I, was built on July 24, 1927, to honor unidentified British and British Commonwealth soldiers who died in the Ypres Salient and have unknown graves. Very soon after the end of the war, thousands of people visited the monument. Over 100,000 people had signed the Menin Gate memorial book at Ypres by 1930, in just three months (Mosse, 1990, p. 154).

The Battle of Gallipoli in 1915 is a significant World War I battle that attracts numerous tourists from both the past and today. The Britinia-Anzac Cemeteries (the Australia and New Zealand Army Corps) on the Gallipoli Peninsula were completed between 1919 and 1930. Visits to this place started in the 1950s. When the Gallipoli Peninsula was declared a Historical National Park in 1973, the region was taken under protection, the region experienced a rise in the number of visitors, especially after the 50th and 75th anniversary celebrations of the Çanakkale War (Slade, 2003). In addition, March 18 Martyrs' Day and Çanakkale Naval Victory are national days celebrated all over Turkey on March 18 every year and are known as important places visited by local and foreign tourists to commemorate their losses. In addition, hundreds of Australians and New Zealanders come to commemorate their ancestors every year between April 24 and 25, coming to the region to organize a ceremony in the "Dawn Rite." Presently, the Gallipoli Peninsula Historical National Park stands as one of Turkey's most frequented locations, drawing millions of annual visitors. These individuals visit to honor the fallen soldiers and gain insights into the region's history. The park is also an important site for researchers and historians who want to study the events that took place during WWI.

Interest in battlefields and this trend have continued with WWII and other conflicts, leading to the development of battlefield tourism, which involves visiting sites associated with war and tragedy. This type of tourism is used today as a pilgrimage and has provided opportunities for remembrance. This trend continued in the twentieth century, with the development of tours of battlefields and the creation of museums and memorials to commemorate the events that took place. Furthermore, between 1919 and 1921, 30 battlefield guidebooks were published (Lloyd, 1998, p. 30). This trend continued to WWII and this day (e.g. Thompson, 2004).

Due to WWII, tourism activities in the WWI regions stopped, and interest in these regions decreased for a long time. However, with the end of WWII, travel started again in the 1950s to commemorate the losses, and the battlefields were opened to tourism in the late 1960s and early 1970s. In the 1970s, it was seen that tourism on the battlefields was revived (Miles, 2012). The reason for the revival of battlefield tourism at these dates is possible: the children of people who fought or died in the war are now old enough to retire and want to visit their graves and places of conflict. Additionally, increased interest in the anniversaries of wars of those who lost their ancestors, especially the interest sparked by several 1914 anniversaries (the 50th in 1964, the 60th in 1974, and the 70th in 1984) and the rise in the 1970s in the number of books and magazines published about the conflict, may have had an impact. In addition, the incorporation of WWI into the British history curriculum leads to thousands of students annually visiting the Western Front. In 2010, over 47% of all visitors to the In Flanders Fields Museum in Ypres, totaling 50,320 individuals, were school-children from 1,057 British schools (Haycock, 2005). This highlights the significance of the museum as an educational resource for young people and the enduring relevance of battlefield sites as a training ground for military personnel. The museum's popularity among schoolchildren and the British Army's continued use of battlefield sites for training demonstrates the lasting impact of World Wars I and II on both historical memory and contemporary practices.

WWII was highly influential in the spread of battlefield tourism both in Europe and elsewhere, for example, WWII such as Pearl Harbor and Hiroshima in the Pacific. Numerous like these important places, including WWII battlefields, consistently attract large numbers of visitors (Cooper, 2006). Also, there has been a notable increase in battlefield tourism following relatively recent conflicts such as the Vietnam War (Henderson, 2000). After the 1970s, the increasing economic well-being of people and the accessibility and affordability of travel also contributed to the increase in visits to battlefields and war memorials, contributing to the development of battlefield tourism. It can be said that the films shot during these periods were effective in the development of tourism in the battlefield. With the developments in the late 1970s, the number of battlefield tours increased and battlefield tours became more popular. This trend continued into the 1980s as more people became interested in learning history through experiential travel. He wanted to see the places in the movies they watched. He wanted to recognize and remember his history. Today, battlefield tours continue to be a preferred means for individuals to connect with history and gain a deeper understanding of past events. In addition, technological developments and animations that allow visitors to experience the reality of historical events in a way that was not possible before have made it easier for people to interact with these places. This has led to increased interest in battlefield tourism and increased awareness of the importance of preserving these sites for future generations.

In the 2000s, it was seen that the demand for active battlefields, which is the third level of battlefield tourism for the ongoing wars, had increased. The tourism business called "War Zone Tours (WZT)," which organizes travel to active battlefields and was established in 1993, organizes tours to more than 50 security-risk sites in the world (WZT, 2023). This company, which organizes tours to dangerous sites upon the request of people, organizes the most tours in Iraq, Beirut, Mexico, and African countries. The company makes sure its clients are safe by giving them experienced guides and the right gear. They also offer customized tours based on the interests and preferences of their clients. The enterprise employs local security experts, guides, captains (vehicle drivers), and expert teams from 20 different countries (WZT, 2023). This ensures that clients have a personalized and authentic experience while also supporting the local economy and promoting cultural exchange. The enterprise's commitment to safety and expertise in various regions around the world make it a top choice for adventurous travelers.

Today, battlefield tourism has gained widespread popularity as a means for individuals to explore history, honor those who participated in battles, and provide economic benefits to local communities. Many countries have developed battlefield tours and museums that offer visitors a unique educational experience. Tourist destinations such as Waterloo, Gettysburg, Pearl Harbor, Iwo Jima, Normandy, the Western Front, and the Dardanelles attract millions of visitors who appreciate and preserve their historical significance. As a result, battlefield tourism has become an important segment of the tourism industry because of the support of tour operators or local tourism organizations that seek to benefit from the historical legacy of war and conflict through active or passive participation.

Conclusion

Battlefields have become a type of tourism with the emergence of wars, which are important turning points in human history, and visiting the places where these wars took place over time. Battlefield tourism has changed over time as a reflection of the changing social structure and sociocultural dynamics from past to present, and differences in motivation sources have been observed. In addition to dark journeys made for reasons such as encountering death, keeping the pain fresh by remembering the pain experienced, or individuals connecting with the past, there have also been battlefields that reach wider audiences, such as commemoration, respect, and the development of a sense of unity, honoring heroes who served their nation, educational, or enjoyable discovery visits.

War-related tourist attractions form an important destination category and are often exemplified by "dark" motivation. The interpretation of war and the complex relationship between battlefield tourism and the concept of death are still debated in studies, understanding and classification of battlefield tourism. While some studies classify battlefield tourism within "dark tourism," some studies argue against classifying it only as "dark tourism." Those who oppose its definition only as dark tourism argue that travel to battlefields takes place as a means to understand the realities of war, to honor and remember those who fought and died in wars, or for ethical purposes. Battlefield tourism, despite its undeniable connection to the bleak aspect of death, is now seen as a vehicle for enlightenment and uplift. The postwar revival of pilgrimages to battlefields is a testament to this.

Consequently, this chapter summarizes the history of battlefield tourism. It aims to provide a basis for reflecting, remembering, and understanding the impact of war on individuals and societies. Examining the history of battlefield tourism reveals that various motivations shape this form of travel; it develops supply potentials in response to demand, and it continues to exist as an important type of tourism according to the social understanding of the ongoing wars.

References

Ashworth, G. J., & Isaac, R. K. (2015). Have we illuminated the dark? Shifting perspectives on "dark" tourism. *Tourism Recreation Research, 40*(3), 316–325.

Baldwin, F., & Sharpley, R. (2009). Battlefield tourism: Bringing organized violence back to life. In R. Sharpley & P. Stone (Eds.), *The darker side of travel: The theory and practice of dark tourism* (pp. 186–207). Channel View Publication.

Bigley, J. D., Lee, C. K., Chon, J., & Yoon, Y. (2010). Motivations for war-related tourism: A case of DMZ visitors in Korea. *Tourism Geographies, 12*(3), 371–394.

Biran, A., & Hyde, K. F. (2013). New perspectives on dark tourism. *International Journal of Culture, Tourism and Hospitality Research, 7*(3), 191–198.

Blom, T. (2000). Morbid tourism e a postmodern market niche with an example from Althorp. *Norsk Geografisk Tidsskrift e Norwegian Journal of Geography, 54*(1), 29–36.

Bowman, M. S., & Pezzullo, P. C. (2010). What's so "dark" about "dark tourism"?: Death, tours, and performance. *Tourist Studies, 9*(3), 187–202.

Bryant, C. W. (2009). *10 most dangerous places you should visit.* https://adventure.howstuffworks.com/10-most-dangerous-places

Butler, R., & Suntikul, W. (2013). *Tourism and war.* Routledge.

Carrigan, A. (2014). Dark tourism and postcolonial studies: Critical intersections. *Postcolonial Studies, 17*(3), 236–250.

Casbeard, R., & Booth, C. (2012). Postmodernity and the exceptionalism of the present in dark tourism. *Journal of Unconventional Parks, Tourism and Recreation Research, 4*(1), 2–8.

Casella, E. C., & Fennelly, K. (2016). Ghosts of sorrow, sin and crime: Dark tourism and convict heritage in Van Diemen's Land, Australia. *International Journal of Historical Archaeology, 20*(3), 506–520.

Cheal, F., & Griffin, T. (2013). Pilgrims and patriots: Australian tourist experiences at Gallipoli. *International Journal of Culture, Tourism and Hospitality Research, 7,* 227–241.

Chronis, A. (2005). Co-constructing heritage at the Gettysburg Storyscape. *Annals of Tourism Research, 32*(2), 386–406.

Cooper, M. (2006). The Pacific War battlefields: Tourist attractions or war memorials? *International Journal of Tourism Research, 8*(3), 213–222.

Coughlin, M. (2014). Sites of absence and presence: Tourism and the morbid material culture of death in Brittany. In B. Sion (Ed.), *Death tourism: Disaster sites as recreational landscape* (pp. 183–204). Seagull.

Dann, G. M. S., & Potter, R. B. (2001). Supplanting the planters: Hawking heritage in Barbados. *International Journal of Hospitality & Tourism Administration, 2*(3/4), 51–84.

Dunkley, R., Morgan, N., & Westwood, S. (2011). Visiting the trenches: Exploring meanings and motivations in battlefield tourism. *Tourism Management, 32*(4), 860–868.

Foley, M., & Lennon, J. J. (1996). JFK and dark tourism: A fascination with assassination. *International Journal of Heritage Studies, 2*(4), 198–211.

Friedrich, M. (2016). Heritage interpretation of the dead as a tool for peace and reconciliation: The case of visitor development at Rwanda's post-conflict memorial scape. Unpublished PhD thesis, University of Central Lancashire.

Gibson, D. (2006). The relationship between serial murder and the American tourism industry. *Journal of Travel and Tourism Marketing, 20,* 45–60.

Hall, J., Basarin, J., & Binney, L. L. (2010). An empirical analysis of attendance at a commemorative event: Anzac Day at Gallipoli. *International Journal of Hospitality Management, 29*(2), 245–253.

Hanink, D., & Stutts, M. (2002). Spatial demand for national battlefield parks. *Annals of Tourism Research, 29*(3), 707–719.

Hartmann, R. (2014). Dark tourism, thanatourism and dissonance in heritage tourism management: New directions in contemporary tourism research. *Journal of Heritage Tourism, 9*(2), 166–182.

Haycock, R. G. (2005). The relevance and role of the battlefield tour and the staff ride for armed forces in the 21st century. *Defence Studies, 5*(1), 5–14.

Henderson, J. (2000). War as a tourist attraction: The case of Vietnam. *International Journal of Tourism Research, 2*(3), 269–280.

Johnston, T. (2013). Mark Twain and the innocents abroad: Illuminating the tourist gaze on death. *International Journal of Culture, Tourism and Hospitality Research, 7*(3), 199–213.

Kamin, D. (2014). The rise of dark tourism: When war zones become travel destinations? https://www.theatlantic.com/international/archive/2014/07/the-rise-of-dark-tourism/374432/

Korstanje, M., & George, B. (2015). Dark tourism: Revisiting some philosophical issues. *E-Review of Tourism Research, 12*(1/2), 127–136.

Lennon, J. J., & Foley, M. (1996). Editorial: Heart of darkness. *International Journal of Heritage Studies, 2*(4), 195–197.

Lennon, J. J., & Foley, M. (1999). Interpretation of the unimaginable: The US Holocaust Memorial Museum, Washington, DC, and "dark tourism". *Journal of Travel Research, 38*(1), 46–50.

Lennon, J. J., & Foley, M. (2000). *Dark tourism: The attraction of death and disaster.* Continuum.

Lisle, D. (2016). *Holidays in the danger zone: Entanglements of war and tourism.* University of Minnesota Press.

Lloyd, D. W. (1998). *Battlefield tourism – Pilgrimage and commemoration of the Great War in Britain, Australia and Canada, 1919–1939.* Berg.

Mac Cannell, D. (1999). *The tourist.* MacMillan.

Miles, W. F. S. (2002). Auschwitz: Museum interpretation and darker tourism. *Annals of Tourism Research, 29*(4), 1175–1178.

Miles, S. T. (2012). Battlefield tourism: Meanings and interpretations. Unpublished PhD thesis. Philosophy College of the Arts University of Glasgow.

Miles, S. T. (2014). Battlefield sites as dark tourism attractions: An analysis of experience. *Journal of Heritage Tourism, 9*(2), 134–147.

Mosse, G. L. (1990). *Fallen soldiers: Reshaping the memory of the World War.* Oxford University Press.

Murphy, B. (2015). Dark tourism and the Michelin World War 1 battlefield guides. *Journal of Franco-Irish Studies, 4*(1/8), 1–9.

Piekarz, M. (2007). Hot war tourism: The live battlefield and the ultimate adventure holiday. In C. Ryan (Ed.), *Battlefield tourism: History, place and interpretation* (pp. 153–169). Elsevier.

Prideaux, B. (2007). Echoes of war: Battlefield tourism. In C. Ryan (Ed.), *Battlefield tourism: History, place and interpretation* (pp. 39–50). Routledge.

Rojek, C. (1993). *Ways of escape, modern transformations in leisure and travel.* Palgrave Macmillan.

Rojek, C. (1997). Indexing, dragging and the social construction of tourist sights. In C. Rojek & J. Urry (Eds.), *Touring cultures: Transformations of travel and theory* (pp. 52–74). Routledge.

Rundquist, S. (2014). *Swedish dad takes gamer kids to warzone.* http://www.thelocal.se/20140808/swedish-dad-takeskids-towar-zone

Schaffer, S. (2016). From Geisha girls to the atomic bomb dome: Dark tourism and the formation of Hiroshima memory. *Tourist Studies, 16*(4), 351–366.

Seaton, A. V. (1996). Guided by the dark: From thanatopsis to thanatourism. *International Journal of Heritage Studies, 2*(4), 234–244.

Seaton, A. V. (1999). War and thanatourism: Waterloo 1815–1914. *Annals of Tourism Research, 26*(1), 130–158.

Seaton, A. V. (2000). Another weekend away looking for dead bodies... Battlefield tourism on the Somme and in Flanders. *Tourism Recreation Research, 25*(3), 63–77.

Seaton, A. V. (2009a). Beckford and the tourists: Gothic performances at Lansdown Tower, Bath. *The Beckford Journal, 15*, 61–82.

Seaton, A. V. (2009b). Thanatourism and its discontents: An appraisal of a decade's work with some future issues and directions. In T. Jamal & M. Robinson (Eds.), *The Sage handbook of tourism studies* (pp. 521–542). Sage.

Seaton, A. V. (2010). Purposeful otherness: Approaches to the management of thanatourism. In R. Sharpley & P. R. Stone (Eds.), *The darker side of travel. The theory and practice of dark tourism* (pp. 75–108). Channel View Publications.

Seaton, T. (2018). Encountering engineered and orchestrated remembrance: A situational model of dark tourism and its history. In P. R. Stone (Editor-in-Chief), R. Hartmann, T. Seaton, R. Sharpley, & L. White (Eds.), *The Palgrave handbook of dark tourism studies* (pp. 9–31). Palgrave Macmillan.

Shackley, M. (2001). Potential futures for Robben Island: Shrine, museum or theme park? *International Journal of Heritage Studies, 7*(4), 355–363.

Sharpley, R. (2005). Travels to the edge of darkness: Towards a typology of dark tourism. In C. Ryan, S. Page, & M. Aicken (Eds.), *Taking tourism to the limit.* Elsevier.

Sharpley, R. (2009). Shedding light on dark tourism: An introduction. In R. Sharpley & P. R. Stone (Eds.), *The darker side of travel: The theory and practice of dark tourism* (pp. 3–22). Channel View.

Slade, P. (2003). Gallipoli thanatourism: The meaning of ANZAC. *Annals of Tourism Research, 3*(4), 779–794.

Smith, V. (1996). War and its attractions. In A. Pizam & Y. Mansfeld (Eds.), *Tourism crime, and international security issues* (pp. 247–264). John Wiley.

Smith, V. (1998). War and tourism: An American ethnography. *Annals of Tourism Research, 25*(1), 202–227.

Somaiya, R. (2013). *Japanese Man vacations on Syrian front lines.* The New York Times. https://archive.nytimes.com/thelede.blogs.nytimes.com/2013/01/03/japanese-man-vacations-on-syrian-front-lines/

Stone, P. R. (2006). A dark tourism spectrum: Towards a typology of death and macabre related tourist sites, attractions and exhibitions. *Tourism, 54*(2), 145–160.

Stone, P. R. (2011). Dark tourism: Towards a new post-disciplinary research agenda. *International Journal of Tourism Anthropology, 1*(3/4), 318–332.

Thi Le, D.-T., & Pearce, D. G. (2011). Segmenting visitors to battlefield sites: International visitors to the former demilitarized zone in Vietnam. *Journal of Travel & Tourism Marketing, 25*, 451–463.

Thompson, C. (2004). *The 25 best World War II sites: European theater*. Greenline Publications.

Vonow, B. (2017). *What is dark tourism? Travelers visiting war zones and disaster areas – Here's what we know*. The Sun. https://www.thesun.co.uk/news/2303847/dark-tourism-travel-popular-destinations/

Winstone, M. (2010). The holocaust sites of Europe. A historical guide. I.B. Tauris.

WZT. (2023). *War Zone Tours, the original high-risk tour operator*. http://www.warzonetours.com/

An Examination of Battlefield Tourism Along With the Tourism System

Introduction

Wars have continued since the beginning of humanity and have had devastating effects on both individuals and societies. The social effects of wars have continued for many years and have become embedded in social memory along with the areas where the wars took place. Wars leave some traces in geographical areas, and sometimes these traces become a source for later periods. It cannot be said that these scars are only physical. The two great world wars of the 20th century witnessed great suffering. Areas where wars took place throughout history attract the attention of millions of people today.

Tourists' search for authenticity has increased the importance of niche tourism types. Battlefield tourism can be seen as a niche tourism movement whose importance has increased with the information age. Because in today's world, accessing information is not just about printed works. Past wars are reenacted in movies, TV series, and even video games. Thus, interest in wars and the areas where wars are fought is increasing (Akbulut & Ekin, 2018, p. 410).

Battlefields hold a very important place for nations for both respect for history and social memory. With all these, it has become an important tourist product. Today, millions of people visit battlefields for different reasons. Although the reasons for these visits vary, it is possible to say that spiritual and national feelings generally come to the fore.

Tourist satisfaction is very important not only in battlefield tourism but also in other types of tourism. Increasing tourist satisfaction can contribute to increasing tourist flow to the destination. For this reason, in today's world where competition is increasing, destination managers need to make some arrangements to increase tourist satisfaction and increase the flow of tourists to the region. Making transportation to battlefields easier and keeping buildings and businesses (toilets, souvenirs, sitting and resting areas, food and beverage services, etc.) in the area that tourists may need can be given as examples of these regulations.

In this context, supply and demand for battlefields, tourism providers, tourist flows, supporting institutions, and battlefields as an element of tourism development are discussed. The flowchart in Fig. 1 has been drawn to express this process. In this section, in accordance with the flowchart, the titles battlefield tourism supply and demand, battlefield tourism intermediaries, battlefield tourism tourist flows, battlefield tourism supporting institutions, and battlefield tourism as an agent of tourism development are included.

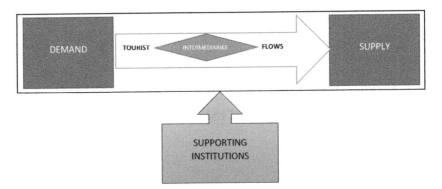

Fig. 1.   Flowchart for Examining Battlefield Tourism With Tourism
System. *Source:* Created by editors.

Chapter 5

Battlefield Tourism Supply and Demand

Özgür Saribas

İzmir Katip Çelebi University, Türkiye

Abstract

While the battlefield means danger to some people, it may mean excitement and adrenaline for others. Battlefields can also carry the meanings of a mirror of history, a place of commemoration, and respect. At the same time, it is a market and marketing area for travel providers that respond to changing human needs. Many studies mention that battlefields can mean different things for each individual. This section gives the supply and demand size of battlefield tourism that will meet all these meanings. The supply and demand for the battlefields are tried to be expressed by giving both the place of the visit-oriented research on the battlefields in the literature and the protected and surviving battlefields and related structures in the world.

Keywords: War and tourism; battlefield tourism; war tourism; battlefield tourism supply; battlefield tourism demand; battlefield destinations

Introduction

It is difficult to determine the supply and demand of battlefield tourism. Today, there are many different discourses and scopes related to battlefield tourism. Battlefield tourism covers different fields of study in different pieces of literature. Battlefield tourism is expressed in association with areas such as war, history, death, memorial days, and dark tourism, and there are debates and different opinions on this issue. For example, in some studies, battlefield tourism is defined as a category of dark tourism. Upton (2015) states that "dark tourism is about the dark side of travel and has the potential to provoke deeper emotions and feelings. It is often defined as travel to places associated with death. Therefore, battlefield tourism is a category of dark tourism. Battlefield tourism experiences have the potential to provoke life-or-death thinking." Another example can be given in the context of war and tourism. There are many studies on the relationship between

Battlefield Tourism, 101–114

Copyright © 2024 Özgür Saribas

Published under exclusive licence by Emerald Publishing Limited

doi:10.1108/978-1-83909-990-820241008

war and tourism (Cooper, 2006; Henderson, 2000; Hertzog, 2012; Iles, 2006; Smith, 1998; Šuligoj, 2017; Winter, 2011a, 2011b). According to literature, the development of battlefield tourism started after the World War I (Hertzog, 2012; Winter, 2011a, p. 164). According to Smith (1998, p. 204), "the theoretical orientation of the anthropologist Turney-High defines war as a dynamic social process and therefore war parallels with the dynamics of tourism." War is a situation that affects a culture deeply and changes lives irreversibly. Culture and behavior differ as "before the war," "during the war," and "after the war." War affects human activities and memory so profoundly, yet despite the horror and destruction, it constitutes one of the largest tourist attraction categories in the world (Smith, 1996, p. 248; Smith, 1998, p. 205). Iles (2006, p. 162) examined contemporary tourist performance, exploring how they interact with the battlefield landscape and the role of the tour guide in establishing and managing their creative and emotional encounters with the region. It is possible to give such examples for other categories associated with battlefield tourism. From a perspective in this context, it is necessary to evaluate the supply and demand for battlefield tourism in a vast scope, and for this, the literature on the field should be reviewed. In the literature, battlefield tourism is intensely studied, and the discussions on it continue. All these researches show that battlefield tourism has a large place in the literature and is also the subject of research in many countries of the world. Some of these countries can be listed as follows:

USA (Alexandra et al., 2014; Floyd et al., 1997; Gatewood & Cameron, 2004; Gibson, 2006; Hanink & Stutts, 2002; Henderson, 2000; Levitt, 2010; Melstrom, 2014; Seaton, 2000; Smith, 1998), UK (Adams, 2005; Bloom, 2000; Miles, 2014), Belgium (Iles, 2006; Seaton, 1999; Winter, 2011a, 2011b, 2019), France (Dunkley et al., 2011; Foulk, 2016; MacCarthy & Willson, 2015; Seaton, 2000; Winter, 2011b, 2012, 2019), Vietnam (Henderson, 2000; Le & Pearce, 2011), Spain (Holguín, 2005), Japan (Cooper, 2006), Scotland (Knox, 2006), Korea (Bigley et al., 2010; Lee, 2006), Turkey (Ağaoğlu, 2012; Akbulut & Ekin, 2018; Alaeddinoğlu & Aliağaoğlu, 2007; Basarin & Hall, 2008; Çakar, 2018; Hall et al., 2010; Hyde & Harman, 2011; Kılıç & Akyurt, 2011; Kurnaz et al., 2013; Lockstone-Binney et al., 2013; West, 2008; Yeneroğlu-Kutbay & Aykaç, 2016; Yeşildağ & Atay, 2011; Ziino, 2006), Australia (Clarke & Eastgate, 2011; Herborn & Hutchinson, 2014; McKay, 2013; Rofe, 2012), Georgia (Gentry, 2007), Southeast Asia, Thailand, Singapore and Vietnam (Lunn, 2007), Cambodia (Hughes, 2008), the Western Front in France and Belgium (Iles, 2008), Taiwan (Kuo et al., 2016; Lee, 2016; Zhang, 2010), Denmark (Daugbjerg, 2011), Canada (Walby & Piche, 2011), South Africa (Venter, 2011), Colombia (Ojeda, 2013), Sweden (Engström & Boluk, 2012), New Zealand (Coats & Ferguson, 2013), Sri Lanka (Pieris, 2014), Sarajevo (Volcic et al., 2014), and Croatia (Šuligoj, 2017).

Supply and Demand for Battlefield Tourism Is Increasing

When the countries that are the subject of the above-mentioned studies are examined, it is possible to see different parts of the world such as Australia,

Belgium, Colombia, Cambodia, Canada, Denmark, France, Georgia, the United States of America, Spain, Turkey, the United Kingdom, South Korea, South Africa, Taiwan, Singapore, Vietnam, Japan, Sweden, Sri Lanka, Sarajevo, Scotland, and Croatia. All these countries that are the subject of research provide tourism supply and are among the regions that are desired to be traveled extensively. Another indicator that indicates that the supply and demand for battlefield tourism spread over a very comprehensive area is the areas to which the subject is related. When the above studies are examined, it is seen that battlefield tourism is associated with various concepts. These concepts can be expressed as: war, crime, violence, terror, corpse, serial murder, massacre, sanctified landscape, monument, battlefield parks, national parks, genocide, ghosts and ghost walks, religious cross, dark tourism, bullets and knives, criminal history museums, tourism of sadness, military installations, rural dystopias, diaspora, lands of remembrance and spaces of conscience, invasions, Dracula, dark journey, and colonialism. All of these show the scope of battlefield tourism, and it creates an intense supply and demand area worldwide.

Battlefield tourism strengthens its place in the literature with a growing demand potential and, as seen above, is the subject of many types of research. These studies can be extended, and in addition to all these researches, there are also books, book chapters, and master's and doctoral theses related to battlefield tourism. These studies also reveal the interest in battlefield tourism. In direct proportion to the interest in the literature, it is seen that the supply and demand for battlefield tourism have increased in various parts of the world. The relationship between battlefields and the tourism industry has developed until today and become a more complete structure. Battlefields have expressed a fascinating and inspiring nature over the years. It was seen and wondered as a memorial site for many. Curiosity, better understanding, and experience can be expressed as the driving forces behind battlefield tourism (Venter, 2011, p. 1). According to Seaton (2019, p. 299), tourism has been one of the areas that benefited most from the creative forces of war. He also mentions countless examples worldwide of battlefields, monuments, museums, forts, and other war-related sites that have become tourist resources. Battlefields present impressive scenery, leisure activities, and monuments (Winter, 2012, p. 248). Over time, battlefield tourism has become an important component of national and international tourism (Hall et al., 2011). Foulk's (2016) study shows that "battlefield tourism produces tangible results that reflect positively on the French tourism industry in general." At the same time, it is mentioned that significant investments have been made in the structures that feed this niche market, particularly since the end of the 1990s and the beginning of the 21st century. More than 2000 financial gifts played a role in the creation of the Visitor Center in Thiepval. In addition to these, similar organizations are supported by private companies such as "HSBC," "British American Tobacco," and "Unilever," local and national governments, "The British Foreign and Commonwealth Office," and many other organizations such as the "European Union." This is just one of the examples we come across in the context of battlefield tourism and tourism. With the investments made in battlefields and increasing curiosity and interest, the demand to visit battlefields is increasing. It is also possible to find many studies in the literature explaining this situation. For example, according to the study of Winter (2012), the people who mourn in the area have difficulties due to the tourists coming to the battlefields (Lloyd, 1998 in Winter, 2012, p. 249). According to Kuo et al. (2016, p. 103), the number of battlefield tourists arriving in Taiwan has seen a rapid increase in recent years. Basarin and Hall (2008) mention that since 1925 for Anzac Day visits Gallipoli, which is an important visitation site for Anzacs, the number of visits increased significantly until 2008, and this number will reach 50,000 by 2015. Today, this figure is expressed in hundreds of thousands. At the same time, many battlefields in the world are heavily visited. These battlefields have also been the subject of numerous studies, for example, the Anzac Day commemoration event in Gallipoli, Turkey (Hall et al., 2011, p. 419), Kinmen battlefields in Taiwan (Kuo et al., 2016, p. 103), and Moores Creek National Battlefield (Floyd et al., 1997, p. 391).

Battlefields and Associated Places to Visit Around the World

The foundation, known as the "Commonwealth War Graves Commission" (CWGC), was founded during World Wars I and II. It is an intergovernmental organization created to register and preserve the graves and memorial sites of members of the Commonwealth of Nations military service during World Wars. The data provided by this organization present statistics on memorial sites created in various countries of the world after the wars. Even looking at the data of this organization alone, it is possible to see the size of the supply for battlefield tourism in the world. According to the data obtained from this organization, there are around 23,000 war memorials and war cemeteries all over the world (cwgc.org). Museums, houses, cemeteries, monuments, memorials, parks, and campsites that can be associated with battlefield tourism in some countries are compiled below.

It is possible to say that there is a great deal of supply and demand for battlefield tourism in the world. The compiled areas are also compatible with the studies in the literature. In many countries, as seen in Table 5.1, there are places to visit battlefields and related areas such as monuments, tombs, museums, and prisons. In addition to the countries listed above and the battlefields they provide, there are many battlefields around the world. When the visits to these areas are also evaluated, it is possible to say that the supply and demand for battlefield tourism overlap.

Table 5.1. Some Battlefields and Associated Places to Visit Around the World.

Countries	Battlefields/Battlefield Tourism Regions, Places	
Turkey	• Helles Memorial • Green Hill Cemetery • Twelve Tree Copse Cemetery • V Beach Cemetery • Istanbul (Ferikoi) Protestant Cemetery • Lone Pine Memorial	• The Nek Cemetery, Anzac • Skew Bridge Cemetery • Hill 60 Cemetery • Plugge's Plateau Cemetery, Anzac • 4th Battalion Parade Ground Cemetery • Canterbury Cemetery, Anzac

Table 5.1. *(Continued)*

Countries	Battlefields/Battlefield Tourism Regions, Places
	• Twelve Tree Copse (New Zealand) Memorial • Beach Cemetery, Anzac • Haidar Pasha Cemetery, Memorial, Cremation Memorial • Johnston's Jolly Cemetery • Seddel-Bahr Military Grave • Chanak Consular Cemetery • Izmir (Bornova) British Protestant Cemetery • Redoubt Cemetery, Helles • Pink Farm Cemetery, Helles • Chunuk Bair (New Zealand) Memorial • Quinn's Post Cemetery, Anzac • Courtney's and Steel's Post Cemetery • Baby 700 Cemetery, Anzac • Chunuk Bair Cemetery, Anzac • Hill 60 (New Zealand) Memorial • The Farm Cemetery, Anzac • Lancashire Landing Cemetery • 7th Field Ambulance Cemetery • Hill 10 Cemetery • Embarkation Pier Cemetery • Lone Pine Cemetery • No. 2 Outpost Cemetery • Anzac Walker's Ridge Cemetery • Lala Baba Cemetery • Ari Burnu Cemetery, Anzac • Anzac New Zealand No. 2 Outpost Cemetery • Shrapnel Valley Cemetery • Shell Green Cemetery • Ankara Municipal Cemetery • Azmak Cemetery, Suvla
Germany	• Bergen-Belsen and Anne Frank's Memorial • Sachsenhausen Concentration Camp • Battle for the Reichstag; Ravensbrück Concentration Camp (Hitlers Bunker, Ravensbrück Concentration Camp) • Wehrmacht Headquarters Bunkers; Battle of the Halbe Pocket (Zossen-Wünsdorf) • Hürtgen Forest • Siegfried Line • Remagen • Seelow Heights • Tollense valley battlefield

(Continued)

Table 5.1. *(Continued)*

Countries	Battlefields/Battlefield Tourism Regions, Places
Netherlands	• Siegfried Line; Hürtgenwald (Museum, Cemetery etc.) • Rheinberg War Cemetery • Arnhem Landing Grounds and Oosterbeek (Oosterbeek Church, Arnhem Memorial, Arnhem Airborne Museum) • Reichswald Forest and The Rhineland (War Cemetery, Liberation Museum, Forest War Cemetery, Kleve, Operation Varsity)
Italy	• San Pietro; Italian and French War Cemeteries • Moro River Valley • Melfa River • Monte Cassino; Liri Valley • Dolomites, Italy • Commonwealth War Cemeteries at Agira • Bark West Beach • Monte Assoro • Ortona • Casa Berardi • Coriano Ridge • Savio River
United Kingdom	• Jersey War Tunnels and St. Brelades Bay • Corbieres and Channel Island Military Museum • Dover Castle, Dover, England • Battle of Hastings, England • Hastings, East Sussex, England • The Battle of Towton Nr Towton, North Yorkshire • Bosworth Battlefield Heritage Center and Country Park • Battle of Culloden, Culloden Battlefield and Visitor Center • Inverness, Scotland • Battle of Hastings, Battle Abbey, Battle, East Sussex • Siege of Kenilworth, Kenilworth Castle, Warwickshire • The Battle of Bannockburn, Stirling, Scotland • Killiecrankie Visitor Center, Scotland • Newark Castle and National Civil War Center, Nottinghamshire • Battle of Worcester, The Commandery, Worcestershire
Singapore	• Battle Box – British Army Command Center • Kranji coast • Former Ford Motor Factory • Changi Chapel and Museum • Alexandra Hospital • Kranji War Memorial

Table 5.1. *(Continued)*

Countries	Battlefields/Battlefield Tourism Regions, Places
United States	• Gettysburg Battlefield and National Military Park
	• David Wills House
	• Jennie Wade House
	• Shriver House Museum
	• Antietam National Battlefield
	• Manassas National Battlefield Park
	• Richmond Civil War Day
	• Mount Vernon, Virginia
	• Yorktown, VA
	• Independence Hall, Philadelphia, PA
	• Vietnam Veterans Memorial, Washington DC
	• Big Hole Battlefield, Montana, United States
France	• Beaumont-Hamel Newfoundland Memorial
	• The Somme Battlefields
	• Anniversary of the Battle of Fromelles
	• Anniversary of the Battle of Pozieres
	• Last Post Ceremony at Menin Gate
	• Normandy
	• Vel D'Hiv Monument
	• Dunkirk
Belgium	• In Flanders Fields Museum
	• Château d'Hougoumont
	• Lion's Mound
	• Menin Gate
	• Flanders Field
	• Ypres, Belgium
	• The Ardennes Forest, Wallonia
	• Western Front, France/Belgium
	• Waterloo
Thailand	• Thai-Burma Railway
	• Thai-Burma Railway Center Museum
	• Kanchanaburi War Cemetery,
	• Chungkai Cemetery and adjacent POW Camp
	• Ban Huai Kon Kao Battlefield Memorial
Singapore	• The Kranji War Memorial
	• Causeway
	• Sungei Buloh Wetland Reserve
	• Lim Chu Kang Road

(Continued)

Table 5.1. (*Continued*)

Countries	Battlefields/Battlefield Tourism Regions, Places
	• Sarimbun
	• Kranji War Cemetery
	• Former Ford Factory
	• Johore Battery
	• The Changi Museum
	• Adam Park
Australia	• The Australian War Memorial
	• Western Front Day Tours
	• The Somme and Flanders
	• Fromelles and Pheasant Wood
	• Passchendaele
	• Pozieres
	• Hill 60
	• Polygon Wood
	• Broodseinde
	• Messines
	• Menin Road
	• Hellfire Corner
	• Bullecourt
	• Le Hamel
	• The Ypres Salient
	• Mont Saint-Quentin
	• Peronne, Arras
	• VC Corner
	• Tyne Cot
Japan	• Battlefields of Sekigahara, Japan
	• Okinawa, Japan
	• Hiroshima, Japan
	• Nagakute Battlefield
	• Historic Sekigahara Battlegrounds
Vietnam	• Khe Sanh, Vietnam
	• Long Tan, Vietnam
	• War Remnants Museum
	• Reunification Palace
	• Cu Chi Tunnels
	• Hue Imperial Citadel
	• Vietnam Military History Museum
	• Hoa Lo Prison
	• Ap Bac Battlefield
	• Ashau Valley
	• Cannon Fort, Cat Ba Island
	• Dien Bien Phu Battlefield

Table 5.1. *(Continued)*

Countries	Battlefields/Battlefield Tourism Regions, Places	
Russia	• Borodino, Russia	
	• Stalingrad, Russia	
	• Kubinka and Patriot Park	
South Korea	• The Demilitarized Zone	
	• Panmunjon	
	• Dorosan Station	
	• Imjingak	
	• Korean War Memorial – Yongsan	
	• Independence Hall	
	• The Battle of Hansando, South Korea	
Brazil	• São Luis Fortress	
	• Praça Carlos Telles	
	• Capão da Mortandade	
	• Capão da Mortandade	
	• KSOL Paintball	
	• Forte Marechal Moura de Naufragados	
	• Ponte da Azenha	
	• Grota de Angico	
	• Parque Histórico "Colônia Militar dos Dourados"	
	• Clube de Airsoft Black Ops Operação Theatro	
Some other destinations related to battlefields	• Kapyong, South Korea • Oświęcim, Poland • Pearl Harbor, Hawaii • Mausoleum of Genghis Khan, Inner Mongolia • The Khmer (Angkor) Empire, Cambodia • Singapore: Changi • Shanghai: Hongkou District • Philippines: Bataan • India: Red Hill (Lokpaching) • Siem Reap, Cambodia • Plain of Jars, Laos • Putao, Myanmar	• Old Fort Erie, Fort Erie, Ontario, Canada • Culloden, Scotland • Battle of Stirling Bridge, Scotland • Karelia, Finland • Soča Valley, Slovenia • Thermopylae, Greece • Crete, Greece • El Alamein, Egypt • Isandlwana and Rorke's Drift, South Africa • Honiara, Solomon Islands • Battlefield of Ayacucho, Quinua, Huamanga, Peru

Source: Compiled by the author.

Conclusion

People have participated in travel movements with different motivations throughout history. The needs, expectations, and demands of people and societies have also changed over time. One of the travel motivations that arise in this process is the desire to visit battlefields under the influence of emotional and spiritual triggers. Thus, the desire to go to battlefields appears as a travel motivation from past to present. It would be incomplete to interpret this desire as solely based on individual motivations; visiting battlefields creates an intense demand as a national/social motivation. The supply that will meet such a huge demand that concerns so many societies is also very important. As mentioned in this chapter, the supply and demand density regarding battlefields is at a remarkable level. The issue of supply and demand for battlefields has been addressed and discussed under this title. In this context, a brief look at battlefield tourism was taken and the magnitude of supply and demand in the world was mentioned. It has been emphasized that battlefield tourism is a subject that is also heavily involved in the literature, and then the countries that supply battlefield tourism are included. In the section where the intense demand for battlefields is emphasized, supply and demand for battlefields are discussed together.

World history is full of war, pain, grief, sadness, mourning, and memories. Almost every country has lands built on bloody memories and sadness. These memories are phenomena that should be remembered and respected by nations. From this point of view, it is important to protect, preserve, and remember all these areas for future generations. There are many structures such as battlefields, museums, houses, cemeteries, monuments, parks, and campsites preserved in many places around the world. With the protection and opening of these areas to visitors, supply and demand for battlefield tourism have maintained its existence in every period of history. Today, unfortunately, hot wars continue in different parts of the world, and the pain and sadness brought by losses cause the battlefields to emerge with new stories. It is obvious that these stories and painful experiences will continue. In such a case, battlefields will attract visitors in the future as well.

References

Adams, C. P. (2005). Footprints in the mud: The British Army's approach to the battlefield tour experience. *Defence Studies, 5*(1), 15–26.

Ağaoğlu, Y. S. (2012). Visiting Gallipoli Peninsula: Perception of Australian and New Zealand visitors towards Anzac Day in Turkey. *Gümüşhane Üniversitesi Sosyal Bilimler Elektronik Dergisi, 6,* 212–218.

Akbulut, O., & Ekin, Y. (2018). *Savaş Alanları Turizmi: Birleşik Krallık Savaş Alanları Kaynak Merkezi Örneği ve Kurtuluş Savaşı Alanlarının Turizm Potansiyeli* (pp. 105–141). Türkiye Sosyal Araştırmalar Dergisi.

Alaeddinoğlu, F., & Aliağaoğlu, A. (2007). Savaş Alanları Turizmine Tipik Bir Örnek: Büyük Taarruz ve Başkomutan Tarihi Milli Parkı. Anatolia. *Turizm Araştırmaları Dergisi, 18*(2), 215–225.

Alexandra, D., Alexandru, C., & Larisa, T. (2014). Dark tourism, Romania and Dracula. The perceptions of potential American tourists. *Annals of the University of Oradea, Economic Science Series, 23*(1), 309–319.

Basarin, V. J., & Hall, J. (2008). The business of battlefield tourism. *Deakin Business Review, 1*(2), 45–55.

Bigley, J. D., Lee, C., Chon, J., & Yoon, Y. (2010). Motivations for war-related tourism: A case of DMZ visitors in Korea. *Tourism Geographies, 12*, 371–394.

Bloom, T. (2000). Morbid tourism – A postmodern Market Niche with an example from Althorp. *Norsk Geografisk Tidsskrift – Norwegian Journal of Geography, 54*, 29–36.

Çakar, K. (2018). Experiences of visitors to Gallipoli, a nostalgia-themed dark tourism destination: An insight from TripAdvisor. *International Journal of Tourism Cities, 4*(1), 98–109.

Clarke, P., & Eastgate, A. (2011). Cultural capital, life course perspectives and Western Front battlefield tours. *Journal of Tourism and Cultural Change, 9*(1), 31–44.

Coats, A., & Ferguson, S. (2013). Rubbernecking or rejuvenation: Post earthquake perceptions and the implications for business practice in a dark tourism context. *Journal of Research for Consumers, 23*, 32–65.

Commonwealth War Graves. (2023, November 29). https://www.cwgc.org/visit-us/find-cemeteries-memorials/search-results/?Country=Turkey+(including+Gallipoli) &Lat=0&Lon=0&Lo cality=null&Name=&CasualtiesRange=0&Page=1

Cooper, M. (2006). The Pacific War battlefields: Tourist attractions or war memorials? *International Journal of Tourism Research, 8*, 213–222.

Daugbjerg, M. (2011). Not mentioning the nation: Banalities and boundaries at a Danish war heritage site. *History and Anthropology, 22*(2), 243–259.

Dunkley, R., Morgan, N., & Westwood, S. (2011). Visiting the trenches: Exploring meanings and motivations in battlefield tourism. *Tourism Management, 32*, 860–868.

Engström, C., & Boluk, K. A. (2012). The battlefield of the mountain: Exploring the conflict of tourism development on the three peaks in Idre, Sweden. *Tourism Planning & Development, 9*(4), 411–427.

Floyd, M. F., Jang, H., & Noe, F. P. (1997). The relationship between environmental concern and acceptability of environmental impacts among visitors to two U.S. National Park settings. *Journal of Environmental Management, 51*, 391–412.

Foulk, D. (2016). The impact of the "economy of history": The example of battlefield tourism in France. *Mondes du Tourisme, 12*, 1–21.

Gatewood, J. B., & Cameron, C. M. (2004). Battlefield pilgrims at Gettysburg National Military Park. *Ethnology, 43*(3), 193–216.

Gentry, G. W. (2007). Walking with the dead the place of ghost walk tourism in Savannah, Georgia. *Southeastern Geographer, 47*(2), 222–238.

Gibson, D. C. (2006). The relationship between serial murder and the American tourism industry. *Journal of Travel & Tourism Marketing, 20*(1), 45–60.

Hall, J., Basarin, V. J., & Lockstone-Binney, L. (2011). Pre- and posttrip factors influencing the visitor experience at a battlefield commemorative event: Gallipoli, a case study. *Tourism Analysis, 16*, 419–429.

HallBasarin, J. V. J., & Binney, L. L. (2010). An empirical analysis of attendance at a commemorative event: Anzac day at Gallipoli. *International Journal of Hospitality Management, 29,* 245–253.

Hanink, D. M., & Stutts, M. (2002). Spatial demand for national battlefields parks. *Annals of Tourism Research, 29*(5), 707–719.

Henderson, J. C. (2000). War as a tourist attraction: The case of Vietnam. *International Journal of Tourism Research, 2,* 269–280.

Herborn, P. J., & Hutchinson, F. P. (2014). "Landscapes of Remembrance" and sites of conscience: Exploring ways of learning beyond militarizing "Maps" of the future. *Journal of Peace Education, 11*(2), 131–149.

Hertzog, A. (2012). War battlefields, tourism and imagination. *Via Tourism Review, 1*(1), 1–13.

Holguín, S. (2005). National Spain invites you: Battlefield tourism during the Spanish Civil War. *American Historical Review, 110*(5), 1399–1426.

Hughes, R. (2008). Dutiful tourism: Encountering the Cambodian Genocide. *Asia Pacific Viewpoint, 49*(3), 318–330.

Hyde, K. F., & Harman, S. (2011). Motives for a secular pilgrimage to the Gallipoli battlefields. *Tourism Management, 32,* 1343–1351.

Iles, J. (2006). Recalling the ghosts of war: Performing tourism on the battlefields of the western front. *Text and Performance Quarterly, 26*(2), 162–180.

Iles, J. (2008). Encounters in the fields – Tourism to the battlefields of the western front. *Journal of Tourism and Cultural Change, 6*(2), 138–154.

Kılıç, B., & Akyurt, H. (2011). Destinasyon İmajı Oluşturmada Hüzün Turizmi: Afyonkarahisar ve Başkomutan Tarihi Milli Parkı. *Gaziantep Üniversitesi Sosyal Bilimler Dergisi, 10*(1), 209–232.

Knox, D. (2006). The sacralised landscapes of Glencoe: From massacre to mass tourism, and back again. *International Journal of Tourism Research, 8,* 185–197.

Kuo, N. T., Chang, K. C., Cheng, Y. S., & Lin, J. C. (2016). Effects of tour guide interpretation and tourist satisfaction on destination loyalty in Taiwan's Kinmen battlefield tourism: Perceived playfulness and perceived flow as moderators. *Journal of Travel & Tourism Marketing, 33,* 103–122.

Kurnaz, H. A., Çeken, H., & Kılıç, B. (2013). Hüzün Turizmi Katılımcılarının Seyahat Motivasyonlarının Belirlenmesi. *İşletme Araştırmaları Dergisi, 5*(2), 57–73.

Le, D. T., & Pearce, D. G. (2011). Segmenting visitors to battlefield sites: International visitors to the former demilitarized zone in Vietnam. *Journal of Travel & Tourism Marketing, 28*(4), 451–463.

Lee, Y. (2006). The Korean War and tourism: Legacy of the war on the development of the tourism industry in South Korea. *International Journal of Tourism Research, 8,* 157–170.

Lee, Y. J. (2016). The relationships amongst emotional experience, cognition, and behavioral intention in battlefield tourism. *Asia Pacific Journal of Tourism Research, 21*(6), 697–715.

Levitt, L. (2010). Death on display: Reifying stardom through Hollywood's dark tourism. *The Velvet Light Trap, 65,* 62–70.

Lockstone-Binney, L., Hall, J., & Atay, L. (2013). Exploring the conceptual boundaries of diaspora and battlefield tourism: Australians' travel to the Gallipoli battlefield, Turkey, as a case study. *Tourism Analysis, 18*(3), 297–311.

Lunn, K. (2007). War memorialisation and public heritage in Southeast Asia: Some case studies and comparative reflections. *International Journal of Heritage Studies, 13*(1), 81–95.

MacCarthy, M., & Willson, G. (2015). The business of D-day: An exploratory study of consumer behaviour. *International Journal of Heritage Studies, 21*(7), 698–715.

McKay, J. (2013). A critique of the militarization of Australian history and culture thesis: The case of Anzac battlefield tourism. *Journal of Multidisciplinary International Studies, 10*(1), 1–25.

Melstrom, R. T. (2014). Valuing historic battlefields: An application of the travel cost method to three American Civil War battlefields. *Journal of Cultural Economics, 38*, 223–236.

Miles, S. (2014). Battlefield sites as dark tourism attractions: An analysis of experience. *Journal of Heritage Tourism, 9*(2), 134–147.

Ojeda, D. (2013). War and tourism: The banal geographies of security in Colombia's "Retaking". *Geopolitics, 18*(4), 759–778.

Pieris, A. (2014). Southern invasions: Post-war tourism in Sri Lanka. *Postcolonial Studies, 17*(3), 266–285.

Rofe, M. W. (2012). Considering the limits of rural place making opportunities: Rural dystopias and dark tourism. *Landscape Research, 3*(2), 262–272.

Seaton, A. V. (1999). War and then a tourism: Waterloo 1815–1914. *Annals of Tourism Research, 26*(1), 130–158.

Seaton, A. V. (2000). "Another weekend away looking for dead bodies..." Battlefield tourism on the Somme and in Flanders. *Tourism Recreation Research, 25*(3), 63–77.

Seaton, P. (2019). Islands of "Dark" and "Light/Lite" tourism: War-related contents tourism around the Seto Inland Sea. *Japan Review, 33*(Special Issue: War, Tourism, and Modern Japan), 299–327.

Smith, V. L. (1996). War and its tourist attractions. In A. Pizam & Y. Mansfeld (Eds.), *Tourism, crime, and international security issues* (pp. 247–264). Wiley.

Smith, V. L. (1998). War and tourism: An American ethnography. *Annals of Tourism Research, 25*(1), 202–227.

Šuligoj, M. (2017). Warfare tourism: An opportunity for Croatia? *Economic research-Ekonomska Istraživanja, 30*(1), 439–452.

Upton, A. (2015). *Understanding the reflections of battlefield tourists regarding their experiences to sites associated with WWI and The Vietnam War: An analysis of travel blogs.* Master of International Tourism Management, Auckland University of Technology.

Venter, D. (2011). Battlefield tourism in the South African context. *African Journal of Hospitality, Tourism and Leisure, 1*(3), 1–5.

Volcic, Z., Erjavec, K., & Peak, M. (2014). Branding post-war Sarajevo. *Journalism Studies, 15*(6), 726–742.

Walby, K., & Piche, J. (2011). The polysemy of punishment memorialization: Dark tourism and Ontario's penal history museums. *Punishment & Society, 13*(4), 451–472.

West, B. (2008). Enchanting pasts: The role of international civil religious pilgrimage in reimagining national collective memory. *Sociological Theory, 26*(3), 258–270.

Winter, C. (2011a). Battlefield visitor motivations: Explorations in the Great War Town of Leper, Belgium. *International Journal of Tourism Research, 13*, 164–176.

Winter, C. (2011b). First World War cemeteries: Insights from visitor books. Tourism geographies. *An International Journal of Tourism Space, Place and Environment, 13*(3), 462–479.

Winter, C. (2012). Commemoration of the Great War on the Somme: Exploring personal connections. *Journal of Tourism and Cultural Change, 10*(3), 248–263.

Winter, C. (2019). Pilgrims and votives at war memorials: A vow to remember. *Annals of Tourism Research, 76*, 117–128.

Yeneroğlu Kutbay, E., & Aykac, A. (2016). Battlefield tourism at Gallipoli: The revival of collective memory, the construction of national identity and the making of a long-distance tourism network. *Journal of Tourism, Culture and Territorial Development, 7*(5), 61–83.

Yeşildağ, B., & Atay, L. (2011). Savaş Alanları Turizmi: Gelibolu Yarımadasına Gelen Ziyaretçilere Yönelik Bir Çalışma. *Balıkesir Üniversitesi Sosyal Bilimler Enstitüsü Dergisi, 14*(26), 267–280.

Zhang, J. J. (2010). Of Kaoliang, bullets and knives: Local entrepreneurs and the battlefield tourism enterprise in Kinmen (Quemoy), Taiwan. Tourism geographies. *An International Journal of Tourism Space, Place and Environment, 12*(3), 395–411.

Ziino, B. (2006). Who owns Gallipoli? Australia's Gallipoli Anxieties 1915–2005. *Journal of Australian Studies, 30*(88), 1–12.

Chapter 6

Battlefield Tourism Intermediaries

Kaan Kasaroğlu and Simge Kömürcü Sarıbaş

İzmir Katip Çelebi University, Türkiye

Abstract

Wars all over the world have changed the course of history, affected communities and ways of life, and caused much pain, sadness, and destruction. Today, these areas are seen as tourist attractions and are visited by many people with different motivations every year. In these travels, which are described as battlefield tourism, intermediary institutions serve as a bridge between the consumer and the producer, in other words, between the tourist and the touristic product. In this section, first the factors that have led people to travel throughout history are discussed, and then the history, purposes, activities, and importance and contributions of intermediary institutions within the tourism industry are explained. Afterward, battlefield tourism, a relatively new concept, was mentioned, and the importance of intermediary institutions in travels to battlefields was explained. Finally, intermediary institutions that organize tours to various major battlefields in the world are listed, and brief descriptive information is given about the wars in question and the tours organized to these areas.

Keywords: Tourism; battlefield; intermediaries; wholesalers; retailers

Introduction

Throughout history, human beings have participated in displacement movements with different motivations. These relocations, which were first made for commercial purposes, have diversified over time for religious reasons, participation in wars, health, etc. Although the first relocation movements did not show a touristic purpose, the developing living conditions increased the participation of people in recreational activities. Positive developments such as improving transportation conditions, facilitating access to technology and information, and increases in people's leisure time and income have positively affected tourism activities.

Battlefield Tourism, 115–129
doi:10.1108/978-1-83909-990-820241009

In ancient times, travel for tourism purposes was a service accessible to people with high income, but today it has become an activity that almost everyone can participate in. In particular, the initiation of intermediary institutions, one of the most important operational sectors of tourism, supported the travels of large masses. The outstanding efforts of intermediary institutions, namely travel agencies and tour operators, such as eliminating language problems, offering safer travels, bringing all touristic products together and presenting them to the consumer as a package, and reducing travel costs have facilitated the participation of the masses in tourism activities aimed at their desired motivations.

Wars are considered to be one of the first displacement movements. However, over the years, people's desire to visit places where their ancestors fought and encountered tragic events, and their desire to experience historical developments that they were curious about, made wars and battlefields an important tourist product. In today's world, there is a great travel trend for travels to places where wars have taken place throughout history and to attend commemorations in these places. Travel agencies and tour operators contribute greatly to these trips, which are also supported by the governments of many countries. Intermediary institutions have a great role in providing transportation and accommodation needs of tourist groups with travel demands to these places and in delivering them to all important areas and activities in the destination.

In this section, first of all, the factors that lead people to travel throughout history are briefly examined. Then, the historical development of intermediary institutions and their contribution to tourism are examined. Finally, battlefield tourism, which has become one of the most important touristic motivations, has been mentioned, and the role and importance of intermediary institutions in the travels to the battlefields has been revealed. In this context, examples of intermediary institutions that organize tours to destinations, that are among the most important battlefields of the world, are given and the characteristics of these tours are mentioned.

Tourism Intermediaries

The notion of travel, defined as an act of displacement, has been observed throughout history, with people embarking on journeys for various reasons even before the invention of the wheel. In ancient societies, when settled communities could not meet all their needs independently, they began traveling for shopping purposes, first with their nearby neighbors and eventually to distant cities (Ahipaşaoğlu & Arıkan, 2003, p. 1). In the following periods, it is known that in Egyptian, Greek, and Roman societies, nobles made various touristic trips for entertainment and education, especially for religious and health purposes, and other individuals for spiritual satisfaction (Holland & Leslie, 2018, p. 1; Syratt & Archer, 2003, pp. 1–2).

With the industrial period, agricultural production left its place to industrial production, and in line with economic developments and changes in business life, individuals who lived in cities found the opportunity to spend a part of their income on tourist travels. In addition, with the invention of steam engines during the Industrial Revolution, first ships and then trains began to be used actively. These developments are seen as factors that facilitate transportation and therefore travel. In the subsequent years, with the outbreak of the First World War, tourism movements came to a halt and resumed in 1918. However, during this period, the automobile became a more efficient means of travel compared to journeys by ship and train. Afterward, the use of airplanes in civil aviation and the developments in air transportation, especially during the Second World War, greatly affected travel mobility (Yarcan & Peköz, 1997, pp. 3–4).

In the subsequent years, people started to participate in more travel movements, thanks to the increasing prosperity due to technological developments, the fact that the borders only took on a spiritual meaning depending on the relations of the countries, and the decreasing working hours (Gökdeniz, 1990, p. 44). The increase in the number of people participating in tourism activities has led to a more complex relationship between the tourism supply and the tourists demanding the product. To address this complexity, it has revealed the need for the existence of some intermediary institutions and organizations that will bring together the supply and demand (Yarcan & Peköz, 2001, pp. 1–2). In other words, Study Guide (2011, p. 4) states that the role of intermediaries in the consumption process is to act as a kind of bridge between the producers of a product or service and the ultimate consumer, providing assistance.

Intermediary institutions are generally defined as "a firm or person (such as a broker or consultant) who acts as a mediator on a link between parties to a business deal, investment decision, negotiation, etc" (Business Dictionary, 2023). As can be seen in the definition made, intermediary institutions operate to regulate and support the relationship between supply and demand. When we evaluate in terms of the tourism industry, it is seen that there are three basic structures in the industry: producer, consumer, and intermediary. Here, the producer role consists of accommodation enterprises, transportation services producers, cultural narrators (tourist guides), food and beverage service producers, and entertainment services producers. The consumer side consists of people who purchase or intend to purchase these services. In this process, intermediaries are the ones who connect the producers with the consumers and help the process to progress more uninterruptedly (İçöz & Öter, 2007, p. 77). They can be a wholesaler such as tour operators or brokers, and retailers such as travel agents (Syratt & Archer, 2003, p. 15).

During the distribution chain structure in the tourism industry, producer of the product or service that an individual needs to travel can sell their products directly to consumers or wholesalers. Wholesalers can bundle products and/or sell them to retailers. Retailers also bring the final product to the consumer (Study Guide, 2011, p. 3). However, considering that there are too many producers and consumers in today's tourism and travel industry, the attempt of the producers to sell their products directly to the consumer may lead to a negative situation in terms of money and time. For this reason, intermediaries serve as a bridge between the producer and the consumer, bringing together the touristic products produced at a lower cost (İçöz, 2006, p. 34). As a matter of fact, Kozak (2012, p. 158) lists the reasons for using an intermediary institution in the marketing and distribution process of tourism products as follows:

- Even if the enterprises in the tourism industry have a large structure, it is generally not economically possible to establish a system that aims to reach the consumer directly.
- The expertise of travel intermediaries in this field will enhance marketing efficiency, enabling them to reach consumers more effectively and yield positive results.
- Considering that the tourism industry has an elastic structure and can be greatly affected by developments around the world, making use of intermediary institutions may reduce this risk to some extent.

Considering the characteristics of the tourism industry, unlike a classical industrial product distribution process, in the distribution of touristic products, the consumer, that is, the tourist, has to go to the place where the product is produced. Although there are many institutions and organizations that take the role of intermediaries in the tourism and travel industry, the ones that are most identified with intermediation are travel enterprises (Kotler et al., 2022, p. 114).

Travel businesses; It is defined as commercial organizations that play a binding role between the producer and the consumer of the touristic product, creating the touristic product or only responsible for the distribution. These businesses are divided into two wholesalers and retailers, namely tour operators and travel agencies (Yarcan & Peköz, 1997, p. 6). Firstly, tour operators, often referred to as tour wholesalers, are organizations that act as bridges between tourist product producers and tourists. They organize various services such as transportation, accommodation, food and beverage, recreation, and entertainment individually, and sell them directly or indirectly to consumers as part of a single package (Halloway et al., 2009, p. 539).

It is known that the first attempt at package tours created by tour operators was made by Thomas Cook (Sheldon, 1986, p. 351). In 1841, Cook organized a trip from Leicester to Loughborough for 570 members of the South Midland Temperance Association. After his successful tour attempt, continued to organize tours by chartering trains for certain holidays, and in 1841 he launched his first business under the name Thomas Cook. In 1879, he organized package tours to Europe and the USA for the first time (Syratt & Archer, 2003, p. 4). As can be seen, Thomas Cook ignited the fuse of tour operators and travel agencies at the global level, and after that, some subsequent developments accelerated the course of development of tour operators. Accordingly, individuals who participate in tourist trips started to prefer package tours to minimize uncertainty, smaller and local businesses operating in a certain area grew to become tour operators, and large companies entered the tour operator area in line with the development of the tourism industry are seen like some of the factors that accelerate this process (İçöz, 2006, pp. 203–204).

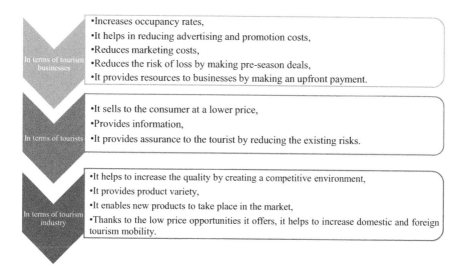

In terms of tourism businesses
- Increases occupancy rates,
- It helps in reducing advertising and promotion costs,
- Reduces marketing costs,
- Reduces the risk of loss by making pre-season deals,
- It provides resources to businesses by making an upfront payment.

In terms of tourists
- It sells to the consumer at a lower price,
- Provides information,
- It provides assurance to the tourist by reducing the existing risks.

In terms of tourism industry
- It helps to increase the quality by creating a competitive environment,
- It provides product variety,
- It enables new products to take place in the market,
- Thanks to the low price opportunities it offers, it helps to increase domestic and foreign tourism mobility.

Fig. 6.1.   Benefits Provided by Tour Operators. *Source:* Çokişler (2017, p. 70).

Tour operators provide many benefits for the tourism industry with their activities. Fig. 6.1 expresses the benefits of tour operators to different stakeholders in the tourism industry.

According to Fig. 6.1, tour operators provide different benefits to different stakeholders involved in tourism due to their nature. In addition, the importance of tour operators in the tourism industry can be seen, given that they are intermediary institutions that guide and support the touristic activities of millions of people from all over the world every year (Kozak, 2012, p. 44). Today, companies such as Schauinsland-Reisen, Alltours, DER Touristik, Ferien Touristik, TUI, FTI Touristik, and Anex Tour are among the world's leading tour operators and continue their activities (Turizm Günlüğü, 2022).

Travel agencies, another intermediary institution, are defined as organizations that operate to meet all the needs of people who want to travel with different purposes and motivations regarding their travel processes (Doğan & Gencan, 2013, p. 71). According to another definition, travel agencies, they are the organizations responsible for programming, presenting, and selling the products of the enterprises in the tourism industry in a way that is most suitable for the national tourism and economy, in favorable conditions to the consumer (İçöz, 2006, p. 71). Although there are different definitions for travel agencies, the definitions generally focus on the following common points (Bahçe, 2006, p. 86):

- They are commercial enterprises acting as an intermediary.
- They have the experience and expertise needed in the travel industry.

- They also provide consultancy services to consumers, i.e., tourists, when necessary during their travel processes.
- Due to the current structure of the tourism industry, the agencies prioritize human relations.
- They usually work on commission.

Travel agencies, which are described as travel intermediaries in the tourism industry (Yarcan & Peköz, 1997, p. 6), have a different structure from tour operators which are another intermediary institution. The differences between travel agencies and tour operators are expressed as follows (İçöz & Öter, 2007, p. 79):

- While the travel agency only plays an intermediary role due to its structure, the tour operator plays both a producer and an intermediary role.
- While travel agencies usually sell products produced and created, the primary job of tour operators is to create package tours.
- Tour operators have a stronger influence on prices, while travel agencies have a low influence on the prices set because they sell manufactured products.
- The risk taken by travel agencies is much lower than by tour operators.
- While the choice of establishment location is important in travel agencies, this does not apply to tour operators operating on a larger scale.

As can be seen, there are some basic structural features that distinguish the two main travel intermediaries, travel agencies and tour operators. One of the most important functions of travel agencies is to ensure that the tourist, who is a consumer during the touristic travel process, reaches the touristic product produced in the easiest way (Çakıcı et al., 2008, p. 70). In addition, these businesses provide services such as arranging tour packages, helping with reservations, making necessary arrangements for transportation, providing information, vehicle rental, ticket sales, travel consultancy, insurance transactions, passport and visa processes, and special events (Doğan & Gencan, 2013, p. 71; Lam & Zhang, 1999, p. 341). And also, according to İçöz (2006, p. 75), travel agencies also have several different local and national functions and duties such as developing tourism, promoting and advertising tourism, and finding new tourism centers. In this context, considering the functions of travel agencies, almost all stakeholders in the tourism industry need travel agencies to market the touristic products they produce in the most appropriate and optimal conditions (Gökdemir & Erdem, 2017, p. 24).

When the relevant literature is examined, it is seen that there are different approaches to the classification of travel agencies. The reason for this is that the legal regulations for travel agencies differ according to the country, but in general, a classification can be made as follows (Bahçe, 2006, p. 93; TURSAB, 2019, pp. 10–11):

(1) Structural Classification

- Major Distribution Agencies: They usually market touristic products produced by tour operators.

- Specialized Agencies: They organize travel for the demands of large companies.
- Independent Agencies: They are agencies that are not affiliated with any institution.

(2) Functional Classification

- Incoming Agencies: They are the welcoming agencies in the destination country.
- Outgoing Agencies: They are usually the agencies that organize tours abroad.

On the other hand, İçöz (2006, pp. 86–88) stated that in addition to the above classifications, travel agencies can also be classified according to the type of service they provide, and he classified as: (a) airline ticket sales agents, (b) tour sales agencies, (c) tour operator representative agencies, (d) car rentals agencies, (e) transportation agencies, (f) congress-meeting agencies, and (g) incentive agencies.

According to another classification found in the literature, travel agencies are divided into three. These are (Sharpley, 2006, p. 80; Study Guide, 2011, p. 4):

(1) Business Travel Agents: They are travel agencies that are more geared toward the business market.
(2) Leisure Travel Agents: These travel agencies usually offer products for leisure travelers. Examples of this are package tours, short holidays and city holidays.
(3) Specialized Travel Agencies: These agencies usually specialize in a particular geography or type of tourism. To give an example for their fields of activity, these agencies are interested in products and/or services for medical tourism and golf tourism, special interest tourism.

It is seen that a clear classification of travel agencies cannot be made and they are categorized under different headings. In addition, today there are travel agencies that cover many different areas from mass tourism activities to more specific special interests and also serve different travel purposes. In the expansion of the activity range of travel agencies, especially in recent years, the change in touristic preferences and habits, and a tendency toward special interest tourism rather than mass tourism activities can be shown (Alaeddinoğlu & Aliağaoğlu, 2007, p. 216). Unlike mass tourism, one of the increasing trends in special interest tourism in recent years is battlefield tourism.

Wars have affected the fate of people and societies throughout history and played a major role in shaping societies (Akbulut & Ekin, 2018a, p. 396; Atay & Yeşildağ, 2010, p. 66). On the other hand, the opening to visit the battlefields where tragic events took place, and the increase in the travels made by people to the battlefields with different motivations found the relationship between the battlefields and tourism (Yeşildağ & Atay, 2011, p. 270). In other words, the tourism industry's constant search for new attractions, combined with an interest in visiting battlefields, has led to the creation of a new and niche market called battlefield tourism (Prideaux, 2007, p. 18).

It is accepted that travels for battlefield tourism started with the Battle of Waterloo in the 19th century (Basarin & Hall, 2008, p. 44). In addition, places such as Normandy, Gettysburg, Verdun, and Gallipoli are considered extremely important areas both historically and touristically and are visited by millions of people every year within the scope of battlefield tourism (Akbulut & Ekin, 2018b, pp. 107–108; Atay & Yeşildağ, 2010, p. 66; Basarin, 2011, p. 51). At this point, it is thought that travel agencies and tour operators that will bring together touristic supply and demand in this niche market formed for battlefields with increasing interest are of great importance. In this context, information on intermediaries operating in battlefields of touristic importance in the world and some of the tours carried out by these institutions are shown in Table 6.1.

Table 6.1 shows the main battlefields, which are of historical and touristic importance in the world and visited by many tourists every year, and the intermediary institutions that organize trips to these areas. The table shows that as well as large-scale and comprehensive tours to the aforementioned battlefields, there are also smaller and local tours. Some information about the battlefields and tours where the tours are organized is given below:

Table 6.1. Intermediary Institutions for Battlefield Tourism.

	Battlefield(s)	Intermediaries
1	Gallipoli	• anzacgallipolitours.com • Leger holidays • Gallipoli Tour Travel Agency • The Cultural Experience Tours & Holidays • Viator • Lutars Turizm • Drabos Tourism • Yeni Abideler Turizm • Ssctur • Hassle-Free Travel Agency
2	Waterloo	• TET Battlefield Tours • Viator • Rifleman Tours • Leger Holidays • The Cultural Experience Tours & Holidays • Cooper's Waterloo Tours • Battlefield Tours • Barrie Friend • Belgium Tour Guide Waterloo • Mat McLachlan Battlefield Tours

Table 6.1. *(Continued)*

	Battlefield(s)	Intermediaries
3	Normandy	• Viator
		• TET Battlefield Tours
		• Barrie Friend
		• Ophorus
		• TourRadar
		• Rifleman Tours
		• Trafalgar
		• Beaches of Normandy Tours
		• NST
		• Adrian Roads
		• Smithsonian
		• Normandy American Heroes
		• Overlord Tour
4	Gettysburg	• Cool Destinations
		• Usaguidedtours
		• Addressinggettysburg
		• Viator
		• Get your guide
		• Destination Gettysburg
		• Past Lane Travels
		• Hickory Hollow Farm
5	Verdun	• The Cultural Experience
		• France Just For You
		• Adrian Roads
		• Sophie Great War Tours
		• Leger Holidays
		• Viator
		• Zeitgeist School Tours
		• Terres de Memoire
		• Royal Journey France
		• Tourisme Grand Verdun
		• Knee Deep Into History
		• Dr Thomson's Tour
		• Ingrid Ferrand
		• Great War Battlefields

Source: Created by authors.

- Located within the borders of Çanakkale province, Gallipoli is one of Turkey's most important battlefield tourism centers. This area of approximately 33,940 hectares is extremely important not only for the Turks but also for the people of New Zealand and Australia, due to the scope of the war. So much so that every year special commemorations and trips are organized for Anzac Day, and thousands of tourists from Australia and New Zealand visit this area (Birdir et al., 2015, p. 14; Topsakal & Ekici, 2014, p. 328). Therefore, it is seen that tours in this area are carried out by local, national and international intermediary institutions for different audiences. When the tours created are examined; It is among the information obtained that tours vary between daily and 1-week tours in terms of duration, there are tours covering only Gallipoli, as well as larger-scale package tours, and tour prices vary according to the scope of the tour.
- The Battle of Waterloo took place on June 18, 1815, between a multinational allied army and the French army under the command of Napoleon, approximately nine miles from the Belgian capital Brussels, and the war resulted in the absolute defeat of the French army and the capture of Napoleon. Today, this area is described as the second most important tourist area of Belgium with the buildings and monuments in it (Seaton, 1999, pp. 130–132). Therefore, the tours organized for this region have been going on for a long time. So much so that the first tour attempt of the Thomas Cook travel agency abroad was for the Battle of Waterloo (Adams, 2007, pp. 3–4). Today, it is seen that both relatively larger international companies and more local businesses organize various tours to this area. In addition, the information that experts on the Waterloo battlefield organize more special and daily tours for this area through local agencies is among the information obtained from their internet addresses.
- II. The Normandy landing, which was shown at the beginning of the events that changed the course of World War II, was carried out on June 6, 1944, when the American and British armies attacked the northern coast of France under German occupation from five different points (Atlas, 2014; Gül, 2007, p. 9). Therefore, it is seen that the tours made here are mostly created under the theme of "heroism" and are preferred by the visitors. The prices of the tours created vary according to the number of days, and these tours are also offered as package tours in a wider scope.
- The Battle of Gettysburg, which took place on July 1–3, 1863, is shown as the most important turning point of the American Civil War. General Robert E. Lee's attacks on the North ended here, and this battle was recorded as the bloodiest battle of the American Civil War. The area where the war took place was later turned into a park and opened to visitors (Greelane, 2019; Historical Events, 2023; National Park Service, 2023). Therefore, many American and foreign tourists visit this area every year for different purposes and motivations. When the travel activities for the area are examined, it is seen that tours are carried out in smaller groups, mostly accompanied by local guides. In addition, it has been observed that some tours are carried out with horses instead of cars, and it is thought that this situation may create an element of attraction.

- The Battle of Verdun, which lasted about 300 days and in which nearly 600 thousand people lost their lives in total, is considered to be one of the longest and bloodiest battles of the First World War. In February 1916, the Germans attacked Verdun, but the French managed to repel this attack together with the people and the army (Hürriyet, 2021; Pazarbaşı, 2008, p. 43). Therefore, this area is extremely important both historically and culturally, and in terms of tourism within the scope of battlefield tourism. In this context, as seen in the table above, many different travel agencies organize trips to this battlefield area. Travel businesses carry out activities for both foreign tourists and local people to visit the region. Some businesses prioritize education and organize tours to the region for students. When the travels are examined, it is seen that areas such as the Douamont Ossuary cemetery, where the bones of 130,000 unidentified soldiers are found, the Mort Homme monument, and the Bois des Caures, the area where the war started, are introduced within the scope of the tours (Andres, 2017).

Conclusion

Intermediary institutions make significant contributions to the development of tourism and the participation of large masses in tourism. When evaluated in terms of battlefield tourism, travel agencies and tour operators have become the organizations preferred by consumers because they facilitate travel. The need for mass travel within a planned program, especially in battlefield tourism, necessitates the existence of intermediary institutions. It is clear that the continuation of the improvements in the existence of intermediary institutions from past to present will support the promotion of battlefields to more potential tourists. The developments in internet technologies and the ease of access to information will support intermediary institutions in reaching more consumers. Intermediary institutions will have great duties in the future in promoting destinations that have historical importance beyond being just a battlefield and in ensuring the desired return from tourism in these destinations.

Bibliography

Adams, P. C. (2007). *Footsteps across time the evolution, use and relevance of battlefield visits to the British armed forces*. Unpublished Doctoral Thesis. Cranfield University.

Addressing Gettysburg. (2023). Experiencing history. https://www.addressing gettysburg.com/

Adrian Roads. (2023). WWI & WW2 battlefield tours. https://www.adrian-roads.com/tours/www1-verdun-1916-and-meuse-argonne-1918-battlefields-tour/

Ahipaşaoğlu, H. S., & Arıkan, İ. (2003). *Seyahat İşletmeleri Yönetimi ve Ulaştırma Sistemleri*. Detay.

Akbulut, O., & Ekin, Y. (2018a). Kültürel miras turizmi olarak savaş alanları turizmi: Türkiye'de yer alan savaş anıtlarının coğrafi bilgi sistemleri analizi. *Hitit Üniversitesi Sosyal Bilimler Enstitüsü Dergisi, 11*(1), 395–420.

Akbulut, E., & Ekin, Y. (2018b). Savaş alanları turizmi: Birleşik Krallık savaş alanları kaynak merkezi örneği ve Kurtuluş Savaşı alanlarının turizm potansiyeli. *Türkiye Sosyal Araştırmalar Dergisi, 22*(1), 105–142.

Alaeddinoğlu, F., & Aliağaoğlu, A. (2007). Savaş alanları turizmine tipik bir örnek: Büyük Taarruz ve Başkomutan Tarihi Milli Parkı. *Anatolia: Turizm Araştırmaları Dergisi, 18*(2), 215–225.

Andres, T. (2017). The 10 best First World War battlefield tours. https://www.telegraph.co.uk/travel/tours/best-first-world-war-battlefield-tours/

Anzac Gallipoli Tours. (2023). http://www.anzacgallipolitours.com/

Atay, L., & Yeşildağ, B. (2010). Savaş alanları ve turizmi. *Aksaray Üniversitesi İktisadi ve İdari Bilimler Fakültesi Dergisi, 2*(2), 65–72.

Atlas. (2014). Normandiya çıkarması: Tarihin 3 boyutu. https://www.atlasdergisi.com/gundem/normandiya-cikarmasi-tarihin-3-boyutu.html

Bahçe, A. S. (2006). *Seyahat işletmelerinin satın alma merkezlerinin yapısı ve bu merkezlerin endüstriyel satın alma kararlarını etkileyen faktörler üzerine bir araştırma.* Unpublished Doctoral Thesis. Anadolu University.

Barrie Friend. (2023). Battlefield tours. http://bf-battlefieldtours.co.uk/waterloo.html

Basarin, V. J. (2011). *Battlefield tourism – Anzac day commemorations at Gallipoli: An empirical analysis.* Unpublished Doctoral Thesis. Deakin University.

Basarin, V. H., & Hall, J. (2008). The business of battlefield tourism. *Deakin Business Review, 1*(2), 45–55.

Battlefield Tours. (2023). Waterloo. https://www.battlefieldtours.co/waterloo-battlefield-tours

Beaches of Normandy Tours. (2023). World War II tours. https://www.beachesofnormandy.com/

Belgium Tour Guide Waterloo. (2023). Guided tour in Waterloo. https://www.belgium-tour-guide.com/private-tour-in-waterloo-t-1257.php

Birdir, K., Dalgıç, A., Güler, O., & Kayaalp, Y. (2015). Hüzün turizmi: Gelibolu Yarımadası Tarihi Milli Parkını ziyaret eden yabancı turistlerin deneyimleri. *Journal of Tourism and Gastronomy Studies, 3*(4), 12–23.

Business Dictionary. (2023). www.businessdictionary.com

Çakıcı, A. C., Atay, L., & Harman, S. (2008). İstanbul'da faaliyet gösteren seyahat acentalarının pazarlama karması kararları üzerine bir araştırma. *İstanbul Ticaret Üniversitesi Sosyal Bilimler Dergisi, 7*(13), 69–87.

Çokişler, N. (2017). Seyahat İşletmeciliği. In A. Akbaba, Z. Öter, M. E. Güler, & V. Altıntaş (Eds.), *Turizm İşletmeciliği Endüstriyel ve Yönetsel Boyutlar.* Detay.

Cool Destinations. (2023). Gettysburg battlefield self-guided driving tour. https://www.cooldestinations.com/activity/gettysburg/gettysburg-battlefield-self-guided-driving-tour/

Cooper's Waterloo Tours. (2023). https://www.waterlootours.co.uk/

Destination Gettysburg. (2023). https://destinationgettysburg.com/

Doğan, N. Ö., & Gencan, S. (2013). Seyahat acentası yöneticilerinin bakış açısıyla en uygun otel seçimi: Bir analitik hiyeraşi prosesi (AHP) uygulaması. *Erciyes Üniversitesi İktisadi ve İdari Bilimler Fakültesi Dergisi, 4*(1), 69–88.

Dr Thomson's Tour. (2023). http://www.drttours.co.uk/verdun-and-argonne.html

Drabos Travel. (2023). Çanakkale Şehitlik Turu. https://www.drabostravel.com/canakkale-sehitlik-turu

France Just For You. (2023). World war history tour of France. https://www.france-justforyou.com/tours/world-war-history-tour-of-france

Gallipoli Tour Travel Agency. (2023). https://www.gallipolitour.com/itinerary/gallipoli-day-trip-from-istanbul/

Get Your Guide. (2023). Gettysburg tours. https://www.getyourguide.com/gettysburg-l32570/tours-tc1/?visitor-id=PWJLW6RLYS20PT5L3376CQC1SPUBGKCD& locale_autoredirect_optout=true

Gökdemir, S., & Erdem, S. H. (2017). Internet usage in travel agencies and social media. *COMU International Journal of Social Sciences*, *2*(3), 23–38.

Gökdeniz, A. (1990). Paket turlar ve üretim safhaları. *Anatolia: Journal of Tourism Research*, *7*(1), 44–48.

Great War Battlefields. (2023). Home. http://greatwarbattlefields.com/

Greelane. (2019). Gettysburg Savaşı'nın önemi. https://www.greelane.com/tr/be%C5% 9Feri-bilimler/tarih-ve-k%C3%BClt%C3%BCr/significance-of-the-battle-of-gettysburg-1773738/

Gül, O. (2007). *Normandiya çıkarması D-Day 6 Haziran 1944*. Unpublished Master Thesis. Yeditepe University.

Halloway, J. C., Humphreys, C., & Davidson, R. (2009). *The business of tourism* (8th ed.). Pearson.

Hassle-Free Travel Agency. (2023). Anzac house. http://www.anzachouse.com/

Hickory Hollow Farm. (2023). https://www.hickoryhollowfarm.com/

Historical Events. (2023). Gettysburg Uluslararası Askeri Parkı, Pensilvanya. https:// www.tarihiolaylar.com/tarihi-olaylar/gettysburg-uluslararasi-askeri-parki-pensilvanya-1037

Holland, J., & Leslie, D. (2018). *Tour operators and operations. Development, management and responsibility*. CABI International.

Hürriyet. (2021). Verdun savaşı, tarihi ve özeti. https://www.hurriyet.com.tr/egitim/verdun-savasi-tarihi-ve-ozeti-verdun-muharebesi-taraflari-nedenleri-ve-sonuclari-kisaca-bilgi-41802534

İçöz, O. (2006). *Seyahat Acentaları ve Tur Operatörlüğü Yönetimi* (5th ed.). Turhan Kitabevi.

İçöz, O., & Öter, Z. (2007). Turizmde tur operatörlüğü ve seyahat acentaları yönetimi. In O. İçöz (Ed.), *Genel Turizm*. Turhan Kitabevi.

Ingrid Ferran. (2023). Discover Verdun and the sites of the Great War. http://verdun-fuehrungen-macht-ingrid.com/en/

Knee Deep Into History. (2023). Battlefield tours. https://kneedeepintohistory.com/verdun-1916-4-day-3-night-tour-23-26-may-2023/

Kotler, P., Bowen, J. T., & Baloglu, S. (2022). *Marketing for hospitality and tourism* (8th ed.). Pearson.

Kozak, N. (2012). *Turizm Pazarlaması* (4th ed.). Detay.

Lam, T., & Zhang, H. Q. (1999). Service quality of travel agents: The case of travel agencies in Hong Kong. *Tourism Management*, *20*, 341–349.

Leger Holidays. (2023). https://www.legerbattlefields.co.uk

Lutars Turizm. (2023). https://www.lutarsturizm.com/

Mat McLachlan Battlefield Tours. (2023). *Battlefields of Belgium tour*. https://battletours.com/the-battlefields-of-belgium-campaigns/

National Park Service. (2023). https://www.nps.gov/index.htm

Normandy American Heroes. (2023). Single-day or a la-carte tours showcase the best of Normandy. https://www.normandyamericanheroes.com/en/a-la-carte

NST. (2023). Normandy sightseeing tours. https://www.normandy-sightseeing-tours.com/

Ophorus. (2023). Battlefield tours. https://www.ophorus.com/category/8/battlefields

Overlordtour. (2023). https://www.overlordtour.com/?cn-reloaded=1

Past Lane Travels. (2023). Gettysburg horseback tour. https://pastlanetravels.com/gettysburg-horseback-tour/

Pazarbaşı, A. (2008). *Birinci Dünya Savaşı'nın 1917 yılı*. Unpublished Master Thesis. Sakarya University.

Prideaux, B. (2007). Echoes of war: Battlefield tourism. In C. Ryan (Ed.), *Battlefield tourism. History, place and interpretation* (pp. 17–27). Elsevier.

Rifleman Tours. (2023). Tours. https://www.riflemantours.co.uk/tours/

Royal Journey France. (2023). Historical tours. https://royaljourneyfrance.com/historical-tours/

Seaton, A. V. (1999). War and thanatourism. Waterloo 1815–1914. *Annals of Tourism Research, 26*(1), 130–158.

Sharpley, R. (2006). *Travel and tourism*. SAGE Publications.

Sheldon, P. J. (1986). The tour operator industry. *Annals of Tourism Research, 13*(3), 349–365.

Smithsonian. (2023). Normandy: A one-week stay in France. https://www.smithsonianjourneys.org/tours/normandy-stay/itinerary/

Sophied Great War Tours. (2023). Visiting the battlefields of Verdun. https://www.sophiesgreatwartours.com/battlefieldblog/2021/3/9/visiting-the-battlefields-of-verdun

Ssctur. (2023). Çanakkale turları. https://www.ssc.com.tr/canakkale-turlari

Study Guide. (2011). *CHT diploma in tourism management, travel agency and tour guide operations*. Confederation of Tourism & Hospitality.

Syratt, G., & Archer, J. (2003). *Manual of travel agency practise* (3rd ed.). Elsevier Butterworth-Heinemann.

Terres de Memoire. (2023). WWI and WWII battlefields tours. https://www.terresdememoire.com/our-tours/ww1-tours/verdun-tour/

TET Battlefield Tours. (2023). Battlefield tours. https://tetbattlefieldtours.com

The Cultural Experience Tours and Holidays. (2023). https://www.theculturalexperience.com

Topsakal, Y., & Ekici, R. (2014). Dark tourism as a type of special interest tourism: Dark tourism potential of Turkey. *Akademik Turizm ve Yönetim Araştırmaları Dergisi, 1*(2), 325–330.

Tourisme Grand Verdun. (2023). Verdun the battlefield tour. https://en.tourisme-verdun.com/sejour/post/the-battlefield-tour

Tourradar. (2023). WWII D-Day landing beaches & battle of Normandy. https://www.tourradar.com/t/129310

Trafalgar. (2023). The treasures of France including Normandy. https://www.trafalgar.com/en-us/tours/the-treasures-of-france-including-normandy?tab=itinerary&optionId=573

Turizm Günlüğü. (2022). 2021'in en iyi tur operatörleri belli oldu. https://www.turizmgunlugu.com/2022/01/25/en-iyi-tur-operatorleri-touristik-aktuell/

TURSAB. (2019). *Turizme Giriş. Seyahat acentacılığı ve tur operatörlüğü.* TÜRSAB Akademi.

Usa Guided Tours. (2023). Gettysburg, PA private tour. https://usaguidedtours.com/dc/tour/gettysburg-pa-private-tour/

Viator. (2023). https://www.viator.com

Yarcan, Ş., & Peköz, M. (1997). *Seyahat İşletmeleri* (2nd ed.). Boğaziçi Üniversitesi Yayınları.

Yarcan, Ş., & Peköz, M. (2001). *Seyahat İşletmeleri.* Boğaziçi Üniversitesi Yayınları.

Yeni Abideler Turizm. (2023). https://www.canakkalegezitur.com/

Yeşildağ, B., & Atay, L. (2011). Savaş alanları turizmi: Gelibolu yarımadasına gelen ziyaretçilere yönelik bir çalışma. *Balıkesir University the Journal of Social Sciences Institute, 14*(26), 267–280.

Zeitgeist School Tours. (2023). Historical and battlefield travel for students. https://www.zeitgeisttours.com/

Chapter 7

Battlefield Tourism Tourist Flows

Fatih Çavuşoğlu

Kutahya Dumlupinar University, Türkiye

Abstract

People's motivation to travel varies from person to person. They may tend to
different types of tourism with different travel motivations. In this context,
this chapter aims to explore reasons for the flow of tourists to battlefield
destinations by examining the travel motivations of people who participate
in battlefield tourism. In general, it can be said that motivations such as
interest in history, interest in battlefields, provide historical information to
children, curiosity, escape stress, boredom and daily routine life, spiritual,
experience and emotional motives, etc., lead people toward battlefield
tourism.

Keywords: Dark tourism; cultural tourism; battlefield tourism; battlefield
tourist flow; battlefield tourists' travel motivation

Introduction

Tourism is generally considered as a phenomenon that needs peace in order to
improve. In recent years, tourism gradually has been offered as playing a significant part in the encouragement of understanding among different cultures and
consequently as a compel for world peace. Nevertheless, tourism has maintained
to exist in times of war in addition to peace. It is possible to find places where
tourism has benefited in times of war just as other places have suffered (Butler &
Suntikul, 2013, p. 1). The increase in the level of welfare and education
throughout the world has increased the demand for cultural tourism. Cultural
tourism can provide a sociocultural interaction with tourists' desire to recognize
and see the cultures of different nations. The demand for cultural tourism is
increasing day by day in line with the desire to learn the cultural values of
different nations. For this reason, cultural values have an important place in
tourism activities. With the increasing number of tourists, traditional tourism

Battlefield Tourism, 131–137
doi:10.1108/978-1-83909-990-820241010

types such as sea sand sun; cultural tourism, dark tourism, battlefield tourism, etc., expanding to include niche products and experiences (Akbulut & Ekin, 2021, p. 156; Beydilli et al., 2017, p. 253). This is an important opportunity for destinations with battlefields and their managers. It is important to know the travel motivations of battlefield tourists for destination managers who want to attract more tourists to their battlefield destinations.

In this chapter of the book, first, the concept of tourist flow is mentioned. Afterward, it is aimed to reveal the factors that cause the tourist flow toward the battlefields by referring to the travel motivations of the tourists on the battlefields.

Tourist Flows

Tourism includes the mobility of people through time and space between their homes and destinations or just within destinations. Understanding the tourist flows and the factors affecting the time and space relationships of tourists in destinations is very important for the development of infrastructure and transportation services, the development of touristic products, the sustainability of the tourism industry and the management of the cultural, environmental, and social effects of tourism (McKercher & Lew, 2004, p. 36).

International tourist flow is mainly determined by the demand factors in the countries that send tourists and the supply factors in the countries that receive tourists. Spendable income, spare time, expenditure of holiday, relative rate of destination, relative exchange rate, and marketing are important factors in demand for international tourism flow. On the other hand, reachability and pull factors of destination, infrastructure and facilities of destination, accommodation options, service quality, and the competitiveness of price, image of the destination, catastrophes, risks, and crises of destination are arbiter factors that affect international tourist flow. Besides cultural distance, common language, cultural connection, and hospitableness of the local people are the most important sociocultural factors for international tourist flows. Peace, security, and health standards of destinations also play critical roles in international tourist flows to certain destinations (Gidebo, 2021, p. 16). According to McKercher and Lew (2004, p. 46), tourist flows are affected by many different factors, such as the distance of demand, the sociocultural structure of tourists, their spendable income, their leisure time, and how they choose to spend this leisure time. The intensity of tourist flow to any destination is related to complex spatial differences in terms of tourist attractions, accessibility in terms of transportation, tourism service, and government policy (O'Hare & Barrett, 1999, p. 60).

Tourism broadly relies on climatic and natural resources. For instance, destinations that have warmer climates generally create preferred environments for recreation and leisure tourists. Natural resources like fresh water, beaches, and forests are vital prerequisites for tourism. This has increased apprehensions that tourist flows will alter to the advantage or disadvantage of destinations, which is the most important apprehension for local and national economies because tourism is one of the biggest economic sectors of the world and of huge significance for many touristic destinations (Gössling & Hall, 2006, p. 163). In this context, it can be stated that tourist flows toward special interest tourism types such as battlefield tourism can reduce apprehensions about the environment and economy of local or national people.

Battlefield Tourist Flows

Wars have had multiple effects on the lives of societies. Tourism activity has also been under the various effects of wars and has been affected by wars. Another contribution of wars to tourism activity is the emergence of military attractions. Battlefields, castles, navy ports, and military museums can be shown among the most important military attractions. A type of tourism that emerges depending on these attractions is battlefield tourism (Aliagaoglu, 2008, p. 88).

Battlefield tourism is an important concentration field within the area of study of thanatourism/dark tourism. Battlefield tourism concentrates especially on famous war sites, war monuments, battlefields, and graveyards (Chen & Tsai, 2017, p. 82). Contrary to almost any other form of tourist experience, battlefield tourism constitutes deep emotional feelings to tourists. Battlefields are the remembrance of the past. The importance of the battlefields is multi-natured and frequently gauged against scales, such as national identity, the seek for freedom, and a reminder of defeat. Battlefields also display several extents that include the battlefield itself, measurement of the consequences on the victor and the over-comer, the impact on participants, and the consequences on their families (Prideaux, 2007, p. 18).

The heritage of wars affects destinations and facilities, whether through the devastating outcomes of bombs and shelling, or the building of defensive molds, which have an existence in the destination. Castles and other consolidations were being built, adapted, and beautified in the 19th and 20th centuries. These war remnants are significant pull factors for patriotic, cultural, or battlefield tourists (Walton, 2013, p. 64).

The flow of tourists toward battlefield tourism is realized by tourists who have different travel motivations. The main reason to visit a battlefield may have been since it is on the drive to another destination, someone's recommendation, or due to a rambling sense of the battlefield's historical significance. According to Gatewood and Cameron (2004, pp. 198–199), the most common reason for tourists to visit battlefields is casual interest in history or battlefields. Another reason for tourists to visit battlefields is serious interest in history or battlefields. For some battlefield tourists, battlefields are a good place for a family tour. In such tours, parents can provide information to their children about the history of the battlefields they visit. For other battlefield tourists, battlefield tourism is seen as an important tourism activity that can be visited as a group.

Winter (2011, pp. 174–175) asserts that the dominant visitor type for battlefield sites is tourists and not pilgrims. Battlefield tourists expect to be involved in commemoration activities and education about the war. Thus, they should not be defined in opposition to pilgrims. Battlefields are places in which dark tourists, along with other tourists, can find some sense of bond with the endeavors of so many others, who were members of their families, citizens of their nation, or ordinary people who fought the war, and as such, battlefield tourists can pull together to make meaning in their own lives.

According to Slade (2003, p. 792), tourists do visit a battlefield, but the battlefield represents a time and place where their countries fought. Battlefield tourists' motives are concerned with nationhood. Broadly, they come to visit the destination in which their nation's constructing stories happened. Akbulut and Ekin (2019, p. 172) state that battlefield sites still mean sites of death, sadness, and destruction for the people. And so battlefields' interpretation has shifted from a nationalist point of view to understanding and remembrance.

Hyde and Harman (2011, p. 1348) express that tourists' motives for joining battlefield tourism are spiritual, nationalistic, family, friendship, and just traveling to their destination. The faith of a tourist in a pilgrimage site is a crucial element of the battlefield experience. Visiting a battlefield site is more closely tied to the national identity of tourists.

Bigley et al. (2010, p. 386) allege that battlefield tourists' motivation can be stated by five main motivation factors. These factors are opposing political regime motivation; knowledge/appreciation of history, culture, and security motivation; curiosity/adventure motivation; war and consequences motivation; and nature-based motivation. Among these factors, it is possible to evaluate nature-based tourism motivation as a pull motivation factor and other factors as a push motivation factor. Kurnaz et al. (2013, p. 63) state that the battlefield tourists' motivation can be explained by four push factors. These factors are dark tourism motivation, personal motivation, war motivation, and escape motivation. According to these factors, dark tourism motivation means that battlefield tourists want to see a destination where their ancestors fought or died and to feel people who fought or died there. Personal motivation includes that battlefield tourists feel necessary to visit a destination, want to see new and different things, want to know local culture closely, and are curious about the region where war emerged. War motivation factor involves battlefield tourists who want to visit museums, monuments, battlefield sites, and tombs of their relations who died in the war. Finally, escape motivation comprises that battlefield tourists want to escape stress, boredom, daily routine life, and intense work pace. Chen and Tsai (2017, p. 90) assert that tourists' motivations that enable tourists to flow into battlefields can be explained by five travel motivations. These travel motivations are personal motives, spiritual motives, experience motives, physical motives, and emotional motives. They also state that battlefield tourists of older age desire to go to battlefields more than young tourists.

Clarke and Eastgate (2011, p. 31) state that tourists who join the battlefield tours conceive the tour as a pilgrimage, allowing the achievement of long-held personal targets and constituting their reminiscence and legacy to praise their nation or family history. According to Le and Pearce (2011, p. 456), interest in battlefield sites and exhibitions, learning something about the history and war, wanting to explore battlefield sites, being curious about war-related areas, seeking for novelty, and experiencing something new and different are the factors that push the tourists to the battlefields.

Battlefield tourist flow can depend on variable reasons. The reasons that push the tourists to the battlefield sites are gratitude for the sacrifice made, respect for the soldiers who fought in the war, understanding the war, remembering the martyrs, visiting war-related monuments and tombs, a better understanding of the historical perspective, interest in history, to see the land where the soldier fought in the war, and to gain experience by visiting the battlefields (Yesildag & Atay, 2012, p. 276). Okuyucu and Erol (2018, p. 142) express that the main push motivation factors for battlefield tourists are commemorative ceremonies, national feelings, understanding of dead and martyrs, curiosity about history, respect for the historical legacy, visiting monuments and museums, and having a family member who died or was injured at the war.

According to Hall et al. (2010, pp. 250–252), accessibility of the battlefield, transportation facilities in the battlefield destination, rubbish management/ collection and toilet facilities in the battlefield sites, and availability of food and drink facilities in the battlefield destination are the most crucial factors for battlefield tourists. If these amenities or opportunities are available on the battlefield sites, tourists can be more satisfied. In addition to this, it can be expressed that accommodation facilities are also more important for battlefield tourists. Okuyucu and Erol (2018, p. 135) assert that transportation and accessibility, the presence of souvenirs that tourists can buy, toilet facilities, and areas for sitting and resting on the battlefield sites are more important for tourists' satisfaction. The absence of these factors in the region or the lack of these services may negatively affect tourist satisfaction and consequently may cause tourists not to visit the same destination again.

Battlefield tourists can feel a strong emotional reaction when experiencing authentic battlefield sites. Battlefield sites can evoke glamorousness in tourists and affect their curiosity and historical understanding of the war. Battlefield tourists who feel positive and peaceful emotions produce high comprehension at battlefield sites. If battlefield tourists perceive historical and spatial comprehension at the battlefield sites where *they* visit, they are most probably to revisit and recommend them to others (Lee, 2016, pp. 712–713). Tourists who have positive feelings about their battlefield visit experience can recommend the destination to their family, friends, or other people who live around them. They may want to come back to the same destination. And they can also make a plan to visit other battlefield sites (Yesildag & Atay, 2012, p. 277).

Tourists who visit a battlefield for the first time anticipate learning something about the history and battles fought there. This type of tourist can rarely be disappointed. But tourists who have come to the battlefield before can be emotionally touched because they pretty much reflect on the battlefield and conceive of the battlefield's importance (Gatewood & Cameron, 2004, p. 213). Battlefield tourists can get some experience and benefits from their visit to any battlefield site. These kinds of experiences and benefits can be expressed as learning about history and war, understanding people who died in the war and so understanding nowadays, understanding the struggle for the nation, fulfillment of spiritual duty, understanding ancestors' tough lives and fortifying of family ties (Okuyucu & Erol, 2018, p. 146).

Any tourist flow takes place toward a certain destination. Not only in battlefield tourism but also in other types of tourism, the local people who live in the destination have a significant impact on the development of tourism in the region. The local people need to have a positive perspective toward tourists to develop tourism in the region. The fact that local people do not want to see tourists in the region where they live is not very valid for dark and battlefield tourism. Local people understand the sorcery that death and tragedy may exert over tourists and ought not to be ignored, as a confrontation with death allows for catharsis, admittance, and a means of feeling sad (Coats & Ferguson, 2013, p. 32).

Conclusion

Tourist flow, in the simplest terms, refers to tourist mobility to a certain destination or region. The constant flow of tourists to any destination is important for the well-being of the local people who live in the destination. From this point of view, it can be stated that destinations with battlefields, which can be seen as an important touristic product, should provide tourist flow to their destinations. At this point, an important task falls on the destination managers to ensure a continuous flow of tourists. It can be stated that determining the factors that push tourists to visit a battlefield, knowing why tourists come to a battlefield, and knowing the facilities that tourists expect from a battlefield site are important information that can contribute to the advertising and promotion of the destination. It can be stated that organizing commemoration events on battlefields, providing products and services that tourists may need on battlefields, and facilitating transportation services can increase the satisfaction of tourists during their visit to the battlefields. Tourists who are satisfied with their visit to the battlefield may make suggestions for others to visit and may want to revisit the same destination. This situation can make tourists flow toward the battlefield constantly.

References

Akbulut, O., & Ekin, Y. (2019). Battlefield tourism: The potential of Badr, Uhud, and the Trench (Khandaq) battles for Islamic tourism. In A. Jamal & K. Griffin (Eds.), *Islamic tourism management of travel destinations* (pp. 168–180). CABI International.

Akbulut, O., & Ekin, Y. (2021). A conceptual study on social memory, cultural heritage and battlefield tourism. *International Journal of Contemporary Tourism Research*, (Special Issue), 150–159.

Aliagaoglu, A. (2008). A typical place to battlefield tourism: Gallipoli Peninsula Historical National Park. *Milli Folklor, 20*(78), 88–104.

Beydilli, E. T., Güven, Ö. Z., & Akça, İ. (2017). Evaluation of the historical mansions that place in Kutahya in content of cultural tourism. *Eurasian Academy of Social Science Journal*, (Special Issue), 252–259.

Bigley, J. D., Lee, C. K., Chon, J., & Yoon, Y. (2010). Motivations for war-related tourism: A case of visitors in Korea. *Tourism Geographies, 12*(3), 371–394.

Butler, R., & Suntikul, W. (2013). Tourism and war: An Ill wind. In R. Butler & W. Suntikul (Eds.), *Tourism and war* (pp. 1–11). Routledge.

Chen, C. M., & Tsai, T. H. (2017). Tourist motivation about a battlefield: A case study of Kinmen. *Tourism Geographies, 21*(1), 78–101.

Clarke, P., & Eastgate, A. (2011). Cultural capital, life course perspectives and western front battlefield tours. *Journal of Tourism and Cultural Change, 9*(1), 31–44.

Coats, A., & Ferguson, S. (2013). Rubbernecking or rejuvenation: Post earthquake perceptions and the implications for business practice in a dark tourism context. *Journal of Research for Consumers, 23*, 32–65.

Gatewood, J. B., & Cameron, C. M. (2004). Battlefield pilgrims at Gettysburg National Military Park. *Ethnology, 43*(3), 193–216.

Gidebo, H. B. (2021). Factors determining international tourist flow to tourism destinations: A systematic review. *Journal of Hospitality Management and Tourism, 12*(1), 9–17.

Gössling, S., & Hall, M. (2006). Uncertainties in predicting tourist flows under scenarios of climate change. *Climatic Change, 79*(3), 163–173.

Hall, J., Basarin, V. J., & Lockstone-Binney, L. (2010). An empirical analysis of attendance at a commemorative event: Anzac Day Gallipoli. *International Journal of Hospitality Management, 29*, 245–253.

Hyde, K. F., & Harman, S. (2011). Motives for a secular pilgrimage to the Gallipoli battlefields. *Tourism Management, 32*, 1343–1351.

Kurnaz, H. A., Ceken, H., & Kilic, B. (2013). Determination of dark tourism participants' travel motivations. *Isletme Arastirmalari Dergisi, 5*(2), 57–73.

Le, D. T. T., & Pearce, D. G. (2011). Segmenting visitors to the battlefield sites: International visitors to the former demilitarized zone in Vietnam. *Journal of Travel & Tourism Marketing, 28*(4), 451–463.

Lee, Y. J. (2016). The relationships amongst emotional experience, cognition, and behavioral intention in battlefield tourism. *Asia Pacific Journal of Tourism Research, 21*(6), 697–715.

McKercher, B., & Lew, A. A. (2004). Tourist flows and the spatial distribution of tourists. In A. A. Lew, C. M. Hall, & A. M. Williams (Eds.), *A companion to tourism* (pp. 36–48). Blackwell Publishing.

O'Hare, G., & Barrett, H. (1999). Regional inequalities in the Peruvian tourist industry. *The Geographical Journal, 165*(1), 47–61.

Okuyucu, A., & Erol, F. (2018). Motivation, feelings and experiences towards battle fields tourism: Metristepe and Inonu war grave – The case of Bozuyuk. *Cografi Bilimler Dergisi, 16*(1), 135–151.

Prideaux, B. (2007). Echoes of war: Battlefield tourism. In C. Ryan (Ed.), *Battlefield tourism history, place and interpretation* (pp. 17–26). Elsevier.

Slade, P. (2003). Gallipoli thanatourism: The meaning of ANZAC. *Annals of Tourism Research, 30*(4), 779–794.

Walton, J. K. (2013). War and tourism: The nineteenth and twentieth centuries. In R. Butler & W. Suntikul (Eds.), *Tourism and war* (pp. 64–74). Routledge.

Winter, C. (2011). Battlefield visitor motivations: Explorations in the Great War town Ieper, Belgium. *International Journal of Tourism Research, 13*, 164–176.

Yesildag, B., & Atay, L. (2012). Battlefield tourism: A survey with the visitors of Gallipoli battlefields. *Balikesir Universitesi Sosyal Bilimler Dergisi, 15*, 267–280.

Chapter 8

Battlefield Tourism Supporting Institutions

Buğcan Güvenol and Mehmet Emre Güler

İzmir Katip Çelebi University, Türkiye

Abstract

Throughout history, battlefield sites have continued to develop within the scope of tourism activities, primarily through the support of both official and nonofficial institutions. The nature of these institutions may vary depending on their country or type. In this section, examples of institutions are examined in a general framework according to countries and the activities undertaken by these institutions to support battlefield tourism. Examples can be further multiplied, but it should be kept in mind that the ministries of the countries, especially those related to tourism, or the local administrations where the battlefield is located, will support this type of tourism rather than the examples given. In conclusion, institutions generally contribute to battlefield sites by organizing commemorative events, tours, and educational programs, safeguarding areas through restoration efforts, and disseminating information about these sites. All these activities carried out by these institutions not only contribute to battlefield tourism but also serve to raise awareness among individuals about battlefield sites.

Keywords: Supporting institutes; official institutes; government; civil society organizations; foundations; associations; battlefield; tourism

Introduction

Wars have caused horrific deaths in the areas where they have taken place, destroyed the natural and artificial environment, and destroyed cultural heritage sites that were at the forefront of tourism movements in prewar periods. However, all these deaths and environmental destruction caused by wars have paradoxically turned into an attraction for tourism activities. For all these reasons, battlefields have become symbolic places from past to present (Ekin & Akbulut, 2018). Countries, on the other hand, make various efforts both to preserve and transfer

Battlefield Tourism, 139 155

Copyright © 2024 Buğcan Güvenol and Mehmet Emre Güler

Published under exclusive licence by Emerald Publishing Limited

doi:10.1108/978-1-83909-990-820241011

their cultural heritage to future generations and to ensure the continuity of tourism activities in the regions where the battlefields are located. In this context, there are some institutions in countries that play a leading role in the realization of these efforts by directly or indirectly supporting battlefield tourism. These institutions can essentially be categorized into two distinct themes: official and nonofficial institutions. While official institutions can be considered the ministries of the countries, field administrations under the ministries, migration and veterans' offices, directorates, commissions, and bureaus; nonofficial institutions can be considered civil society organizations, foundations, and associations. In this section, which examines the institutions that support battlefield tourism, the importance of official and nonofficial institutions for battlefields is briefly mentioned, as examples of some official and nonofficial institutions that can be accessed by the country and that have efforts directly related to the activities carried out in battlefields are given.

Supporting Institutions

Battlefields commonly give visitors a chance to interact with history and culture, enhancing their comprehension of historical events and contributing to the healing journey of those impacted by wars (García-Madurga & Grilló-Méndez, 2023). Battlefields play an important role in many tourism activities with the support of governments, nongovernmental organizations, various foundations, and associations. Commemoration ceremonies are at the forefront of these activities. Beyond such ceremonies, specialized events can also be orchestrated as part of the broader spectrum of tourism activities (Atay & Yeşildağ, 2010). While tourism activities associated with battlefields have been present since the Battle of Waterloo, organized visits to such sites saw a substantial increase after World War I, propelled by the tragic loss of innumerable lives (Holguín, 2005). From a conceptual perspective, battlefield tourism can be expressed as a subset within the realm of cultural heritage tourism (Akbulut & Ekin, 2018). Cultural and natural heritage are resources that create unique tourist attractions for countries, but it is not easy to know how to preserve their value and ensure their development in the future within the scope of sustainable tourism (Hoang, 2021). There are various concerns about how the impacts of battlefields, which can also be referred to as cultural heritage, on cultural and historical sites in the context of tourism are managed. The increasing popularity of battlefield tourism has led to an increase in the number of visitors to the area. This increase is likely to put pressure on both the battlefields themselves and on some of the communities surrounding them. Therefore, it is important to understand and manage all impacts to ensure the sustainability of battlefields (García-Madurga & Grilló-Méndez, 2023). According to White and Livoti (2013), if archaeologists are to effectively manage and preserve the heritage of battlefields, they need to be competent not only in their technical competence in their field but also in military and various procedures and planning. In this context, it is thought that in addition to the support of institutions for battlefields, people working on battlefields should also have various competencies.

Countries have wanted to protect their battlefields with various institutions and practices and transfer them to future generations. It is stated that national parks are the most effective way to protect battlefields (Aliağaoğlu, 2008). As an illustration, the National Park Service, which was established in 1916 in the United States, has conducted extensive studies on battlefields over time (Bearss, 1987). In a similar vein, in Türkiye, the Gallipoli Peninsula to Historical National Park was declared in 1973 (Atay & Yeşildağ, 2010). In this context, Gallipoli has become the most visited battlefield region in Türkiye, and the fronts, cemeteries, and monuments in the region have been preserved (Topsakal & Ekici, 2014). Since 2014, to preserve the historical texture of the region and pass it on to future generations, this region has transitioned from being a national park to administered as the Çanakkale Wars Gallipoli Historical Site Presidency under the auspices of Türkiye's Ministry of Culture and Tourism (Çanakkale Wars Gallipoli Historical Site Presidency, n.d.). The British Government established the Imperial War Graves Commission (IWGC) by Royal Charter on May 21, 1917. The official name of the commission today is the Commonwealth War Graves Commission (CWGC). The commission carried out many studies on wars, cemeteries, and memorials. For instance, the official website of the commission enables users to locate war memorials and cemeteries spanning over 150 countries from both World Wars I and II. In 2019/20, it received funding from various countries (*the United Kingdom, Canada, Australia, Australia, New Zealand, South Africa, and India, respectively*) in proportion to the number of graves to support all its work, and it also has a foundation (Commonwealth War Graves Commission, n.d.). In other words, the CWGC has an undeniable importance in commemorating those who died in World Wars I and II (Maggio, 2018). English Heritage, on the other hand, registered England's battlefields in 1995. This practice carried out by the English Heritage institution was the first official attempt to pay attention to the battlefields as a cultural and historical resource of the United Kingdom (Banks & Pollard, 2011). When the literature is examined, it is seen that there are also applications on battlefields with the cooperation of different countries or different institutions in countries. For instance, in the Netherlands, monuments from World War II can be seen with the Liberation Route (Gieling & Ong, 2016). The Liberation Route is organized by the European Liberation Route Foundation and certified Cultural Route of the Council of Europe. The route includes countries such as Germany, Belgium, England, the Netherlands, France, and Belgium. Thus, the cultural route has the opportunity to show people the war memories, battlefields, and memorials of the countries affected by World War II by bringing them together in a European context (Martens, 2022). The Adam Park Project (TAPP) is a project conducted through a partnership between the National Heritage Board of Singapore, the National University of Singapore, and the Singapore Heritage Society and is the first archeological survey of a battlefield in Singapore (Cooper, 2011).

It is thought that the official institutions of the countries support tourism activities in the region with various practices related to the wars and battlefields they have experienced in the past. Examples of official institutions that support battlefield tourism by country are given in Table 8.1.

Table 8.1. Official Institutions Supporting Battlefield Tourism by Country.

Country	Name of Institution	Information About the Institution
The United States	The National Park Service (NPS)	The NPS is a bureau of the US Department of the Interior. The NPS protects battlefields, military parks, and historic sites that commemorate the service of American veterans. The NPS maintains information and studies on battlefields such as the US–Mexican War, the French and Indian War, the War of 1812, World War II, and the Civil War. There are also efforts to protect battlefields inside or outside National Parks. For example, the NPS supports the protection of battlefields and armed conflict sites beyond national park boundaries through the American Battlefield Protection Program (ABPP). In addition, the official website of the NPS includes descriptions of battlefields. In addition to all these statements, the NPS also contributes to the commemoration of those who lost their lives while serving in the US military, for example, events are organized for Memorial Day, which will take place on May 29, 2023
Australia	Australian War Memorial (AWM)	Combining a mausoleum, a world-class museum, and an extensive archive, the AWM was established by the Australian War Memorial Act 1980. The purpose of the memorial is to commemorate the sacrifices of Australians who have died in combat or operational service and all those who have served Australia in times of conflict. It provides information on the memorial, including planning tours, commemorations, video-assisted events, exhibitions, and information on the wars. The unit's official website also features collections of war relics and maps of the battlefields. For example, the location of the Sphinx, one of the battlefields in Gallipoli, Türkiye, is shown on the map

Table 8.1. *(Continued)*

Country	Name of Institution	Information About the Institution
	Australian Government Department of Veterans Affairs (DVA)	Established in memory of those who have served the Australian people. The DVA takes care of maintaining battlefields and cemeteries. For instance, the department's Australian War Graves Office works in Australia, Papua New Guinea, and the Solomon Islands. It also builds and maintains official Australian memorials overseas. The DVA notes that much evidence of the battle can be found in the sea around the Gallipoli/Türkiye battlefield and that this underwater evidence can provide visitors with the opportunity to dive and explore the wartime heritage of Gallipoli. The department also supports travel to Villers-Bretonneux (France) and Gallipoli (Türkiye) for Anzac Day services and provides information to those wishing to attend dawn services
Canada	Parks Canada	Located in a 450,000 km² area, Parks Canada is responsible for the management of national parks, historical sites, and protected areas in Canada under the Canadian government. In this context, it is effective in the protection of its battlefields. As an example, it promotes battlefields such as Vimy Ridge National Historic Site, Fort Louisbourg National Historic Site, and Windmill National Historic Site and encourages people to travel
	The National Battlefields Commission (TNBC)	TNBC is affiliated with the Government of Canada and protects and develops the battlefield park in Quebec City, including the Plains of Abraham. The Commission shares information transparently to better hold everyone accountable for what is being done. In addition, the commission offers a variety of events and recreational activities involving the battlefields in the Plains of Abraham

(Continued)

Table 8.1. *(Continued)*

Country	Name of Institution	Information About the Institution
Türkiye	T.C. Tarım ve Orman Bakanlığı Doğa Koruma ve Milli Parklar Müdürlüğü (Republic of Türkiye Ministry of Agriculture and Forestry General Directorate of Nature Conservation and National Parks)	The directorate protects many areas such as national parks, natural parks, natural monuments, and wetlands. Some parks within the national parks (such as Sakarya Battlefield Historical National Park, Kop Mountain Defense Historical National Park, and Malazgirt Battlefield Historical National Park) are the battlefields of the past. Therefore, the protection of these parks directly contributes to the transfer of battlefields to future generations and tourism activities
	T.C. Kültür ve Turizm Bakanlığı (Republic of Türkiye Ministry of Culture and Tourism)	Republic of Türkiye Ministry of Culture and Tourism not only protects all areas suitable for tourism activities in Türkiye but also develops various strategies and plans for the development of these areas. The Ministry supports battlefield tourism through films from its archive, virtual museums including battlefields, and announcements of events held around the world related to battlefields
	Çanakkale Savaşları Gelibolu Tarihi Alan Başkanlığı (Çanakkale Wars Gallipoli Historical Site Presidency)	Çanakkale Wars Gallipoli Historical Site Presidency is an organization of the Republic of Türkiye Ministry of Culture and Tourism. The Presidency's mission is to preserve the Gallipoli Historical Site, where the Gallipoli Battles took place, with all its values and turn it into an open-air museum. The Presidency is responsible for the protection, preservation, promotion, transfer to future generations, and management of the historical site. In addition, various activities are organized under the leadership of the Presidency, and the official website provides visuals and information about the monuments, museums, castles, and martyrdoms in the area

Table 8.1. *(Continued)*

Country	Name of Institution	Information About the Institution
Germany	Der Beauftragten Der Bundesregierung für Kultur und Medien (The Federal Government Commissioner for Culture and the Media)	The Federal Government for Culture and Media is particularly involved in commemorating the consequences of the Nazi regime and supporting the preservation of various memorials in the country. It also develops new formats in education with the "Youth Remembers" program and supports Nazi memorials and documentation centers
France	Ministère des Armées (The Ministry of Armed Forces)	The Ministry supports battlefield tourism through its activities. For example, the Ministry has developed a policy of "Remembrance Tourism" as part of the promotion of France's civil and military architecture. This policy is supported by local authorities, museums, and countries that share a common memory with France. An official website has also been created as part of *Chemins de Mémoire*. The website introduces visitors to museums, necropolises, battlefields, monuments, and thematic routes and provides information about them. It also organizes various defense training
	Center Des Monuments Nationaux – CMN (National Monuments Center)	The CMN reports to the Ministry of Culture and is mandated by the Heritage Act with four main missions about the monuments for which it is responsible. These missions are to protect, restore, and maintain the monuments and cultural assets under its responsibility; revitalize the monuments and make them accessible to as many people as possible; contribute to the inclusion of national monuments in cultural life and the development of tourism through activities such as exhibitions and performances; publish books on relevant topics
South Korea	The War Memorial of Korea	The Korean War Memorial is a national institution established in 1989. It organizes exhibitions, training, cultural events, and tours

(Continued)

Table 8.1. *(Continued)*

Country	Name of Institution	Information About the Institution
Japan	Japan National Tourism Organization (JNTO)	JNTO undertakes various activities to attract foreign tourists to Japan. Websites for Japanese tourism (*Japan Travel*) have been created with different language options. The website includes information on the Nagakute and Sekigahara wars
Belgium	Visitflanders	Visit Flanders is part of the Flemish government and aims to develop Flanders as a destination for tourism. In this context, one of the types of tourism it supports can be considered as battlefield tourism. For instance, on its official website, the institution shares information about battlefields and offers suggestions for tours, especially for Canadians, Irish, and Australians
	War Heritage Institute	The War Heritage Institute preserves and presents historic war heritage (battlefields and collections). The Institute supports sites such as the Death Pit in World War I and the Fort Breendonk National Monument in World War II; organizes commemorative trips abroad, workshops, exhibitions, and intergenerational meetings; shares examples of books on the wars. In addition, the federal organization War Heritage Institute has established *Belgium, Battlefield of Europe* network. Belgium, Battlefield of Europe shares information and organizes programs on museums, battlefields, and events to visit

Source: Compiled by the authors.

Table 8.1 gives examples of some official institutions that support battlefield tourism by country. When the table is examined, it is seen that even if there are differences between institutions, there are also similarities in terms of activities to support battlefields in general. Institutions mostly protect the ruins, monuments, sites, and cemeteries for future generations and especially organize commemorative events. In addition, although not included in the table, it is thought that there may be a wide range of institutions that indirectly support battlefields. For instance, the US Department of Veterans Affairs was established with the mission to fulfill President Abraham Lincoln's promise to support those who served in the US military and support the families, caregivers, and survivors of those who served. The Department provides training and health services and organizes memorial services at various cemeteries (U.S. Department of Veterans Affairs, n.d.). Cultural Heritage Agency of the Netherlands (official name is Rijksdienst voor het Cultureel Erfgoed) is part of the Ministry of Education, Culture, and Science. It maintains a register of national monuments in the country. It also implements practices for the protection and restoration of monuments (Cultural Heritage Agency of the Netherlands, n.d.). Another institution in the Netherlands, the Netherlands Institute of Military History (NIMH), is affiliated with the Dutch Ministry of Defense. It deals with the history of the period from the 80 Years War to the present day. The Institute manages the military historical collection, conducts scientific studies, and provides training and conferences (The Netherlands Institute of Military History, n.d.). The National Office for Veterans and Victims of War (ONaCVG), on the other hand, works for the recognition of war-affected persons and the restoration of the effects of war, solidarity, civic awareness for younger generations, peace promotion, commemoration, care and restoration, and memory work. It also shares information on monuments and necropolises in different cities in France, offers guided tours, and organizes commemorative action (The National Office for Veterans and Victims of War, n.d.).

Examples could be multiplied to expand the scope of such institutions. It is thought that these institutions can indirectly enhance public awareness by emphasizing past wars, veterans, cemeteries, memorials, training, and more, thereby fostering the development of tourism activities centered on battlefields. In addition to official institutions, Table 8.2 presents instances of nonofficial institutions supporting battlefield tourism and their activities by country.

Table 8.2. Nonofficial Institutions Supporting Battlefield Tourism by Country.

Country	Name of Institution	Information About the Institution
The United States	Gettysburg Foundation	A philanthropic and educational organization that works in partnership with the National Park Service to preserve Gettysburg National Military Park and Eisenhower National Historic Site and educate the public about their importance. Founded in the United States, the foundation offers specialized resources and unique experiences to tell the story of the 1863 Battle of Gettysburg and to provide tours of the battlefield. It organizes many exhibitions, tours, museum visits, and general and special events

(Continued)

Table 8.2. *(Continued)*

Country	Name of Institution	Information About the Institution
	The American Battlefield Trust	Preserving America's sacred battlefields educates the public about what happens in war and why it matters. Considered the leading heritage land conservation organization in the United States, they have saved more than 56,000 acres of battlefields in 24 states to date with the support of their members and partners. They also strive to create opportunities for people to experience battlefields firsthand
	The Great War Association (GWA)	In Newville, Pennsylvania, USA, it strives to keep the history of World War I alive and honor the men who fought in it through battle re-enactments and educational events. The Association has 45 units that regularly participate in its events and about 700 members representing various units from different countries. The Association recreates many of the sights and sounds of the Great War. In addition to various special events across the country, the GWA is the owner of the Caesar Krauss Great War Memorial Site. Here, the GWA has recreated part of the Western Front as it originally appeared in 1917–1918
	Shenandoah Valley Battlefields Foundation	The Foundation is located in Virginia, USA, and its primary mission is to preserve and promote important historical and cultural sites associated with the Shenandoah Valley Campaign of the American Civil War. To this end, the Foundation organizes guided tours, promotes the 11 battlefields and museums, and provides information for people interested in visiting these sites

Table 8.2. *(Continued)*

Country	Name of Institution	Information About the Institution
	Friends of the National World War II Memorial	It is a nonprofit organization based in Washington, DC. It was founded in 2007 by the creators of the World War II Memorial. It organizes many virtual and face-to-face trainings, conferences, and memorial days. For example, it organizes a tour to Italy from October 10 to 16, 2023, including cemeteries and battlefields
	Virginia World War II Heritage Alliance	Virginia World War II Heritage Alliance is a cooperative association of nonprofit foundations, organizations, museums, and monuments. Identifying World War 2 Heritage Routes, securing legislation that supports the establishment, promotion, and maintenance of World War 2 Heritage Routes, and maintaining and increasing visitation among alliance members are among the missions of the association
	Kernstown Battlefield Association	It was founded in July 1996. The association shares information about the battles of Kernstown and organizes special events throughout the year
	Georgia Battlefields Association	It was founded in March 1995. Its objectives are the acquisition, study, preservation, and dissemination of information about the battlefields where the Civil War took place. It organizes guided tours
	Princeton Battlefield Society	The institution which aims to raise public awareness about the Battle of Princeton and to preserve and restore the battlefields conducts battlefield tours

(Continued)

Table 8.2. *(Continued)*

Country	Name of Institution	Information About the Institution
England	The Western Front Association	The Western Front Association was founded in 1980 to maintain the interest in the period 1914–1918 and to perpetuate the memory, courage, and comradeship of those who served their country in the Flanders region of France and Belgium during World War I. It organizes many events related to the battlefield. It also offers its members the opportunity to meet other people to exchange information and publishes journals regularly
	Commonwealth War Graves Commission (CWGC)	The CWGC is a global organization that cares for war graves at 23,000 locations in more than 150 countries and territories, commemorating the sacrifices of approximately 1.7 million people in the Commonwealth. The organization was established by Royal Charter. The commission has built around 2,500 war cemeteries and plots. It also erected tombstones at graves and, where there are no remains, inscribed the names of the deceased on permanent monuments. The global estates are managed by a multinational and multilingual workforce of around 1,300 people. The organization works to ensure that all those who have fallen are remembered equally and has created information centers, volunteering opportunities, and educational programs designed to educate future generations
	The Battlefields Trust (TBT)	An approved charity run by volunteers to help preserve research and interpret Britain's battlefields. TBT campaigns locally and nationally to prevent inappropriate development and destruction of battlefields. It offers its members a quarterly magazine, a growing range of battlefield walking events, and online talks by experts in their field

Table 8.2. *(Continued)*

Country	Name of Institution	Information About the Institution
	War Memorials Trust	A charity working to protect war memorials in the United Kingdom. It works to protect war memorials, estimated to number more than 100,000 across the country, from neglect, destruction, or damage due to adverse weather conditions
	English Heritage	It looks after more than 400 historic monuments, buildings, and sites, ranging from world-famous prehistoric sites to great medieval castles, Roman forts to Cold War bunkers. English Heritage operates as a charity independent of the government and has offices in Swindon and London. English Heritage's vision is for people to experience the story of England where and how it happened. It organizes events and tours of battlefields and shares up-to-date news
	Gallipoli Association	The Gallipoli Association was founded in London/UK to perpetuate the memory of the Gallipoli Campaign. The main focus of the association is the education of young people from all countries that once participated in this war. Thus, it aims to raise public awareness about the Gallipoli Campaign and to ensure that all the people involved are not forgotten. To this end, the association organizes training, publishes a magazine, shares information about commemorative events, and invites battlefield tours. Membership continues to grow worldwide, and the association currently has over 1,000 members. The majority of members are descendants of veterans

(Continued)

Table 8.2. *(Continued)*

Country	Name of Institution	Information About the Institution
Ireland	The Somme Association	It was established in 1990 to coordinate research into Ireland's role in the First World War and to ensure that the sacrifices of all those from Ireland who served in the war and their families are continued, honored, and commemorated. There is also a Friends of the Somme organization to support the work undertaken by the Somme Association. This institution has more than 800 members from countries as diverse as Canada, South Africa, Hong Kong, and Australia. The Somme Association organizes a variety of interactive educational tours about the First World War and in particular the Battle of the Somme and Ireland's role in it. It also organizes exhibitions and events, both on-site and in other locations
Spain	The Wellington Society of Madrid	Founded in 1979, the association organizes battlefield tours in countries such as Spain, Portugal, France, and Belgium. The association provides participants with opportunities such as narrating local legends, walking along the war route, and examining war zones and special collections derived from battles during the conducted tours
India	United Service Institution of India	The United Service Institution of India was established in 1870 to promote interest and knowledge in the art, science, and literature of the Defense Services. The organization promotes battlefield tours and conducts activities, especially for young people, to teach them about the war period. In addition, an international conference "GALLIPOLI REVISITED" was organized in partnership with the Indian Council of World Affairs (ICWA) on April 22–23, 2021

Source: Compiled by the authors.

Table 8.2 provides examples of some nonofficial institutions that support battlefield tourism by country. When the table is examined, it is seen that the institutions that can be reached are mostly located in the United States and that these have efforts to support battlefields similar to the institutions in Table 8.1. In general, the institutions provide training, conservation activities, special events, and tours related to war and battlefields. In addition, although not included in the table, it is thought that there may be a wide range of institutions that indirectly support battlefields. For instance, the National World War I Museum and Memorial in the United States is a nonprofit institution dedicated to honoring those who served in the First World War. The institutions aim to encourage the public by interpreting the history of World War I, conducting exhibitions and educational programs targeting diverse audiences, and implementing practices to collect and preserve historical artifacts to professional standards (The National WWI Museum and Memorial, n.d.). The National D-Day Memorial Foundation, also operating in the United States, is on a mission to preserve the lessons learned from D-Day and its legacy. It organizes activities such as virtual and face-to-face training, memorial days, and guided tours (The National D-Day Memorial Foundation, n.d.). Similar institutions to those expressed through examples also prioritize the significance of the occurred wars and can organize various training programs. Consequently, individuals will probably possess a heightened awareness of wars and battlefields in the future.

Conclusion

Although institutions that support battlefield tourism can be divided into two categories, their efforts for these sites generally share similar characteristics. They organize events such as commemoration ceremonies, walks, and educational tours; carry out preventive activities against the possibility of damage to battlefields; carry out various restoration works; conduct research on battlefields; share up-to-date information on these areas. In addition, some institutions contribute to raising people's awareness of battlefields through their work in war cemeteries, support for the families of war veterans and martyrs, and informative training on wars. As a result, with all these activities, institutions protect and develop battlefields for future generations and thus support battlefield tourism both directly and indirectly. When considering official institutions, it should not be forgotten that countries, particularly the ministries related to tourism or local administrations in regions where a battlefield is located, could implement practices such as promotion, advertising, and marketing to promote battlefield sites that can also be regarded as cultural heritage, or they could undertake necessary protective and supportive efforts to enhance existing tourism activities.

References

Akbulut, O., & Ekin, Y. (2018). Kültürel miras turizmi olarak savaş alanları turizmi: Türkiye'de yer alan savaş anıtlarının coğrafi bilgi sistemleri analizi. *Hitit Üniversitesi Sosyal Bilimler Enstitüsü Dergisi, 11*(1), 395–420. https://doi.org/10. 17218/hititsosbil.397914

Aliağaoğlu, A. (2008). Savaş alanları turizmi için tipik bir yer: Gelibolu yarımadası tarihi milli parkı. *Milli Folklor Dergisi, 20*(78), 88–104.

Atay, L., & Yeşildağ, B. (2010). Savaş alanları ve turizmi. *Aksaray Üniversitesi İktisadi ve İdari Bilimler Fakültesi Dergisi, 2*(2), 65–72.

Australian Government Department of Veterans Affairs. (n.d.). https://www.dva.gov. au/

Australian War Memorial. (n.d.). https://www.awm.gov.au/

Banks, I., & Pollard, T. (2011). Protecting a bloodstained history: Battlefield conservation in Scotland. *Journal of Conflict Archaeology, 6*(2), 124–145. https://doi. org/10.1179/157407811X13027741134148

Bearss, E. C. (1987). The national park service and its history program: 1864–1986: An overview. *The Public Historian, 9*(2), 10–18. https://doi.org/10.2307/3377327

Belgium, Battlefield of Europe. (n.d.). https://belgiumbattlefield.be/nl

Çanakkale Wars Gallipoli Historical Site Presidency. (n.d.). https://canakkale tarihialan.gov.tr/

Centre Des Monuments Nationaux. (n.d.). https://www.monuments-nationaux.fr/

Chemins de Mémoire. (n.d.). https://www.cheminsdememoire.gouv.fr/fr

Commonwealth War Graves Commission. (n.d.). https://www.cwgc.org/

Cooper, J. (2011). Chosen ground—The significance, objectives and progress of the Adam park project (TAPP). *Journal of Conflict Archaeology, 6*(1), 22–41. https:// doi.org/10.1179/157407811X12958710480380

Cultural Heritage Agency of the Netherlands. (n.d.). https://www.cultureelerfgoed.nl/

Der Beauftragten Der Bundesregierung für Kultur und Medien. (n.d.). https://www. bundesregierung.de/breg-de/bundesregierung/bundeskanzleramt/staatsministerin-fuer-kultur-und-medien

Ekin, Y., & Akbulut, O. (2018). Battlefield tourism: An examination of events held by European institutions and their websites related to battlefields. *International Journal of Contemporary Economics and Administrative Sciences, 8*(1), 73–123.

English Heritage. (n.d.). https://www.english-heritage.org.uk/

Friends of the National World War II Memorial. (n.d.). https://www.wwiime morialfriends.org/

Gallipoli Association. (n.d.). www.gallipoli-association.org

García-Madurga, M.-Á., & Grilló-Méndez, A.-J. (2023). Battlefield tourism: Exploring the successful marriage of history and unforgettable experiences: A systematic review. *Tourism and Hospitality, 4*(2), 307–320. https://doi.org/10.3390/ tourhosp4020019

Georgia Battlefields Association. (n.d.). http://www.georgiabattlefields.org/

Gettysburg Foundation. (n.d.). https://www.gettysburgfoundation.org/

Gieling, J., & Ong, C.-E. (2016). Warfare tourism experiences and national identity: The case of Airborne Museum 'Hartenstein' in Oosterbeek, the Netherlands. *Tourism Management, 57*, 45–55. https://doi.org/10.1016/j.tourman.2016.05.017

Hoang, K. V. (2021). The benefits of preserving and promoting cultural heritage values for the sustainable development of the country. *E3S Web of Conferences, 234*, 00076. https://doi.org/10.1051/e3sconf/202123400076

Holguín, S. (2005). "National Spain invites you": Battlefield tourism during the Spanish civil war. *The American Historical Review, 110*(5), 1399–1426. https://doi.org/10.1086/ahr.110.5.1399

Japan National Tourism Organization. (n.d.). https://www.jnto.go.jp/

Japan Travel. (n.d.). https://www.japan.travel/en/au/

Kernstown Battlefield Association. (n.d.). http://www.kernstownbattle.org/

Maggio, A. (2018). The memory of war: The role of the commonwealth war graves commission in the identification and memorialisation of missing and unknown soldiers from WW1. *Limina. A Journal of Historical and Cultural Studies, 23*(2), 31–42.

Martens, D. (2022). The experience of common European heritage: A critical discourse analysis of tourism practices at cultural routes of the council of Europe. *Journal of European Landscapes, 3*(3), 45–59. https://doi.org/10.5117/JEL.2022.3.82504

Ministère des Armées. (n.d.). https://www.defense.gouv.fr/

Parks Canada. (n.d.). https://parks.canada.ca/

Princeton Battlefield Society. (n.d.). https://pbs1777.org/

Republic of Türkiye Ministry of Agriculture and Forestry General Directorate of Nature Conservation and National Parks. (n.d.). Milli Parklar. https://www.tarimorman.gov.tr/DKMP/Menu/27/Milli-Parklar

Republic of Türkiye Ministry of Culture and Tourism. (n.d.). https://www.ktb.gov.tr/

Shenandoah Valley Battlefields Foundation. (n.d.). https://www.shenandoahatwar.org/

The American Battlefield Trust. (n.d.). https://www.battlefields.org/

The Battlefields Trust. (n.d.). https://www.battlefieldstrust.com/

The Great War Association. (n.d.). http://www.great-war-assoc.org/

The National Battlefields Commission. (n.d.). https://www.ccbn-nbc.gc.ca/en/

The National D-Day Memorial Foundation. (n.d.). https://www.dday.org/

The National Office for Veterans and Victims of War. (n.d.). https://www.onac-vg.fr/

The National Park Service. (n.d.). https://www.nps.gov/index.htm

The National WWI Museum and Memorial. (n.d.). https://theworldwar.org/

The Netherlands Institute of Military History. (n.d.). https://www.nimh.nl/

The Somme Association. (n.d.). https://www.sommeassociation.com/

The War Memorial of Korea. (n.d.). https://www.warmemo.or.kr/

The Wellington Society of Madrid. (n.d.). https://wellsoc.org/

The Western Front Association. (n.d.). https://www.westernfrontassociation.com/

Topsakal, Y., & Ekici, R. (2014). Dark tourism as a type of special interest tourism: Dark tourism potential of Turkey. *Akademik Turizm ve Yönetim Araştırmaları Dergisi, 1*(2), 325–330.

United Service Institution of India. (n.d.). https://www.usiofindia.org/

U.S. Department of Veterans Affairs. (n.d.). https://www.va.gov/

Virginia World War II Heritage Alliance. (n.d.). https://www.wwiiheritagealliance.org/

Visitflanders. (n.d.). https://www.visitflanders.com/en

War Heritage Institute. (n.d.). https://warheritage.be/

War Memorials Trust. (n.d.). https://www.warmemorials.org/

White, C., & Livoti, T. (2013). Preserving cultural heritage in time of conflict: A tool for counterinsurgency. In J. D. Kila & J. A. Zeidler (Eds.), *Cultural heritage in the crosshairs: Protecting cultural property during conflict* (pp. 195–218). Brill.

Chapter 9

Battlefield Tourism as an Agent of Tourism Development

Eben Proos and Johan Hattingh*

Central University of Technology, South Africa

Abstract

Battlefield tourism is a growing field in tourism research. However, it focuses primarily on an activity known as Dark Tourism, the visiting of places where tragedies or death took place. It includes the development of these sites as well. Cemeteries, internment sites, and memorials relating to death and depravity are the main features of battlefield tourism. Tourism development relies primarily on good infrastructure and an attractive (tourism) environment. As a niche tourism market, battlefield tourism can actively enhance the tourism product proposition of a destination. Identifying battlefield sites, incorporating them into battlefield tourism routes, and developing them as tourist attractions can act as an agent of tourism development. Battlefield tourists are mostly retired and have time to travel. They are also highly educated and fall into the high-income group. They are primarily interested in visiting existing battlefields, which indicates that battlefield tourism has the potential to act as an agent of tourism development and growth. For battlefield tourism developers, it would be essential to know their target market. Key factors in developing a successful tourism development plan for battlefield tourism are study preparation, determination of objectives, data gathering, analysis and synthesis, policy and plan formulation, recommendations, implementation, and monitoring. Battlefields need interpretation, development, marketing, and even commercializing to act as "storyteller(s)" of the past, add value to the more extensive tourism offering of a specific area, and act as an agent of tourism development.

Keywords: Battlefield tourism; tourism development; battlefield route(s); Dark Tourism; thanatourism

---

*Deceased

Battlefield Tourism, 157–172
Copyright © 2024 by Emerald Publishing Limited
All rights of reproduction in any form reserved
doi:10.1108/978-1-83909-990-820241012

Introduction

Worldwide there is an increase in individuals interested in destinations associated with war and destruction, or "Dark Tourism" (Proos, 2019, p. 11; Sharpley & Stone, 2009, p. 5). "Dark Tourism" is visiting places where tragedies or death took place. It includes the development of these sites as well. Cemeteries, internment sites, and memorials relating to death and depravity are the main features of battlefield tourism. Battlefield tourism is a growing field in tourism research. The aim of this chapter is to bring knowledge and insight into battlefield tourism as an agent of tourism development. This chapter will provide information on topics such as Dark Tourism as a Growing Niche Tourism Market, Battlefield Tourism Attractions Across the World, The Role of Battlefield Tourism in the Tourism Landscape, and Key Factors of a Thriving Tourism Development Plan for Battlefield Tourism.

Dark Tourism as a Growing Niche Tourism Market

Worldwide an increase in the interest in visiting places associated with war and destruction or "Dark Tourism" is visible (Acha-Anyi, 2018, p. 374; Boateng et al., 2018, p. 104; Dark Tourism: The Demand for new Experiences, 2017; Proos, 2019, p. 11; Proos & Hattingh, 2020; Sharpley & Stone, 2009, p. 5). "Dark" in the context of "Dark Tourism" is not meant literally, but metaphorically, as in a dark chapter of history. The fascinating aspects that tourists find about dark tourism are the history and humanity (Proos, 2019, p. 12). Foley and Lennon (1996) coined the term "Dark Tourism" and is also the title of their book *Dark Tourism* (Lennon & Foley, 2000; Sharpley & Stone, 2009, p. 12). "Dark Tourism" is defined as "apparent disturbing practices and morbid products (and experiences) within the tourism domain" (Stone, 2006, p. 146). "Dark Tourism" is further identified as "visitations to places where tragedies or historically noteworthy deaths have occurred and that continue to impact our lives" (Chang, 2017, p. 1; Tarlow, 2005, p. 48). "Dark Tourism" is also associated with traveling to places associated with death and suffering in one way or another (Acha-Anyi, 2018, p. 374; Proos, 2019, p. 12).

Visitations to battlefields, murder and massacre sites, places where celebrities have passed away, graveyards, internment sites, memorials, events and exhibitions featuring relics, and reconstruction of death all form part of "Dark Tourism" (Dark Tourism: The Demand for new Experiences, 2017; Miles, 2014, p. 136; Proos, 2019, p. 12). Various authors refer to "Dark Tourism" in different terms, including thanatourism, fatal attraction, death spots, a heritage that hurts, or atrocity heritage tourism (Ashworth, 2004, p. 95; Beech, 2000, p. 30; Chang, 2017, p. 1; Lennon & Foley, 2000; Miles, 2014; Moeller, 2005, p. 14; Podoshen, 2013, p. 264; Proos, 2019, p. 12; Rojek, 1993; Seaton, 1996). Interest in this phenomenon is growing, and research about the topic is increasing (Dunkley et al., 2011, p. 860; Proos, 2019, p. 12; Proos & Hattingh, 2019, 2020).

It can be argued that there has always been a close link between tourism and death. Pilgrims, as the first tourists, were motivated to visit the tombs of the saints and sites closely associated with them, including their places of death. Evidence suggests that tourists were present at the Battle of Waterloo (Seaton, 1999), and the First Battle of Bull Run in the American Civil War (Miles, 2012, p. 32). Popular examples of "Dark Tourism" include tourists viewing sites of the brutality of World War 1 and World War 2 battlefields in northern France, Chernobyl in Ukraine, the Auswitch-Birkenau concentration camp in Poland, Robben Island in South Africa, and the National 9/11 Memorial & Museum, "Ground Zero" in New York, USA.

Tourists that visit "Dark Tourism" sites (known as dark tourists) have an apparent motivation. These motivations could be classified into five categories (Miles, 2012, p. 32; Proos, 2019, p. 13; Proos & Hattingh, 2020; Seaton, 1996):

(1) those who travel to be a spectator at public enactments of death (which is quite rare in the contemporary context);
(2) those who travel to see sites of individual or mass deaths after they have occurred. This can include visiting the death sites of celebrities (e.g., JF Kennedy) or battlefield sites (e.g., the Anglo-Zulu and Anglo-Boer War battlefields of South Africa);
(3) those who travel to memorials or burial sites, which could include cemeteries, memorials, tombs, and resting places of famous individuals like the cemetery tourist attractions at Highgate (London) and Père-Lachaise (Paris);
(4) those who travel to witness the symbolic representation of death at distinct sites. The Tower of London serves as an example;
(5) those who travel for purposes of re-enactment or the simulation of death. Battlefield re-enactment, with its origins in the gladiatorial combats of ancient Rome, is an example of this category. (Miles, 2012, p. 32; Proos & Hattingh, 2020; Sharpley & Stone, 2009)

Motivations to travel differ from one tourist to the next (Dunkley, 2007, p. 66; Proos, 2019, p. 14; Swarbrooke & Horner, 1999). Dunkley (2007, p. 72), Ryan (2007, p. 251), Kim and Butler (2014), Van Der Merwe (2014, p. 123), Proos (2019, p. 14), and Proos and Hattingh (2020) identified the following categories of motivation:

• Special interest: personal interest in a particular site or war due to a family link with the event.
• Thrill/risk seeking: being part of the re-enactment of a battle.
• Validation: forming approval for the event.
• Authenticity: representation of the event from all perspectives.
• Self-discovery: learning about the experiences of one's ancestors involved or killed in that conflict.
• Iconic sites: some sites are classified as a "must-see" for tourists.
• Convenience: a battlefield is situated close by and forms part of the tourist's itinerary.
• Morbid curiosity: people interested in the macabre.

- Pilgrimage: people who lost loved ones in a particular event and now want to find out more about the event.
- Remembrance and empathy: young and old tied together.
- Contemplation: thinking history through for one's reflection.
- Legitimization: creating national pride.
- Economic resurgence: creating economic opportunities through employment.
- Discovery of heritage: where locals discover a sense of identity through past histories.
- Acts of remembrance: honoring people who died in the quest for one's freedom.
- Personal aspirations: seeking social or political prestige.

The relationship between tourism and death has received attention from some scholars, and it has now become a mainstream research topic (Boateng et al., 2018, p. 104; Hartmann, 2014, p. 170; Light, 2017, p. 276; Miles, 2014, p. 134; Podoshen, 2013, p. 264; Podoshen et al., 2015, p. 331; Proos, 2019, p. 15; Proos & Hattingh, 2020). "Dark Tourism" has caught the media's attention (Seaton & Lennon, 2004) and has become a regular topic in newspapers, magazines, and television programs (Light, 2017, p. 276). A prime example of the growing interest in "Dark Tourism" worldwide is the popular television show featured on Netflix, *Dark Tourist* (Eloff, 2018; Proos, 2019, p. 15; Proos & Hattingh, 2020).

Battlefield Tourism Attractions Across the World

Battlefield tourism can act as an agent of tourism development as it adds to the tourism product base of tourism destinations. Across the world, there are many examples of battlefield tourism attractions. This is due to past conflicts that shaped the future of the world. Examples of past conflicts include the Crusades (1096–1271), the Anglo-Scottish Wars (Wars of Scottish Independence) (1229–1346), the Hundred Years War (1337–1453), the Qing Dynasty Conquest Of The Ming Dynasty (1618–1683), the Battle of Culloden (1746), the Napoleonic Wars (1803–1815), the American Civil War (1861–1865), World War 1 (1914–1918), the Chinese Civil War (1927–1950), World War 2 (1939–1945), and the Vietnam War (1954–1975). South Africa also experienced great wars in its history including Colonial and frontier conflicts (1795–1906), Voortrekker battles (1836–1848), Anglo-Zulu War (1879), and the South African War (1899–1902) (Von der Heyde, 2013, 2017).

There are multiple well-known battlefield tourism attractions in the United States of America. These include:

- Manassas National Battlefield Park (the site of two Civil War battles),
- Antietam National Battlefield (a reminder of the single bloodiest day on American soil),
- Gettysburg National Military Park in Pennsylvania, where legendary combat sites such as Devil's Den and Little Round Top are still visible. (Conners, 2020; Godbey, 2017; National Geographic, 2010; US National Park Service, 2020)

Various European battlefields have also drawn global attention; these include:

- The Battle of Waterloo (where the Duke of Wellington defeated Napoleon Bonaparte),
- The Battle of the Bulge in the Ardennes Forest,
- The Normandy D-Day Landing Beaches (where the most significant land, air, and sea invasion in all of history occurred during World War II on June 6, 1944). (AutoFrance, 2020; History.com Editors, 2019a, 2019b; Worral, 2015)

Asian examples of battlefield tourism attractions in Vietnam include:

- The Reunification Palace (the finishing point of the Vietnam War),
- The War Remnants Museum in Ho Chi Minh City (where permanent and revolving exhibitions document different facets of the war),
- The Cu Chi Tunnels (a massive network of underground tunnels that once served as a command post for North Vietnamese forces) (Rodgers, 2019),
- Chinese battlefield attractions include the Military Museum of the Chinese People's Revolution in Beijing. (Travel China Guide, 2020)

South Africa and its rich war history offer a plethora of developed and underdeveloped battlefield tourism attractions. Attractions include battlefields, cemeteries, monuments, museums, and concentration camps. Battlefield tourism routes are popular in South Africa and include the KwaZulu-Natal Battlefields Route and the newly developed Magaliesberg Battlefields Route (Battlefields Route KwaZulu Natal, 2020; Ramela, 2018; Solomon Edwardian Guest House, 2020). The Battle of Isandlwana (January 22, 1879), southeast of Dundee in northern KwaZulu-Natal, and the Battle of Rorke's Drift (January 22, 1879) form part of the Anglo-Zulu War (1879) battlefield attractions in South Africa. The South African War 1899–1902 offers many battlefield attractions for tourists. Battlefield attractions include sites such as the Magersfontein (December 11, 1899), Colenso (December 15, 1899), Spioenkop (January 24, 1900), and the Battle of Sannaspos (March 31, 1900) outside of Bloemfontein to name a few. The well-known National Woman's Memorial in Bloemfontein is also a must-see for battlefield tourists. This monument commemorates the 26,370 women and children who died in British concentration camps during the South African War and also has a well-established museum on sight that provides tourists with detailed information on the war (1899–1902) (Grobler, 2018; LeMaitre, 2017; Von der Heyde, 2013).

As illustrated above, ample examples of battlefield tourist attractions are found worldwide. Thus, the opportunity for tourism development exists as it is seen as a creator of jobs, provides foreign income, and acts as the ignitor of further tourism growth. Therefore, battlefield tourism routes could assist in and serve as an agent for tourism development.

The Role of Battlefield Tourism in the Tourism Landscape

According to Light (2017, p. 276), research into tourism at battlefields and sites associated with war is substantially growing. These sites probably constitute "the largest single category of tourist attractions in the world" (Smith, 1998, p. 205; Stone & Sharpley, 2008, p. 574). For this reason, battlefield tourism has become an essential tourism sector today.

A battlefield is "the land area over which a battle was fought and [where] significantly related activities occurred. A battle is an engagement involving wholly or largely military forces that aimed to inflict lethal force against an opposing army" (Historic Scotland (undated) Inventory of Historic Battlefields, 2009, p. 29; Miles, 2012, p. 59).

According to Venter (2011, p. 1), there is no clear definition of battlefield tourism. However, some definitions are provided in the literature. Battlefield tourism includes "[v]isiting war memorials and war museums, 'war experiences,' battle re-enactments and the battlefield" (Dunkley et al., 2011, p. 860; Van Der Merwe, 2014, p. 123). Battlefield tourism offers sites of cultural memory where "memory becomes institutionalised through cultural means, such as commemorative rituals, memorials, and museums" (Misztal, 2003, pp. 130–131). Similarly, Moeller (2005, p. 6) defines battlefield tourism as explicitly focusing on famous war sites, battlefields, and cemeteries.

When considering war and tourism, it would not seem that they go together at first glance. The world's largest single category of tourist attractions includes the memorabilia of warfare and accompanying products (Sharpley & Stone, 2009, p. 186). Battlefields were referred to as the "punctuation marks" of history by Sir Winston Churchill, Prime Minister of the United Kingdom, from 1940 to 1945 and again from 1951 to 1955 (Miles, 2012, p. 2). According to Sharpley and Stone (2009, p. 186), battlefield tourism has attracted attention from early times (As mentioned, during the Battle of Waterloo in 1815, many spectators visited the battlefield while the battle took place (Holguin, 2005, p. 1400; Klein, 2016; Moeller, 2005, p. 18; Proos, 2019, p. 16; Seaton, 1999, p. 234). The first tour to Waterloo occurred in 1854, establishing battlefield tourism as a new kind of attraction (Seaton, 1999, p. 139). During the 19th and 20th centuries, Waterloo remained Belgium's most popular tourist attraction (Gilks, 2021; Proos, 2019, p. 16; Seaton, 1999, p. 130). Ryan (2007, p. 13) correctly states that battlefield sites can attract hundreds of thousands of tourists annually (Proos, 2019, p. 16).

Extensive research has been undertaken on WWI battlefields, and with 2014 marking the centenary of WWI, many tourists visited these battlefield sites (Clarke & Eastgate, 2011; Winter, 2012). Civil War battlefield sites, including Gettysburg (1863), are extremely popular, attracting over 3 million visits a year (Miles, 2012, p. 4; Page & Connell, 2020; Proos, 2019, p. 16). Another type of tourism which is gaining in popularity worldwide is cemetery tourism (Marais, 2017, p. 42; Proos, 2019, p. 17).

However, the question lingers: Who are the people visiting battlefields? Van der Merwe (2014, p. 129) addressed this question by investigating the major battlefield routes around Dundee (a coal mining town) in Kwa Zulu Natal, South

Africa. The findings revealed that most battlefields were visited by well-off white males who are retired and have a great deal of time and money to travel (Proos, 2019, p. 17).

Similar results were identified by a study conducted in Great Britain. Similarities included the age distribution indicating a higher preference for visiting battlefields among older age groups and a strong result for the 50–65-year-old category (Miles, 2014, p. 139). This category also has higher disposable income, is educated, and has a specific interest in battlefields and the history of the conflicts (Proos, 2019, p. 17). This is echoed in a recent study by Proos and Hattingh (2020). These similarities of the profile of the respondents include that the respondents are mostly white males who are retired and have a great deal of time to travel. They are also highly educated and fall in the high-income group.

Interestingly, Proos and Hattingh (2020) indicated that the age group 18–30 is starting to demonstrate a more considerable interest in battlefield tourism. Respondents stated that they were most interested in visiting existing battlefields, which suggests that battlefield tourism has the potential to act as an agent of tourism development and growth. This information could serve as a guideline to identify the type of tourist who visits battlefields. For battlefield tourism developers, it would be essential to know their target market. The following section alludes to critical factors of a thriving tourism development plan for battlefield tourism.

Key Factors of a Thriving Tourism Development Plan for Battlefield Tourism

Tourism development can be seen as a long-term process (NDTRSA, 2018, p. 34). When incorporating tourism into a development plan, the development plan must be organized and developed according to a tourism strategy constructed on sound foundations. The development planning process involves a broad cross-section of participants (Cooper et al., 2008, p. 251; Hattingh, 2016; Proos, 2019). To ensure effective and efficient tourism development, tourism planning should be a key focus in all local planning activities (NDTRSA, 2018, p. 34).

In the past, the only planning that went into the tourism development plans focused on aspects such as the most suitable location for development and infrastructural development (Inskeep, 1991, p. 15; NDTRSA, 2017; Page & Connell, 2020; Proos, 2019, p. 100). The careful planning process ensures that all role players know their part in the planning and how they can contribute to the plan's successful implementation (Brokaj, 2014; Martins, 2018; NDTRSA, 2018, p. 39).

Tourism can be developed in many different forms ranging from urban tourism (e.g., the variety of heritage and cultural attractions within an urban context attracts visitors to a specific city, e.g., Cape Town, London, or New York), particular interest and adventure tourism (e.g., specific interest such as birding, 4 × 4 trips or shark cage diving), agritourism (tourism linked to agricultural practices), water-based tourism (e.g., cruise ships), transport-based tourism (e.g., Rovos Rail, Orient Express), religious tourism (linked to specific religious events), and business tourism (attending conferences, meetings, etc.) (NDTRSA, 2018, p. 21; Proos, 2019, p. 101).

Various external factors such as tourism market trends, seasonality, and climate change influence tourism. Therefore, all the mentioned factors must be considered in regional tourism development (Edgell & Swanson, 2013, p. 245; Proos, 2019, p. 101). Tourism development can have positive and negative effects on a region. Thus, tourism development in a region needs to be studied diligently by key role players (NDTRSA, 2018, p. vi; Proos, 2019, p. 101). Positive effects on a region could include job creation, income generation, government revenue, and small business stimulation, while adverse effects could consist of unforeseen social conflicts among community members, disastrous environmental hazards, high cost of development, and over-tourism (Acha-Anyi, 2018, p. 21; Milano et al., 2018; Proos, 2019, p. 101). Many regional developmental problems solution is seen as lying within tourism (Goeldner & Ritchie, 2012, p. 355; Martins, 2018). Tourism development needs to be conducted correctly and effectively (Proos, 2019, p. 102). The following section will discuss tourism development planning to assist battlefield tourism destinations as an agent of tourism development.

Globally, there is no agreement on one fixed definition of "planning" (Dredge & Jenkins, 2007, p. 8). However, planning is not homogeneous and can be understood as giving due consideration to the process and options of achieving defined goals (Acha-Anyi, 2018, p. 22). Inskeep (1991, p. 25) further contends that planning takes place daily. Planning ranges from choosing what to wear to what to eat and stretches as far as decisions made at regional and national planning undertaken by governments. According to Cooper et al. (2008, p. 260) and Proos and Hattingh (2019), planning involves organizing future events to achieve pre-specified objectives.

Inskeep (1991, p. 16), Goeldner and Ritchie (2012, p. 355), Proos (2019, p. 102), and Proos and Hattingh (2019, p. 102) identified that tourism planning is necessary for the following reasons:

- Some governments and the private sector have little or no experience developing their tourism industry. In such cases, a tourism development plan can provide a guideline to ensure the proper development of a proposed battlefield and related tourism route.
- Tourism involves many sectors and thus needs coordination among all these sectors.
- Tourism provides employment opportunities which, in return, assist with addressing regional economic problems that could arise without proper planning.
- Proper planning could ensure that natural and cultural resources for tourism are not destroyed during the tourism development process.
- Planning could be utilized to revitalize outmoded or poorly developed tourism areas.
- Tourism generates a supply of foreign exchange and increases the gross domestic product (GDP) of a region.

- Tourism allows a lesser known region to establish a favorable impression on foreign visitors.
- Tourism assists with the process of modernization through the education of the youth.

As can be deducted from those mentioned above, careful planning could have advantages to destinations such as battlefield destinations concerning tourism development (Inskeep, 1991, p. 17). Battlefield tourism can act as an agent of tourism development. For this reason, a tourism development plan is critical for a region planning to expand and develop its current battlefield tourism offering. Various development plans can be evaluated in the literature. Worldwide battlefield and battlefield routes are popular agents for tourism development (Acha-Anyi, 2018; Cooper et al., 2008; Goeldner & Ritchie, 2012; Hattingh, 2016; Inskeep, 1991). The following section describes the key factors of a successful tourism development plan for battlefield tourism.

Study Preparation

The first step is study preparation concerning the development of a battlefield or related tourism route (Acha-Anyi, 2018, p. 25; Hattingh, 2016, p. 24). This process is conducted in consultation with the private sector and public stake-holders. The development of this route was supported by stakeholders upon their realization that battlefield tourism is a desirable development option for their region. At this stage, a study team will also be selected, and parties such as the government, the private sector, and the local community are part of the study team. The Terms of Reference (TOR) will also be developed in the study preparation step. The TOR should preferably include a time framework and details regarding the development of the battlefields and tourism route and the project's stage (Cooper et al., 2008, p. 261; Hattingh, 2016, p. 24; Inskeep, 1991, p. 49).

Determination of Objectives

Goals and objectives indicate the desired results of developing a battlefield and tourism route and could include socioeconomic benefits and minimizing environmental and sociocultural impacts. The type of survey to be conducted, the formulation of policy, and the plan itself, as well as recommendations, would be determined by the objectives (Inskeep, 1991, p. 51). Objectives of the plan should be realistic, time-bound, and measurable (Acha-Anyi, 2018, p. 27).

The critical question to ask at this stage of the planning process is "why do we want battlefield tourism development" (Cooper et al., 2008, p. 262)? The significant objectives of battlefield tourism development can be:

- to develop a high-quality battlefield tourism product;
- to encourage the use of battlefield tourism for cultural and economic exchange;
- to distribute economic benefits as a result of battlefield tourism;

- to preserve cultural and natural resources as part of tourism development;
- to appeal to a broad cross-section of international and domestic tourists interested in battlefield tourism. (Cooper et al., 2008, p. 262; Hattingh, 2016, p. 25; Proos, 2019, p. 108)

Data Gathering

The data-gathering step in the battlefield tourism planning process entails surveys, although this stage includes quantitative and qualitative data collection methods. The step consists of field surveys of battlefield tourist-related attractions, other facilities and services, transportation, and infrastructure. Other data could consist of existing documents, maps, data, and any other source of information (Inskeep, 1991, p. 52; Proos, 2019, p. 108). At the data gathering stage, the researcher must find out "what data are available," and then the "information gaps" should be filled (Cooper et al., 2008, p. 261; Hattingh, 2016, p. 27; Proos, 2019, p. 108).

The following essential data need to be gathered about battlefield tourism planning (Cooper et al., 2008, p. 262; Hattingh, 2016, p. 26; Inskeep, 1991, p. 50)

- tourist travel patterns,
- tourist accommodation,
- accommodation facilities,
- other tourist facilities,
- land availability and use. (Proos, 2019, p. 108)

For battlefield tourism development planners, good quality data for planning, management, and monitoring purposes are critical (Cooper et al., 2008, p. 263; Proos, 2019, p. 109).

Analysis and Synthesis

After the objectives have been formulated, the analytical framework selected will determine the specific sets of historical data to be collected. The survey data analysis and synthesis could be conducted either quantitatively or qualitatively. After data gathering, the data should be analyzed concerning the following (Cooper et al., 2008, p. 263):

- asset evaluation,
- market analysis,
- development planning,
- impact analyses. (Proos, 2019, p. 109)

The battlefield tourism development plan must address the abovementioned issues before the policy can be formulated (Cooper et al., 2008, p. 264; Proos, 2019, p. 109).

Policy and Plan Formulation

The following step in tourism development is the policy and planning formulation process (Hattingh, 2016, p. 29; Proos, 2019, p. 109). During the planning formulation step, the tourism development policy is determined (Inskeep, 1991; Proos, 2019, p. 109).

First, the policy is formulated on a preliminary basis, and a draft plan is designed. After the policy has been tested for suitability in achieving the objectives of battlefield tourism development and its feasibility of implementation, the policy could be finalized (Cooper et al., 2008, p. 264; Proos, 2019, p. 110). Through the policy, how the objectives can be achieved is communicated. The overall development policy and plan of the country or region should be reflected in the tourism policy to ensure that battlefield tourism is integrated into the tourism sector (Inskeep, 1991, p. 170; Proos, 2019, p. 110; NDTRSA, 1996).

Recommendations

The second last step is the recommendation phase (Hattingh, 2016, p. 29; Proos, 2019, p. 110). The plan's structure can be finalized once the analysis and synthesis have been prepared and the selected policy and plan have been completed. The relevant recommendations can now be made concerning the development of battlefield tourism (Proos, 2019, p. 110). During the recommendation phase, "several recommendations may be put forward for policy choice" (Cooper et al., 2008, p. 261; Proos, 2019, p. 110).

Implementation and Monitoring

The battlefield tourism development plan can now be concluded with the implementation and monitoring phase (Acha-Anyi, 2018, p. 33; Hattingh, 2016, p. 30; Proos, 2019, p. 110). The entire plan needs to be reviewed at this step. Furthermore, the adoption of the plan, the adoption of legislation and regulations, integration of the plan into public and private sector development policies, continuous monitoring, adjustments to the plan and program as required, and, finally, a review and revision of the plan is completed at this step (Hattingh, 2016, p. 30; Inskeep, 1991, p. 50; Proos, 2019, p. 110). Through the monitoring process, both the negative and positive impacts of the tourism development plan can be measured. These impacts can be measured against the expectations and feedback provided by all stakeholders (Acha-Anyi, 2018, p. 33; Proos, 2019, p. 110).

The critical factors of a successful tourism development plan for battlefield tourism are emphasized in Fig. 9.1. It is essential for the tourism developer intending to develop a battlefield and tourism route to appraise the advantages of an in-depth tourism plan. The following six benefits of the successful implementation of a tourism development plan can be highlighted (Edgell & Swanson, 2013, p. 248):

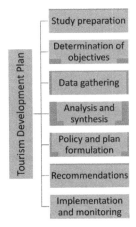

Fig. 9.1.   Key Factors of a Successful Tourism Development Plan for Battlefield Tourism. *Source:* Proos (2019).

(1) The tourism policies of an area or an organization are strengthened.
(2) Tourism planning is future-oriented.
(3) Tourism planning provides a blueprint for future development.
(4) Tourism planning improves the quality of life for residents.
(5) Resources are conserved for future tourism growth.
(6) Marketing success will be achieved through tourism planning.

When considering the results of these advantages, battlefield tourism can prosper.

Conclusion

For battlefield tourism to serve as an agent of tourism development, an in-depth tourism development plan must be designed for battlefield tourism for the above advantages to be affected. On their own, battlefields are unremarkable. It needs interpretation, development, marketing, and commercializing to enrich and become part of the tourism landscape, or they can then act as "storyteller(s)" of the past, add value to the more extensive tourism offering of a particular area, and act as an agent of tourism development.

References

Acha-Anyi, P. N. (2018). In P. N. Acha-Anyi (Ed.), *Introduction to tourism planning & development: Igniting Africa's tourism economy*. Van Schaik Publishers.

Ashworth, G. J. (2004). Tourism and heritage of atrocity: Managing the heritage of South African apartheid for entertainment. In T. V. Singh (Ed.), *New horizons in tourism*. CABI Publishing.

AutoFrance. (2020). The top 4 historic battlegrounds to visit in Europe. https://www. autofrance.net/blog/the-top-4-historic-battlegrounds-to-visit-in-europe/

Battlefields Route KwaZulu Natal. (2020). Battlefields route. https://www. battlefieldsroute.co.za/

Beech, J. (2000). The enigma of holocaust sites as tourist attractions – The case of Buchenwald. *Managing Leisure, 5*, 29–41.

Boateng, H., Okoe, A. F., & Hinson, R. E. (2018). Dark Tourism: Exploring tourist's experience at the Cape Coast Castle, Ghana. *Tourism Management Perspectives, 27*(January), 104–110. https://doi.org/10.1016/j.tmp.2018.05.004

Brokaj, R. (2014). Local government's role in the sustainable tourism development of a destination. *European Scientific Journal, ESJ, 10*(31).

Chang, J. (2017). Tourists' perception of dark tourism and its impact on their emotional experience and geopolitical knowledge: A comparative study of local and non-local tourist. *Journal of Tourism Research & Hospitality, 6*(3).

Clarke, P., & Eastgate, A. (2011). Cultural capital, life course perspectives and western front battlefield tours. *Journal of Tourism and Cultural Change, 9*(1), 31–44.

Conners, V. (2020). Top civil war battlefield tours. https://www.travelchannel.com/ interests/history/articles/top-civil-war-battlefield-tours

Cooper, C., Fletcher, J., Fyall, A., Gilbert, D., & Wanhill, S. (2008). *Tourism principles and practice* (4th ed.). Pearson Education Limited.

Dark Tourism: The demand for new experiences. (2017). https://www.tourism-review. com/dark-tourism-includes-various-niches-news10368

Dredge, D., & Jenkins, J. (2007). *Tourism planning and policy*. John Wiley & Sons Australia, Ltd.

Dunkley, R. (2007). *The thanatourist: Collected tales of the thanatourism experience*. University of Wales.

Dunkley, R., Morgan, N., & Westwood, S. (2011). Visiting the trenches: Exploring meanings and motivations in battlefield tourism. *Tourism Management, 32*(4), 860–868. https://doi.org/10.1016/j.tourman.2010.07.0n

Edgell, D., & Swanson, J. (2013). *Tourism policy and planning yesterday, today, and tomorrow* (2nd ed.). Routledge.

Eloff, H. (2018). Dark tourist channel 24. https://www.channel24.co.za/TV/Reviews/ dark-tourist-20180725

Foley, M., & Lennon, J. (1996). JFK and dark tourism: A fascination with assassination. *International Journal of Heritage Studies, 2*, 198–211.

Gilks, M. (2021). Battlefield monuments and popular historicism: A hermeneutic study of the aesthetic encounter with 'Waterloo'. *Critical Military Studies*. https:// doi.org/10.1080/23337486.2021.1888015

Godbey, H. (2017). Our top 8 favourite American civil war sites to visit today. https:// www.warhistoryonline.com/american-civil-war/top-american-civil-war-sites-to-visit-today.html

Goeldner, C. R., & Ritchie, J. R. B. (2012). *Tourism principles, practices, philosophies* (12th ed.). John Wiley & Sons, Inc.

Grobler, J. (2018). *Anglo-Boer war (South African War) 1899–1902*. 30 South Publishers (Pty) Ltd. www.30degreessouth.co.za

Hartmann, R. (2014). Dark tourism, thanatourism, and dissonance in heritage tourism management: New directions in contemporary tourism research. *Journal of Heritage Tourism, 9*(2), 166–182. https://doi.org/10.1080/1743873X.2013.807266

Hattingh, J. L. (2016). *The Karoo Riveria: A cross border tourism development plan for the middle orange river*. Central University of Technology.

Historic Scotland (undated) Inventory of historic battlefields. (2009). http://www. historic-scotland.gov.uk/index/heritage/battlefields/battlefieldsunderconsideration. htm

History.com. (Eds.). (2019a). *Battle of the bulge*. https://www.history.com/topics/ world-war-ii/battle-of-the-bulge

History.com. (Eds.). (2019b). *D-Day invasion, facts & significance – History*. https:// www.history.com/topics/world-war-ii/d-day

Holguin, S. (2005). "National Spain invites you": Battlefield tourism during the Spanish civil war. *American Histoirical Review*, 1399–1426.

Inskeep, E. (1991). *Tourism planning an integrated and sustainable development approach*. John Wiley & Sons, Inc.

Kim, S., & Butler, G. (2014). Local community perspectives towards dark tourism development: The case of Snowtown, South Australia. *Journal of Tourism and Cultural Change*. https://doi.org/10.1080/14766825.2014.918621

Klein, C. (2016). Battle of Waterloo. http://www.history.com/news/7-things-you-may-not-know-about-the-battle-of-waterloo

LeMaitre, A. (Ed.). (2017). *On route in South Africa explore South Africa region by region* (Third). Jonathan Ball Publishers.

Lennon, J., & Foley, M. (2000). *Dark tourism the attraction of death and disaster*. Continuum.

Light, D. (2017). Progress in dark tourism and thanatourism research: An uneasy relationship with heritage tourism. *Tourism Management, 61*, 275–301. https://doi. org/10.1016/j.tourman.2017.01.011

Marais, C. (2017, February). Tombstone travel in the Karoo. *Country Life*, 38–43.

Martins, M. (2018). Tourism planning and tourismphobia: An analysis of the strategic tourism plan of Barcelona. *Journal of Tourism, Heritage & Services Marketing, 4*(1), 3–7.

Milano, C., Cheer, J., & Novelli, M. (2018). Overtourism: A growing global problem. http://theconversation.com/overtourism-a-growing-global-problem-100029

Miles, S. (2012). Battlefield tourism: Meanings and interpretations. http://theses.gla. ac.uk/3547/1/2012milesphd22.pdf

Miles, S. (2014). Battlefield sites as dark tourism attractions: An analysis of experience. *Journal of Heritage Tourism, 9*(2), 134–147.

Misztal, B. (2003). *Theories of social remembering*. Open University Press.

Moeller, M. (2005). *Battlefield tourism in South Africa with special reference to Isandlwana and Rorke's Drift KwaZulu-Natal* (Issue October). University of Pretoria.

National Department of Tourism Republic of South Africa. (2017). *National tourism sector strategy (NTSS) 2016–2026*. https://www.gov.za/sites/default/files/National %20Tourism%20Sector%20Strategy%20NTSS%202016-2026_a.pdf

National Department of Tourism Republic of South Africa. (1996). *White paper the development and promotion of tourism in South Africa*. Cape Town. http://scnc. ukzn.ac.za/doc/tourism/White_Paper.htm

National Department of Tourism Republic of South Africa. (2018). *Tourism destination planning manual national department of tourism.* https://www.tourism.gov.za/Tenders/Documents/NDT0010-18-TOURISM%20DESTINATION%20PLANNING%20MANUAL.pdf

National Geographic. (2010). *Top 10 civil war sites – National geographic.* https://www.nationalgeographic.com/travel/destinations/north-america/united-states/civil-war-sites/

Page, S. J., & Connell, J. (2020). *Tourism a modern synthesis* (5th ed.). Routledge.

Podoshen, J. S. (2013). Dark tourism motivations: Simulation, emotional contagion and topographic comparison. *Tourism Management, 35,* 263–271. https://doi.org/10.1016/j.tourman.2012.08.002

Podoshen, J. S., Andrzejewski, S. A., Venkatesh, V., & Wallin, J. (2015). New approaches to dark tourism inquiry: A response to Isaac. *Tourism Management, 51,* 331–334. https://doi.org/10.1016/j.tourman.2015.05.008

Proos, E. (2019). *A tourism development plan for the South African war battlefields route in the central Karoo.* Central University of Technology. http://hdl.handle.net/11462/2035

Proos, E., & Hattingh, J. (2019). Advancing heritage tourism in the central Karoo: The South African war battlefields route. *Development Southern Africa, 0*(0), 1–16. https://doi.org/10.1080/0376835X.2019.1698409

Proos, E., & Hattingh, J. L. (2020). Dark tourism: Growth potential of niche tourism in the Free State Province, South Africa. *Development Southern Africa.* https://doi.org/https://www.tandfonline.com/action/showCitFormats?doi=10.1080/0376835X.2020.1847636

Ramela, N. (2018). Magaliesberg battlesfield route to boost tourism while revisiting history. https://www.gauteng.net/blog/new-magaliesberg-battlefields-route-to-benefit-tourism-while-revisiting-history

Rodgers, G. (2019). Vietnam war sites of interest – A virtual tour. https://www.tripsavvy.com/vietnam-war-sites-of-interest-1630012

Rojek, C. (1993). *Way of seeing modern transformation in leisure and travel.* Macmillan.

Ryan, C. (2007). *Battlefield tourism: History, place and interpretation.* Elsevier Ltd.

Seaton, A. (1996). Guided by the dark – From thanatopis to thanatourism. *International Journal of Heritage Studies, 2*(4), 234–244.

Seaton, A. (1999). War and thanatourism. Waterloo 1815–1914. *Annals of Tourism Research.* http://sciencedirect.com/

Seaton, A., & Lennon, J. (2004). Thanatourism in the early 21st century: Moral panic, ulterior motives and alterior desires. In T. V. Singh (Ed.), *New horizons in tourism: Strange experiences and stranger practices* (pp. 63–82). CAB International.

Sharpley, R., & Stone, P. R. (2009). *The darker side of travel.* Chanel View Publications.

Smith, V. (1998). War and tourism: An American ethnography. *Annals of Tourism Research, 25*(1), 202–227.

Solomon Edwardian Guest House. (2020). Kimberley battlefield route. http://www.thesolomon.co.za/battlefield-n12-route—kimberley.html

Stone, P. R. (2006). *A dark tourism spectrum: Towards a typology of death and macabre related tourist sites, attractions and exhibitions.* https://www.mendeley.com/catalogue/selectedworks-dr-philip-stone-2006-dark-tourism-spectrum-towards-typology-death-macabre-related-tour/

Stone, P., & Sharpley, R. (2008). Consuming dark tourism: A thanatological perspective. *Annals of Tourism Research, 35*(2), 574–595. https://doi.org/10.1016/j.annals.2008.02.003

Swarbrooke, J., & Horner, S. (1999). *Consumer behaviour in tourism.* Elsevier Ltd.

Tarlow, P. (2005). Dark tourism: The appealing 'dark' side of tourism and more. In M. Noveilli (Ed.), *Niche tourism: Contemporary issues, trends and cases* (pp. 47–57). Elsevier.

Travel China Guide. (2020). *Military museum of the Chinese people's revolution.* https://www.travelchinaguide.com/attraction/beijing/military-museum.htm

US National Park Service. (2020). *Gettysburg National Military Park.* https://www.nps.gov/gett/index.htm

Van Der Merwe, C. D. (2014). Battlefields tourism: The status of heritage tourism in Dundee, South Africa. *Bulletin of Geography, 26*(26), 121–139. https://doi.org/10.2478/bog-2014-0049

Venter, D. (2011). Battlefield tourism in the South African context. *African Journal of Hospitality, Tourism and Leisure, 1*(3), 1–5.

Von der Heyde, N. (2013). In C. Dos Santos (Ed.), *Field guide to the battlefields of South Africa.* Struik Travel & Heritage.

Von der Heyde, N. (2017). In R. Theron & E. Bowles (Eds.), *Guide to sieges of South Africa.* Struik Travel & Heritage.

Winter, C. (2012). Commemoration of the Great War on the Somme: Exploring personal connections. *Journal of Tourism and Cultural Change, 10*(3), 248–263.

Worral, S. (2015). How the battle of Waterloo changed the world. https://www.nationalgeographic.com/news/2015/06/150616-waterloo-napoleon-wellington-history-world-ngbooktalk/

Index

Printed and bound by CPI Group (UK) Ltd, Croydon, CR0 4YY

21/11/2024

14596799-0001